Governance for Sustainable Development

A Foundation for the Future

Governance for Sustainable Development

A Foundation for the Future

Edited by Georgina Ayre and Rosalie Callway

London • Sterling, VA

First published by Earthscan in the UK and USA in 2005

ISBN: 1-84407-208-8   paperback
       1-84407-207-X   hardback

Typesetting by JS Typesetting Ltd, Porthcawl, Mid Glamorgan
Printed and bound in the UK by Bath Press
Cover design by Yvonne Booth

For a full list of publications please contact:

Earthscan
8–12 Camden High Street
London, NW1 0JH, UK
Tel: +44 (0)20 7387 8558
Fax: +44 (0)20 7387 8998
Email: earthinfo@earthscan.co.uk
Web: **www.earthscan.co.uk**

22883 Quicksilver Drive, Sterling, VA 20166-2012, USA

Earthscan is an imprint of James and James (Science Publishers) Ltd and publishes in association with the International Institute for Environment and Development

A catalogue record for this book is available from the British Library

Library of Congress Cataloging-in-Publication Data

Governance for sustainable development : a foundation for the future /
edited by Georgina Ayre and Rosalie Callway.
        p. cm.
    Includes bibliographical references and index.
    ISBN 1-84407-208-8 — ISBN 1-84407-207-X
    1. Sustainable development—International cooperation. 2.
Sustainable development—Government policy. 3. Environmental
protection—International cooperation. 4. Environmental policy. I.
Ayre, Georgina. II. Callway, Rosalie.
    HC79.E5G658 2005
    338.9′27—dc22

                                                2005004988

Printed on elemental chlorine-free paper

Contents

List of Figures, Tables and Boxes

Figures

Tables

Boxes

List of Contributors

Georgina Ayre is a policy adviser on sustainable development, with a particular expertise in international governance and multi-stakeholder processes. She recently joined the UK Department of the Environment, Food and Rural Affairs (DEFRA), and is predominantly working on environmental sustainability within the United Nations system.

Rosalie Callway is international policy officer at the Local Government International Bureau (LGIB). Her role addresses the ways local government contributes to sustainability and international development. She provides policy analysis, advice and information on international polices of relevance to local government. Rosalie has been working on sustainable development and environmental issues for over ten years. Previously she was head of policy at Stakeholder Forum, where her work focused on the Johannesburg World Summit on Sustainable Development. She also managed the Global Governance Programme where the concept for this book was first developed. She has a BSc in environmental economics and management from the University of York and a Master's degree from the University of Warwick in ecosystems analysis and governance.

Andrew M. Deutz has extensive experience in international environmental law, policy and negotiation, as well as in international conservation and development. He is currently working with the World Conservation Union (IUCN) as their special adviser for global policy, responsible for IUCN's engagement with the United Nations, the World Bank and a variety of other multilateral institutions dealing with sustainable development. Previously within IUCN he served as head of IUCN's Canada Office, with responsibility for political, constituency and fundraising relations in Canada; as international forest policy adviser to the World Bank, facilitating a globe-spanning, two-year review and public consultation process on forest policy and poverty alleviation; and as coordinator of IUCN's Temperate and Boreal Forest Programme, establishing IUCN's forest conservation programme in Russia. Prior to joining IUCN in 1997, Dr Deutz was a research associate at the Woods Hole Research Centre, working on the Kyoto Protocol negotiations on climate change, as well as on international forest policy and the Convention on Biological Diversity (CBD). He holds a doctorate in international environmental law from the Fletcher School of Law and Diplomacy.

Alan W. Hall is the network coordinator for the Global Water Partnership (GWP). He has worked in water-related development for 30 years, mainly in Africa and Asia. His work has involved consultancy, research and project management on rural development and irrigated agriculture, as well as water resources management. He was a principal project officer with the African Development Bank in Abidjan for six years, covering project and policy work throughout Africa. During the 1990s he was the group manager for a research programme for international development at HR Wallingford Ltd focused on water resources. In 1999 he led a team for the Global Water Partnership to develop the Framework for Action presented at the second World Water Forum in The Hague in 2000. From this he established the Dialogue on Effective Water Governance. This dialogue was carried out by GWP, with support from the United Nations Development Programme (UNDP) and the International Council for Local Environmental Initiatives (ICLEI), throughout the GWP network, and has helped to create a different way of thinking among water professionals.

Maria Ivanova is the director of the Global Environmental Governance Project at the Yale Center for Environmental Law and Policy. Her work focuses on international institutions and organizations, environmental policy at the national and global levels, and global governance. She is the co-editor, with Daniel Esty, of *Global Environmental Governance: Options and Opportunities* (Yale School of Forestry and Environmental Studies, 2002) and author and co-author of articles and chapters on governance, globalization and the environment. She has delivered talks at many international conferences and lectured at universities. A Bulgarian national, Maria received a Bachelor's degree in European policy from Mount Holyoke College (*summa cum laude*) and Master's degrees in environmental management and international relations from Yale University. She is currently a doctoral candidate at the Yale School of Forestry and Environmental Studies where she is writing on the development of the international environmental regime with a focus on the United Nations Environment Programme (UNEP). Maria has worked at the Environment Directorate of the Organisation for Economic Co-operation and Development (OECD) in Paris on environmental regulatory reform in the New Independent States of the Former Soviet Union. She was also a project manager at the Swedish Environmental Protection Agency in Stockholm, where she developed policies for water quality standard-setting in the Russian Federation.

Maria Figueroa Küpçü specializes in strategic market research and the development of political and corporate advocacy campaigns. She has worked as a senior director at the consulting firm Penn, Schoen and Berland Associates, the Council on Foreign Relations and several United Nations agencies, including the UNDP and the United Nations Centre for Human Settlements (UNCHS). She co-founded the international non-governmental organization (NGO) Youth for Habitat II and helped to foster the active participation of young people in the UN global conferences, including the United Nations Social Summit (Copenhagen, 1995) and the United Nations Habitat II Conference (Istanbul, 1996). Maria's contributions and comments have appeared in various international media, such as the *Voice of America*, *UNDP Human Development Report* (Turkey), *UNDP Poverty Report*, *New India Digest* and *People from Impoverishment to Empowerment* (Kirdar and Silk (eds), 1995, NYU Press, New York).

Robert L. Paarlberg is professor of political science at Wellesley College and associate at the Weatherhead Center for International Affairs at Harvard University. He received his undergraduate degree in political science from Carleton College and his PhD in government from Harvard University. Paarlberg has been a member of the board of directors of Winrock International, a member of the Emerging Markets Advisory Committee at the United States Department of Agriculture, a member of the Board of Agriculture and Natural Resources of the National Academies and a consultant to the International Food Policy Research Institute. He has published books on food trade and diplomacy (*Food Trade and Foreign Policy*, Cornell University Press, 1985), on international agricultural trade negotiations (*Fixing Farm Trade*, Ballinger, 1988), on environmentally sustainable farming in developing countries (*Countrysides at Risk*, Overseas Development Council, 1994), on US foreign economic policy (*Leadership Abroad Begins at Home*, Brookings, 1995) and on the reform of US agricultural policy (*Policy Reform in American Agriculture*, with David Orden and Terry Roe, Chicago University Press, 1999). His latest book, *The Politics of Precaution: Policies toward GM Crops in the Developing World*, was published by the Johns Hopkins University Press in November 2001.

Yasmin von Schirnding is the 'focal point' for Agenda 21 at the World Health Organization (WHO) and manager of the Healthy Environments for Children Alliance at WHO. Prior to this she was director of the former Office of Global and Integrated Environmental Health at WHO, and director of environmental health for Johannesburg. She has also held senior research positions in environmental health at the South Africa Medical Research Council. She holds several postgraduate degrees in the environmental and health sciences, and has published widely on health, environment and development issues. She has held positions on the boards of several professional bodies, including the International Society for Environmental Epidemiology and the International Association for Impact Assessment, and is the recipient of various awards.

Richard Sherman When not on assignment for the *Earth Negotiations Bulletin* (ENB) produced by the International Institute for Sustainable Development (IISD), Richard Sherman serves as the head of the Research and Policy Unit at the Southern African regional office of Global Legislators Organization for a Balanced Environment (GLOBE). His areas of specialty for ENB are climate change, sustainable development and desertification, and he also compiles *CLIMATE-L News* and *WATER-L News* for IISD. From 1998–2001 he was a member of the South African government's climate change delegation and has played an active role in the South African NGO sector since 1995.

Andrew Simms is policy director and head of the Climate Change Programme at the New Economics Foundation (NEF), a board member of Greenpeace, UK, and at The Energy and Resources Institute (TERI), Europe. Previously, he led campaigns for Christian Aid for four years and was one of the original campaigners for the Jubilee 2000 Coalition debt campaign. He has worked for a variety of development and environmental organizations, including Oxfam, the World Development Movement and the International Institute for Environment and Development (IIED), and was national youth speaker for the Green party and an adviser to Michael Meacher as shadow overseas development minister. His publications include several reports published by New Economics Foundation (NEF), on climate change, globalization and localization, development issues, debt and ecological debt, corporate accountability, and genetic engineering and food security. They include *Who Owes Who? Climate Change, Debt, Equity and Survival* (2002); *Up in Smoke – Threats From and Responses to the Impact of Global Warming on Human Development* (2005); *Collision Course – Free Trade's Free Ride on the Global Climate* (2005); *The Price of Power – Poverty, Climate Change, the Coming Energy Crisis and the Renewable Revolution* (2004); and *Free Riding on the Climate – The Possibility of Legal, Economic and Trade Restrictive Measures to Tackle Inaction on Global Warming* (2003). He has been a regular contributor to the International Red Cross's annual *World Disasters Report*. His book *Ecological Debt – The Health of the Planet and the Wealth of Nations* is published by Pluto Press (2005).

Foreword

Over the past five years there has been a growing interest in the systems of govern-ance that determine the way in which the world works. The problems facing the peoples of the world have not gone away since the report *Governance for a Sustain-able Future* was launched by the World Humanity Action Trust (WHAT) in 2000. There is progress in some areas, and awareness of the problems of poverty, AIDS and global tensions of all kinds is growing. And although there are increasing signs of consensus on the actions that are required, implementation of these is slow.

The World Summit on Sustainable Development (WSSD), held in Johannes-burg in 2002, could be called a success in that a large number of people came together to exchange ideas and experience regarding sustainable development. However, the formal debates between government representatives too often feat-ured self-congratulatory statements and a reluctance to commit to clearly defined action. Nevertheless, new targets and a recommitment to the Millennium Develop-ment Goals (MDGs) were eventually agreed. We all have a responsibility to ensure that member states of the United Nations (UN) understand that those goals are minimum targets and that, although achievement of them will go a long way towards solving the problems of the world, further commitment and action is required.

The UN is far from perfect; but it remains our best hope if agreements are to have a chance of succeeding. During the next few years, member states will have to face the issue of how best to adapt the structure of the UN to improve its ability to mould events through international agreements in a more coherent way. In particular, the UN, in common with national governments everywhere, needs to recognize the vital importance of moving beyond just talking about joined-up thinking. We must escape from the mentality of looking at 'everything in little boxes' that for too long has bedevilled policy-making and decision-making at all levels of government in the world.

Following the merger of WHAT with Stakeholder Forum, the work on governance systems has continued, and this book is a product of some of the ideas that are beginning to emerge.

The book makes an important contribution to improving our understanding, and points a way forward. We must all hope that it moves the world a little closer to a sustainable future.

Jack Jeffery
Newcastle
December 2004

Acknowledgements

We would like to give special thanks to each of the authors for their patience and their efforts in contributing to the book. We are very grateful to the reviewers of the book – Andreas Seiter, Bowden King, Jeffery McNeilly, Joanna Phillips, Karla Schoeters, Jim Oatridge, Stephen Turner and Elena Nekeav – for their thoughts and suggestions, which have helped to improve the work. Special thanks go to Jack Jeffrey and Peter Warren from the World Humanity Action Trust (WHAT) for their support and advice in taking forward the work started in their governance report. Thanks also go to Jane and Duncan Gardiner, Barbara Kleiner and Tom Callway for their encouragement throughout the production of the book.

List of Acronyms and Abbreviations

ABS	access and benefit-sharing
ACC	United Nations Administrative Coordination Committee
AIDS	acquired immune deficiency syndrome
BWI	Bretton Woods Institution
CAN	Climate Action Network
CBD	United Nations Convention on Biological Diversity
C&C	Contraction and Convergence
CCA	United Nations Common Country Assessment
CDD	community-driven development
CEB	United Nations Chief Executive Board for Coordination
CEFDHAC	Conférence sur les Ecosystèmes de Forêts Denses et Humides d'Afrique Centrale
CENA	Capacity Enhancement Needs Assessment (World Bank)
CGIAR	Consultative Group on International Agricultural Research (World Bank)
CITES	Convention on International Trade in Endangered Species of Wild Fauna and Flora
CMA	Catchment Management Agency
CMH	Commission on Macroeconomics and Health
CMS	Convention on the Conservation of Migratory Species of Wild Animals
CO_2	carbon dioxide
COP	Conference of the Parties
CSD	United Nations Commission on Sustainable Development
DEFRA	UK Department of the Environment, Food and Rural Affairs
DESA	United Nations Department for Social and Economic Affairs
ECA	Economic Commission for Africa
ECA	export credit agency
ECE	Economic Commission for Europe
ECLAC	Economic Commission for Latin America and the Caribbean
ECOSOC	United Nations Economic and Social Council
EHS	environmental health services
EMG	Environmental Management Group (UNEP)

ENB	*Earth Negotiations Bulletin*
ESCAP	Economic and Social Commission for Asia and the Pacific
ESCWA	Economic and Social Commission for Western Asia
EU	European Union
ExIm Bank	US Export Import Bank
FAO	United Nations Food and Agricultural Organization
FCTC	Framework Convention on Tobacco Control
FDI	foreign direct investment
G8	Group of 8 (industrialized countries, including the Russian Federation)
GA	United Nations General Assembly
GAO	US General Accounting Office
GATS	WTO General Agreement on Trade and Services
GAVI	Global Alliance on Vaccines Initiative
GDP	Gross Domestic Product
GEF	Global Environment Facility
GEM	Global Environmental Mechanism
GEO	Global Environment Outlook
GHG	greenhouse gas
GLOBE	Global Legislators Organization for a Balanced Environment
GM	genetically modified
GMO	genetically modified organism
GNP	gross national product
GPA	Global Programme of Action
GPPN	global public policy network
GRI	Global Reporting Initiative
GWP	Global Water Partnership
HFA	Health for All strategy
HIPC	Highly Indebted Poor Countries initiative
HYV	high-yielding seed variety
IACSD	Inter-agency Committee on Sustainable Development
IAEA	International Atomic Energy Agency
ICLEI	International Council for Local Environmental Initiatives
ICT	Information Communication Technology
IEA	International Energy Agency
IEG	International Environmental Governance Initiative
IFAD	International Fund for Agricultural Development
IFCS	Intergovernmental Forum on Chemical Safety
IFF	Intergovernmental Forum on Forests
IFI	international financial institutions
IIED	International Institute for Environment and Development
IISD	International Institute for Sustainable Development
ILO	International Labour Organization
IMF	International Monetary Fund
IMO	International Maritime Organization
INWEH	International Network on Water, Environment and Health

IOC	International Oceanographic Commission
IOMC	Inter-organization Programme for the Sound Management of Chemicals
IPCC	Intergovernmental Panel on Climate Change
IPF	Intergovernmental Panel on Forests
IPM	integrated pest management
IRENA	International Renewable Energy Agency
ISEF	International Sustainable Energy Fund
ISEO	International Sustainable Energy Organisation
IUCN	World Conservation Union
IULA	International Union of Local Authorities
IWRM	integrated water resource management
JBIC	Japanese Bank for International Cooperation
JPOI	Johannesburg Plan of Implementation
LA21	Local Agenda 21
LEHAP	Local Environment and Health Action Plan
LGIB	Local Government International Bureau
LPP	Livestock Production Programme (UK)
MDB	multilateral development bank
MDG	Millennium Development Goal
MEA	Multilateral Environmental Agreement
MoU	memorandum of understanding
MSD	multi-stakeholder dialogue
MSF	Médecins Sans Frontières
MSP	multi-stakeholder participation/process
NAAEC	North American Agreement on Environmental Cooperation
NAFTA	North American Free Trade Agreement
NARS	national agricultural research systems
NCD	non-communicable disease
NCSD	national committee (or council) for sustainable development
NEAP	national environmental action plan
NEF	New Economics Foundation
NEHAP	national environmental health action plan
NEPAD	New Plan for African Development
NGO	non-governmental organization
NPT	Nuclear Non-proliferation Treaty
NRG4SD	Network of Regional Governments for Sustainable Development
NSSD	national strategies for sustainable development
OAU	Organization for African Unity
ODA	Official Development Assistance
OECD	Organisation for Economic Co-operation and Development
OPIC	US Overseas Private Investment Corporation
PA21	Philippine Agenda 21
PCB	polychlorinated biphenyl
PCSD	Philippine Council for Sustainable Development
PIC	Prior Informed Consent

POPs	Persistent Organic Pollutants
PPP	public–private partnership
PRSP	poverty reduction strategy paper
PRSP	poverty reduction strategy process
PT	Workers' party (Brazil)
R&D	research and development
RENEW	Renewable Energy Now through Export Finance Worldwide initiative
RPS	Renewable Portfolio Standard
SADC	Southern African Development Community
SIDS	Small Island Developing State
SME	small to medium enterprise
TB	tuberculosis
TERI	The Energy and Resources Institute
TNC	transnational corporation
TRIPS	Trade-related Intellectual Property Rights Agreement
UK	United Kingdom
UN	United Nations
UNAIDS	Joint United Nations Programme on HIV/AIDS
UNCED	United Nations Conference on Environment and Development
UNCHS	United Nations Centre for Human Settlements
UNCTAD	United Nations Conference on Trade and Development
UNDAF	United Nations Development Assistance Framework
UNDP	United Nations Development Programme
UNECE	United Nations Economic Commission for Europe
UNEO	United Nations Environment Organization
UNEP	United Nations Environment Programme
UNESCO	United Nations Educational, Scientific and Cultural Organization
UNFCCC	United Nations Framework Convention on Climate Change
UNFPA	UN Population Fund
UN-Habitat	United Nations Human Settlements Programme (*formerly* UNCHS (Habitat))
UNHCHR	United Nations High Commissioner for Human Rights
UNICEF	United Nations International Children's Fund
UNIDO	United Nations Industrial Development Organization
UNIFEM	United Nations Development Fund for Women
UNITAR	United Nations Institute for Training and Research
UNU	United Nations University
US	United States
WBCSD	World Business Council for Sustainable Development
WEC	World Energy Council
WEF	World Economic Forum
WEHAB	water, energy, health, food and agriculture, biodiversity
WEO	World Environment Organization
WFP	World Food Programme

WHAT	World Humanity Action Trust
WHO	World Health Organization
WIDER	World Institute for Development Economics Research
WIPO	World Intellectual Property Organization
WMA	Water Management Area
WMO	World Meteorological Organization
WRI	World Resources Institute
WSSD	World Summit on Sustainable Development
WTO	World Trade Organization
WWF	World Wide Fund for Nature

Introduction

1

Introduction: Setting the Scene

Rosalie Callway

The tragedy of the commons develops in this way. Picture a pasture open to all. It is to be expected that each herdsman will want to keep as many cattle as possible on the commons . . . as a rational human being, each herdsman seeks to maximize his gain . . . the rational herdsman concludes that the only sensible course for him to pursue is to add another animal to his herd. And another; and another. . . But this is the conclusion reached by each and every herdsman sharing the commons. Therein is the tragedy. Each man is locked into a system that compels him to increase his herd without limit – in a world that is limited. Ruin is the destination towards which all men rush, each pursuing his own best interest in a society that believes in the freedom of the commons. Freedom in a commons brings ruin to all. . .

But what does 'freedom' mean? When men mutually agreed to pass laws against robbing, mankind became more free, not less so. Individuals locked into the logic of the commons are free only to bring on universal ruin: once they see the necessity of mutual coercion, they become free to pursue other goals. I believe it was Hegel who said, 'Freedom is the recognition of necessity' (Hardin, 'The tragedy of the commons', 1968).

The past

Governance is the framework of social and economic systems and legal and political structures through which humanity manages itself (WHAT, 2000).

In 1996 the World Humanity Action Trust (WHAT), a think tank looking at global governance issues, was established in the UK by Sir Austin Bide and Sir Maurice Laing. Sir Austin warned of:

. . . the cumulative effect of the growing array of threats to world security. Global population growth, the international trade in illicit drugs, pollution and climate change, globalization of markets and increasing pressure on resources.

In order to address such challenges, WHAT established three special commissions, aptly named the WHAT commissions, to examine the current institutional frameworks of three natural resource topics: water, biodiversity and agriculture, and fisheries.

A varied group of international academics, scientists and political analysts gathered together and were asked to assess to what degree the governance systems within these sectors supported or restricted the sustainable utilization of natural resources. They were further invited to propose mechanisms to enhance the governance frameworks. The final results of the three working commissions were presented in a single report in 2000, *Governance for a Sustainable Future*. Many of the barriers to good governance are probably just as relevant now as they were when the report was first published (see Box 1.1).

Governance for a Sustainable Future (WHAT, 2000) makes a series of recommendations for strengthening the global governance architecture and for enhancing the national governance of natural resources (see Box 1.2). Perhaps the most critical recommendation of the report is a twofold requirement: the urgent need for greatly enhanced *horizontal* and *vertical* mechanisms of governance. The report noted that institutions at the same level (local, national and international) continue to work in their sectoral silos without adequately taking into account the areas where their work interlinks and impacts on other sectors. This silo mentality undermines the sustainable management of resources, which requires a joined-up or integrated management approach, and necessitates the involvement of a range of institutions and interest groups for their effective use, protection and improvement. Similarly, the report argues that overtly 'vertical' governance systems continue to adopt a predominately top-down system of decision-making without allowing mechanisms of feedback and learning from the 'bottom' or local level. It calls for greater emphasis on drawing from local experiences and the local impacts of global and national policies, as well as enabling more flexible and locally appropriate interpretation of those decisions.

Globally *Governance for a Sustainable Future* (WHAT, 2000) identifies the lack of democratic frameworks in key international institutions, including the International Monetary Fund (IMF), the World Bank, the World Trade Organization (WTO) and other bodies, such as the Organisation for Economic Co-operation and Development (OECD). It calls for an increase in their transparency and strengthening of the democratic frameworks, and urges these bodies to take greater account of the social and environmental implications of their policy-making. It argues for greater coordination across policy areas, as well as better enforcement of non-economic international treaties, such as the Multilateral Environmental Agreements (MEAs). It notes the heavy domination of Western policy-makers and economic paradigms that fail to take account of the complex problems of natural resource management or support for sustainable solutions. A new global ethic and citizen movement is required; but this ethic remains hard to define and promote. Such an ethic would need to be based on widespread public participation in decisions over sustainable resource use, a central message of Agenda 21. It would have to foster commercial markets with a longer-term view, targeting sustainable production and consumption, ethical international relations and sound

Box 1.1 Conclusions from the original *Governance for a Sustainable Future* report

Barriers to good governance

- *Frontier mentality*: the lingering hold on a 'frontier economy' approach despite a reality that necessitates a global commons approach. A frontier economy describes a country that behaves as if there is an inexhaustible supply of natural resources and that financial and man-made capital can substitute lost natural resources (such as coal, timber, plant or fish species) and natural services (for example, water nutrient recycling by wetlands, or coastal protection by mangroves, sea grass and coral reefs).
- *Not developing and listening to sound science*: our interaction with the natural environment is increasingly complex and dynamic, generating greater uncertainty in the assessment of risk and the impacts of unsustainable behaviour. To tackle this complexity requires scientifically rigorous analysis. Yet, scientific research is not keeping up with the impacts of growing environmental pressures. Furthermore, political groups do not always respond to good scientific information that already exists. In part, this is because scientific research is not communicated effectively to decision-makers, but also because science needs to be sufficiently independent of state and commercial interests in order to establish greater openness, trust and confidence in the use of science.
- *Complexity and poor coordination*: failure to achieve integrated resource management (such as water, coastal and forest management) or to agree an agenda between varied stakeholders can stem from organizations which themselves lack coordination. For example, in the United Nations (UN) there are 20 international bodies that deal with water-related issues; but they lack an effective coordinating mechanism to bring this work together. Organizations are also failing to meet the challenge of joined-up problems. For instance, integrated watershed management requires a highly coordinated approach involving diverse stakeholders in various sectors and different levels.
- *The administrative trap*: this problem also undermines coordination across institutions. It recognizes that institutional administration is typically organized vertically within different individual sectors – for example, education, healthcare and agriculture. Horizontal communication and coordination are therefore a real challenge. Too many good international dialogues on sustainable development have failed to result in positive action. The prevalence of these international 'talk shops' is, in part, because of a disjunction between those government ministries who are present at the talks (commonly, environment and development departments) and the absence of those who have the final say (typically, the finance and trade departments). Donor communities can often fail to coordinate effectively with each other. Differing priorities and even competition between bodies can place a heavy burden on the shoulders of the donor receivers. Political, professional and academic systems can reinforce this 'silo' mentality, prohibiting coherent policy-making.

- *Bottom-up disconnection*: poor information flows and understanding between different levels of governance and scales of activity can result in global and national policies that do not capture the local reality or community experience. Long-established traditional systems of community stewardship of common resources and local governance regimes for water abstraction rights or fisheries management are just two examples of effective local management systems that are often missed. Transboundary issues, such as watershed management, require both a bottom-up and top-down approach. Regional organizational structures around ecosystem structure are showing some positive signs of being an effective way of tying the other levels of governance together.
- *No shared ethic*: a lack of common philosophy over natural resource management prohibits the development of workable, mutually agreed, solutions for managing the natural commons. The future of sustainable governance depends not only upon better science to inform policy-making, but also on richer political processes that open up debates about fairness and the long-term implications of different management approaches. The design and implementation of mechanisms for promoting sustainable stewardship of resources, based on a common set of environmental rights and responsibilities, applicable at the individual and institutional level, could help to promote an ethic of 'sustainable stewardship'.

information. The gap between rhetoric and action, particularly in the West, remains huge; however, the report states that 'the realization is spreading among decision-makers and TNC [transnational corporation] leaders that radical change must come in the next decade or so'.

The present

> *There is growing concern about the direction globalization is currently taking...*
> *Its advantages are too distant for too many, whilst its risks are all too real. Corruption is widespread. Open societies are threatened by global terrorism, and the future of open markets is increasingly in question. Global governance is in crisis. We are at a critical juncture, and we need to urgently rethink our current policies and practices* (World Commission on the Social Dimension of Globalization, 2004).

This book aims to take up the baton from where the WHAT *Governance for a Sustainable Future* (2000) report left off and to re-invigorate the debate about good governance. It is not alone. A whole series of processes are currently taking place in an attempt to shift the architecture of various institutions and processes. Globally, we see international bodies such as the Bretton Woods institutions (the World Bank and the IMF), the WTO, the UN, the Group of 8[1] (G8) who are, albeit very slowly, beginning to recognize that they will need to re-orientate

Box 1.2 Governance recommendations

Global reform

- *Global institutional framework: Governance for a Sustainable Future* (WHAT, 2000) encourages joined-up policy-making and mainstreaming of sustainable resource management, the protection of workers' rights and environmental protection in key institutions such as the World Trade Organization (WTO), the World Bank and the International Monetary Fund (IMF). It calls for a strengthening of the United Nations Environment Programme (UNEP) and increasing environmental finance – for example, via the Global Environment Facility (GEF). In addition, it calls on governments, with support from across society, to ratify and implement existing global environmental agreements, such as the Kyoto Protocol to the United Nations Framework Convention on Climate Change (UNFCCC) and the United Nations Convention on the Non-navigational Use of Water. It calls for enhancing the accountability of the UN through establishing a second chamber or People's Assembly, which brings together a wide representation of civil society to enable a more bottom-up view when addressing 'global commons' issues.
- *Rethink the global market system:* there is a need to phase out distorting subsidies that encourage unsustainable harvesting. The perverse subsidy systems in developed countries are crippling countries in sub-Saharan Africa, as well as elsewhere in the developing world. Enhanced market operations to better include environmental and social goods and services with economic systems are also required. In addition, strengthening the regulation of global competition, as well as international tax-gathering and inspection systems, is required in order to encourage the effective regulation and functioning of international trade. *Governance for a Sustainable Future* also calls for the establishment of a global regulatory framework for the operation of transnational corporations, with global standards on the environment and on social and economic behaviour.
- *New development models: Governance for a Sustainable Future* calls for a move away from the Western model of industrial development, taking full account of the need for sustainable resource use and ecological constraints throughout the programmes and policies of international agencies. In addition, it highlights the need for a better understanding of local circumstances and priorities in all countries, as well as for more effective partnerships between countries and across regions – addressing the links between rural and urban areas.
- *Improved international management:* enhancing the transboundary management of water resources and other regional and global commons. This includes spreading good practice experiences, establishing a large sustainable development fund to support the transition to sustainable technologies, and governance and resource management in the South and in transitional economies.
- *Ownership access and common property rights:* seeking more equitable distribution and allocation of rights of access and sustainable use of resources such as

freshwater, fisheries and biodiversity. Establishing private resource rights on their own offers no guarantee of sustainable use and can entrench inequitable patterns of use, as well as being politically and culturally controversial. Thus, alternative models are required, such as common property resource management and tradable permit systems, which are used in certain fisheries and are now becoming established in carbon emission trading.

- *Building networks and changing values:* new networks that connect governments to civil society and link citizens in different sectors and countries are vital for learning about good practice, consensus-building and underpinning good governance systems. Such networks should be strengthened at national and international levels in order to foster commitment and democratization of the global system. Communicating to consumers remains a crucial aspect of changing values. Governments, non governmental organizations (NGOs) and the private sector can play their part in encouraging people to look at their consumption patterns and in leading by example. Formal education could do more to promote sustainable principles and values, as could the media and the internet, making them more accessible to the public as a whole.
- *Monitoring and research:* cross-cutting analysis and research are also essential in order to build up the political debate and organizational capacity needed to confront to the challenges of managing complex joined-up systems, integrated with national sustainable development strategies, regional frameworks and, globally, via coordinating bodies such as the United Nations Commission on Sustainable Development (CSD).

National reform

- *National policy frameworks:* promote national policy change and more coherent national policy by institutionalizing horizontal linkages across sectors and ministries. Encourage partnership arrangements with business and voluntary sectors, as well as bottom-up links between national, regional and local governments, not only to empower local action by citizens and local government, but to redefine the role of national government as a facilitator and collator of strategic cross-disciplinary perspectives.
- *New economic indicators:* establish better sustainability 'signals' to indicate the status of key resources, the economy and society as a whole. These indicators measure resource stocks and flows, and calculate more realistic economic values of natural assets. For developing countries, in particular, international aid agencies should help to stimulate conservation programmes and to ensure that donor programmes within countries take into account their broad sustainable development impacts.
- *Technological improvement, product substitution and eco-efficiency:* governments should promote better production and consumption of natural resources. Environmentally sustainable technologies and socially appropriate technologies should be encouraged in the private sector in order to contribute to key international agreements, such as the Kyoto Protocol.

themselves in order to face up to and meet the challenges of sustainability. The steady push towards market liberalization and globalization contrasts sharply with the voices of protest from those increasingly left further and further behind.

Taking this as our starting point, the first three chapters of the book provide an overview of the three pillars of sustainability: environment, society and economics. They examine the governance and political architecture, demonstrating the considerable crossover between each issue addressed in the section and emphasizing the point that one cannot look at these areas in isolation.

Chapter 3 looks at the foundations of global governance from an environmental perspective and sets the scene for the rest of the book by touching on some of the origins of the concept of governance, as well as examining the international architecture that has developed around environmental issues. Like the original WHAT report, the chapter contrasts the current fragmented and weak environmental bodies with the influence and resources of the global economic institutions. The institutional gaps identified undermine the environmental frameworks and relate to a lack of jurisdiction where key bodies, such as UNEP, lack the mechanisms and authority to tackle environmental disputes and inaction. In addition the chapter touches upon three other critical gaps: poor information, the North–South divide and the implementation gap. The policy implications of addressing these gaps range from a fundamental reform of the current architecture to 'act as a counterbalance' to the economic giants, through to adopting a more multidimensional governance structure, one that is sufficiently flexible to recognize that different environmental issues require action and a response at different levels.

Shifting to the 'problem' of governing the global economy, Chapter 4 puts a special twist on the debate by drawing on linkages of economic frameworks with the Millennium Development Goals (MDGs) and climate change. The chapter argues that the problem can be practically demonstrated by the dichotomy between the demands of the global economic players on the poorest countries to fit into their 'market-shaped box' and the reality for the people in those countries who face death and destitution as a consequence of their governments' spiralling debt repayments. The chapter goes on to present the burgeoning popularity of what Andrew Simms calls 'the conference express', where governments meet, at huge expense, to solve the world's problems through agreeing yet another international declaration: good words that somehow fail to result in action on the ground. Running through six of the eight MDGs, the chapter succinctly demonstrates how a failure to act comprehensively on interrelated global issues, in this instance climate change, will only serve to deepen the numbers of poor, starving, sick, uneducated and excluded. The answer he suggests, like that in Chapter 3, is a reorientation of the economic architecture and a rebalancing of the global system.

In Chapter 5, the third overview chapter, we are presented with emerging forms of social engagement that offer new tools to support sustainable decision-making. Multi-stakeholder processes have gained increasing importance, and it is noted that the role of government has changed from one of 'direct service provider' to one in which they must 'engage and manage external partners'. The chapter comments on the challenges of adopting this new approach to decision-making, as it requires considerable time, resources, transparency, pre-established ground rules, effective facilitation and a clear link with formal decision-making processes. It also looks at the growing prominence of partnerships in the UN, highlighting the challenges of establishing trust and balancing the interests of different groups in the process. Comparing and contrasting examples of participation from global to local spheres, the chapter is unwavering in the view that participation is an essential tool to promote and implement sustainable development action across all spheres of governance.

In Part 2 of the book we look at governance and sustainability through the 'lens' of five thematic issues: water, energy, health, food and agriculture, and biodiversity. These five issues were identified by the UN Secretary General Kofi Annan in 2001 as the most pressing global priorities of our generation, and are more commonly referred to as the WEHAB agenda.

Seeking clarity about the definition of the governance of water, Chapter 6 points out that governance is more than just 'government'. The chapter suggests that governance denotes the interplay between government and society, influencing both formal and informal processes. The chapter looks at the emergence of integrated water resource management (IWRM) as a key tool for sustainable water use, and recognizes that good systems of governance are a prerequisite for IWRM to properly function. Some of the problems of governance that are rife in the water sector are outlined – from the international to local levels. A key challenge pointed to is the transboundary nature of water, traversing national territories, each country with their contrasting water laws and practices. In addition, the chapter notes that financial systems have exacerbated inefficient water management, such as the perverse subsidies for irrigation and agriculture. It comments that private-sector involvement has not always resulted in positive outcomes, in part linked to issues of corruption and poor regulatory capacity. The chapter argues that greater support for strengthening the capacity of local and regional government is needed. It also describes some core principles to further embed good water governance.

Taking on the energy sector in Chapter 7, we find an even stronger view of the market distortions inherent in the international system. The chapter presents to us the overt bias of the development banks and export credit agencies towards the fossil fuel industry and the consequential impact on climate change. It blames part of the problem on a lack of transparency in the international financial community. The chapter expresses hope that the MDGs and commitments set at the World Summit on Sustainable Development (WSSD) may help to shift the priorities of these monetary monoliths to take a stronger focus on promoting renewables and on providing efficient and affordable energy to the poorest in communities. One of the innovations suggested is to create a protocol to the Nuclear Non-proliferation Treaty – a 'renewable energy proliferation treaty' – to begin to legitimize renewables as real energy alternatives. Nationally, it appears that corruption, similar to the water sector, is further exacerbating unsustainable energy practice. At a minimum, the chapter hopes that national energy strategies can be brought in line with broader national sustainable development and poverty reduction strategies. Similarly, it calls for a strengthening of those institutions working to promote renewable energies.

Chapter 8 returns to the issue of institutional complexity in addressing the governance of the health sector. Like the call for IWRM, it is emphasized that inter-sectoral action is essential as 'many of the key determinants and solutions to health and disease lie outside the direct realm of the health sector, in sectors concerned with environment, water and sanitation, agriculture education, employment, urban and rural livelihoods, trade, tourism, industrial development energy and housing'. Outlining a whole range of governance obstacles that continue to block a more integrated approach, the chapter cites insufficient funding, weak administration, poor political commitment and coordination as major barriers in the current system. Giving the example of recent developments in the chemicals industry, the chapter emphasizes that inter-sectoral planning and action are possible. National health action plans are one mechanism, again like IWRM, which it is argued can support a more coordinated approach at a national level. Similarly, the emergence of Local Environment and Health Action Plans (LEHAPs), linked to Local Agenda 21 initiatives, has produced some positive local results in the health sector. Transboundary health problems, such as those caused by air and water pollution, remain a challenge. Chapter 8 notes that, in this case, inter-jurisdictional mechanisms are required. The recommendations tie in very closely with the original WHAT report in calling for greater horizontal and vertical linkages. Crucially, the chapter calls for national and local capacity-building, involving both government institutions and stakeholders.

Turning to look at agriculture and food security, Chapter 9 describes the innumerable governance failures at national and local levels, which, for developing and industrialised countries alike, have resulted in varying degrees of unsustainable farming. At one end of the scale, the chapter points to poverty and environmental damages derived from unsuitable farming techniques in many parts of Africa and Asia. On the other end, intensive farming, excessive use of pesticides and distorting subsidies across Europe, North America, Japan and elsewhere are punishing the environment and society in another way. It is argued that taking a rural 'public good' approach could improve governance in the agricultural sector. Various activities are referred to in favour of promoting farm productivity, food security and the rural environment. Further calls are made for anti-corruption measures or democratization to assist the accountability of institutions and the greater inclusion of key groups such as women in policy-making. Global institutions such as the WTO have been slow to shift these distortions. The chapter further criticizes the impact of the World Bank's structural adjustment processes on developing countries for indirectly reducing government investment in critical public goods such as education, health and infrastructure. Interestingly, the chapter finds that the greatest change needs to come from national rather than global levels.

Finally, we come to Chapter 10 on biodiversity. Here we find a crystallization of many of the issues presented to us in the previous chapters. The chapter takes us on a journey from global to local governance issues relating to biodiversity. It provides several examples of the impacts of other sectors on biodiversity, demonstrating yet again the interconnection between policies and institutions across various sectors. Within the UN, it is argued that good governance will require connections to be made between the Millennium Development Goals and the sustainable development agenda. The chapter presents a real institutional challenge for the development arm of the UN. The example is cited of the Monterrey Financing for Development conference, which barely made any general environment connections and certainly did not address biodiversity. Similarly, when the chapter turns to the trade agenda, the tussle to link trade with wider sustainability concerns continues. Looking more regionally, the chapter appears more hopeful that cooperation might be possible, listing a number of recent process strategies that have emerged in support of biodiversity governance. One challenge pointed to at the national level, like the other WEHAB issues, is that of linking the biodiversity agenda to broader sustainable development processes. Locally, capacity-building needs again to come to the fore, as the chapter talks about communities being unprepared to take on integrated management approaches required at the local level. The chapter ends by making the point that the links between biodiversity and geopolitical security are poorly recognized or understood. This is a point that could be applied to each of the WEHAB issues. Surely the unsustainable governance of each of these basic areas of need can only exacerbate the problems of instability, conflict and insecurity.

The future

The choice is clear. We can correct the global governance deficit in the world today, ensure accountability and adopt coherent policies that forge a path for globalization that is fair and just, both within and between countries; or we can prevaricate and risk a slide into further spirals of insecurity, political turbulence, conflicts and wars (World Commission on the Social Dimension of Globalization, 2004).

The key point of the WHAT *Governance for a Sustainable Future* report – moving from principles to action – is also the key challenge set at the World Summit on Sustainable Development in Johannesburg, in 2002, the ten-year follow-up to the Rio Earth Summit. At the WSSD, governments, international agencies and representatives from across society asked the question: why have we only seen pockets of success when it comes to implementing sustainable development? The challenges and barriers preventing progress appear to be the same problems that the WHAT commission summarized. First, there is a continued dominance of economic policies over and above social and environmental priorities. Second, and perhaps more fundamentally, we have enjoyed the cumulative effect of a whole set of governance failures: from weak vertical and horizontal institutional coordination, to a growing democratic deficit; from poor support for and communication of good science and information, to an underlying lack of political will and understanding of how to effectively implement sustainable policies. Of course, a perfect system of governance is something of a utopian goal. However, as the WHAT report highlights, we have long known about many of the more obvious problems and we have had at our disposal many of the mechanisms that will solve them.

Both the WHAT report and this book call for a sense of urgency. At the opening of the 12th session of the UN Commission on Sustainable Development (CSD) in May 2004 the UN Secretary General Kofi Annan said: 'The natural resource base is under siege. Unsustainable patterns of consumption and production are still the norm. Progress in slowing deforestation and biodiversity loss has been glacial. The AIDS epidemic is an enormous and still growing burden.'

However, it seems that current international events have shifted the attention of the international community away from the vital long-term concerns of sustainable development back towards more divisive geopolitical short-termism. As Annan pointed out, high-level political attention has been diverted 'by the recent emphasis given to terrorism, weapons of mass destruction, and the war in Iraq'. He argues: 'However understandable that focus might be, we cannot lose any more time, or ground, in the wider struggle for human well-being. Just as we need balanced development, so do we need a balanced international agenda.'

Perhaps at the heart of the problem is the fact that sustainable development continues to be thought of as 'an issue' – a passing fashionable catchphrase, something that one addresses amongst a whole plethora of other global concerns and priorities. This totally misses the point. It is sustainable development that *defines* how we *do* good governance. Sustainable development is a *process*. It is a method of structuring our thinking, our decisions and our actions in order to ensure that we achieve the inherent principles and values of good governance. Sustainable development is the blueprint upon which all systems of governance should be based.

The following chapters seek to present this approach from the perspective of different issues. Each chapter presents central questions that we must begin to address if we are to take seriously the need for change.

Note

1   G8 is defined as the Group of 8 industrialized countries: the UK, Canada, France, Germany, Italy, Japan, Russia and the US.

References

Hardin, G. (1968) 'The tragedy of the commons'. *Science*, vol 162, pp1243–1248

NGLS (Non-governmental Liaison Service) (2004) 'World Commission says globalization can and must change, calls for rethink of global governance'. Non-governmental Liaison Service news item, 24 February 2004

UN (United Nations) (2004) 'Secretary-general's remarks to the UN Commission on Sustainable Development'. New York, 28 April 2004, Secretary General, Office of the Spokesman, available at www.un.org/apps/sg/sgstats.asp?nid=899

WHAT (World Humanity Action Trust) (2000) *Governance for a Sustainable Future*. Report by the World Humanity Action Trust, Stakeholder Forum publication, available at www.stakeholderforum.org/policy/governance/future.pdf

World Commission on the Social Dimension of Globalization (2004) Report of the Commission, ILO, February 2004, available at www.ilo.org/public/english/fair globalization/report

2

Outcomes from the World Summit for Sustainable Development

Georgina Ayre and Rosalie Callway

The Johannesburg Plan of Implementation (JPOI) is the key document agreed at the Johannesburg World Summit on Sustainable Development (WSSD). The final agreement was seen by many as flawed, lacking somewhat in terms of structure and coherent objectives. However, the agreement did manage to produce more than was expected, taking into account the political climate under which it was negotiated in 2002. Within the JPOI's 11 chapters there are a number of clear time-bound targets and softer commitments for undertaking action in support of sustainable development. Chapter XI on 'Institutional frameworks for sustainable development' deals exclusively with issues of governance. The chapter presents a set of commitments that support enhancing governance systems for sustainable development at all levels.

This chapter aims to provide a broad overview of the outcomes from the WSSD and addresses some of its possible strategic implications in terms of the future implementation of the commitments made.

There are several potential strategic implications from the JPOI that global and regional institutions, as well as national, regional and local government, will have to face should they rise to the challenges posed by Johannesburg. These implications are addressed in the chapter under the following headings: partnerships; institutional strengthening and capacity-building; integrated management and ecosystem approach; legal and regulatory frameworks; horizontal coordination and cooperation; vertical coherence; and good governance.

Broad outcomes

What actually happened at the summit? Over 20,000 people attended the global meeting, including 10,000 government delegates, 8000 representatives from the major groups[1], 2000 from the business sector and 4000 people from the media. It was described as having an atmosphere 'something like a zoo'. The United Nations (UN) spent an estimated US$1.2 million on administering the entire two weeks. So what was agreed to justify all these people and expense?

There were three official outcomes – the 'Type I' government agreements, which included the Johannesburg Plan of Implementation (JPOI) (see Box 2.1), a 'Political Declaration' and a set of 'Type II' partnership for sustainable development initiatives. The JPOI produced new global sustainability targets and some more generalized commitments (see Table 2.1), whilst governments and stakeholder groups also presented their own initiatives and commitments (see Box 2.2).

Time-bound targets

A recommitment to each of the Millennium Development Goals (MDGs) agreed at the Millennium Development Summit in 2000 is made in the JPOI. There are also over 20 new time-bound targets in the agreement (see Table 2.1). However, many of these targets are weakly worded and lack clear action-orientated obligations. Two further time-bound targets, on renewable energy and energy subsidies, were negotiated out of the text.

Another target was also controversial. The five-year review of Rio in 1997 committed governments to 'the formulation and elaboration of national strategies for sustainable development' by the year 2002. This date was revised at Johannesburg to a later commitment of 2005. The US was criticized during the summit for its lack of willingness to commit to this, as well as other time-based targets. However, as one US official stated, 'I don't know of a single goal that has protected a child from a waterborne disease or provided energy to a village. Goals do not by themselves bring about change or results.' One might sympathize with this view. It seems pointless to agree to a target that will, in reality, never be met. The European Union (EU) argued, on the other hand, that targets are valuable in that they create benchmarks and political momentum, and provide an end goal that can then be broken down into intermediate steps and work programmes in order to make the targets deliverable.

Relationship between the World Trade Organization and the United Nations

At the WSSD, Multilateral Environmental Agreements (MEAs) and international trade agreements were pitted head to head. Since Rio+5 in 1997 there has been much discussion about the possible conflict between the World Trade Organization (WTO), MEAs and other environmental protection measures. On the one hand, this debate has fueled some support for the establishment of an environmental body to act as a counterbalance to the WTO; on the other hand, it has resulted in developed countries being accused of eco-protectionism, preventing developing countries from accessing their trading markets. However, this is an area that remains unresolved. Language was agreed in Johannesburg to promote 'mutual supportiveness' between the two international regimes, which essentially retained the status

---

Box 2.1 Structure of the Johannesburg Plan of Implementation

I   *Introduction*: the United Nations Conference on Environment and Development (UNCED); sustainable development for all; partnerships; good governance; peace, security, stability and respect for human rights and fundamental freedoms;

II   *Poverty eradication*: including eradicating poverty; drinking water and sanitation; energy services for sustainable development; contribution of industrial development to poverty eradication and sustainable natural resource management; slum dwellers; and child labour;

III   *Changing unsustainable patterns of consumption and production*: including sustainable consumption and production; corporate environmental and social responsibility and accountability; sustainable development in decision-making; energy; transport; minimizing waste and maximizing reuse, recycling and use of environmentally friendly alternatives; and the sound management of chemicals;

IV   *Protecting and managing the natural resource base of economic and social development*: including water; conservation of oceans, seas, islands and coastal areas; vulnerability, risk assessment and disaster management; climate change; agriculture; United Nations Convention to Combat Desertification; mountain ecosystems; sustainable tourism development; biodiversity; forests; and mining, minerals and metals;

V   *Sustainable development in a globalizing world*;

VI   *Health and sustainable development*;

VII   *Sustainable development of Small Island Developing States (SIDS)*;

VIII   *Sustainable development for Africa*;

IX   *Other regional initiatives*: including sustainable development in Latin America and the Caribbean, Asia and the Pacific, West Asia, and Economic Commission for Europe regions;

X   *Means of implementation*;

XI   *Institutional framework for sustainable development*: strengthening the institutional framework for sustainable development at the international, regional and national levels, as well as participation of major groups.

---

quo. The ongoing debate over the superiority of MEAs and the WTO, and the ability of countries not signatory or members to either the WTO or a particular MEA illustrates the tension and institutional overlap, in relation to the resolution of disputes between international agreements, which exist in the UN and in other multilateral bodies such as the WTO. Unfortunately, the WSSD did little to move the debate beyond this impasse.

Table 2.1 *World Summit on Sustainable Development (WSSD) time-bound targets*

Issue	Targets
Poverty eradication	• Poverty: halve, by the year 2015, the proportion of the world's people whose income is less than US$1 a day (JPOI II.7.a) [1]. • Hunger: halve, by the year 2015, the proportion of people who suffer from hunger (JPOI IV.40.a) [1]. • Slums: by 2020, achieve a significant improvement in the lives of at least 100 million slum dwellers, as proposed in the Cities without Slums initiative (JPOI II.11) [1]. • Poverty fund: establish a World Solidarity Fund to eradicate poverty and to promote social and human development in developing countries (JPOI II.7.b).
Water and sanitation	• Drinking water: halve, by the year 2015, the proportion of people without access to safe drinking water (JPOI II.8 and IV.25.a) [1]. • Sanitation: halve, by the year 2015, the proportion of people who do not have access to basic sanitation (JPOI IV.25.a) [2]. • Integrated management: develop integrated water resources management and water efficiency plans by 2005 (JPOI IV.26) [2].
Sustainable production and consumption	• Production and consumption: encourage and promote the development of a ten-year framework of programmes to accelerate the shift towards sustainable consumption and production (JPOI III.15).
Energy	• Access: improve access to reliable, affordable, economically viable, socially acceptable and environmentally sound energy services and resources, sufficient to achieve the MDGs, including the goal of halving the proportion of people in poverty by 2015 (JPOI II.9) [2]. • Supply: diversify energy supply and substantially increase the global share or renewable energy in order to increase the renewable contribution to total energy supply (JPOI III.20.e). • Markets: remove market distortions, including restructuring of taxes and phasing out harmful substances. Improve functioning, transparency and information about energy markets with respect to both supply and demand, with the aim of achieving greater stability and ensuring consumer access to energy services (JPOI III.20.p). • Efficiency: establish domestic programmes for energy efficiency with the support of the international community. Accelerate the development and dissemination of energy efficiency and energy conservation technologies, including the promotion of research and development (JPOI III. 20.b, c, h, i, k and III.21).
Chemicals	• Health: aim, by 2020, to use and produce chemicals in ways that do not lead to significant adverse effects on human health and the environment (JPOI III.23) [2].

Table 2.1 *Continued.*

Issue	Targets
	• International agreements: promote the ratification and implementation of relevant international instruments on chemicals and hazardous waste, including the Rotterdam Convention so that it can enter into force by 2003 and the Stockholm Convention so that it can enter into force by 2004 (JPOI III.23.a) [2].
	• Management: further develop a strategic approach to international chemicals management, based on the Bahia Declaration and Priorities for Action beyond 2000, by 2005 (JPOI III.23.b) [2].
	• Classification: encourage countries to implement the new globally harmonized system for the classification and labelling of chemicals as soon as possible, with a view to having the system fully operational by 2008 (JPOI III.23.c) [2].
	• Renew commitment to the sound management of chemicals and of hazardous wastes throughout their life cycle (JPOI III.23).
Oceans and fisheries	• Ecosystem approach: encourage the application, by 2010, of the ecosystem approach for the sustainable development of the oceans (JPOI IV.30.d) [2].
	• Fish stocks: on an urgent basis, and where possible by 2015, maintain or restore depleted fish stocks to levels that can produce the maximum sustainable yield (JPOI IV.31.a) [2].
	• Fishing: put into effect the United Nations Food and Agriculture Organization (FAO) international plans of action by the agreed dates: for the management of fishing capacity by 2005; and to prevent, deter and eliminate illegal, unreported and unregulated fishing by 2004 (JPOI IV.31.d).
	• Tools: develop and facilitate the use of diverse approaches and tools, including the ecosystem approach, the elimination of destructive fishing practices, the establishment of marine protected areas consistent with international law and based on scientific information, including representative networks by 2012 (JPOI IV.32.c) [2].
	• Reporting: establish by 2004 a regular process under the UN for global reporting and assessment of the state of the marine environment (JPOI IV.36.b) [2].
	• Subsidies: eliminate subsidies that contribute to illegal, unreported and unregulated fishing and to overcapacity (JPOI IV.31.f).
	• Governance: establish an effective, transparent and regular inter-agency coordination mechanism on ocean and coastal issues within the UN system (JPOI IV.30.c).
Atmosphere	• Ozone: facilitate implementation of the Montreal Protocol on Substances that Deplete the Ozone Layer by ensuring

Table 2.1 *Continued.*

Issue	Targets
	adequate replenishment of its fund by 2003/2005 (JPOI IV.39.b) [2].
	• Access to alternatives to ozone-depleting substances: improve access by developing countries to alternatives to ozone depleting substances, by 2010, and assist them in complying with the phase-out schedule under the Montreal Protocol (JPOI IV.39.d) [2].
Biodiversity	• Biodiversity loss: achieve, by 2010, a significant reduction in the current rate of loss of biological diversity (JPOI IV.40).
Forests	• Assessment: intensify efforts on reporting to the United Nations Forum on Forests to contribute to an assessment of progress in 2005 (JPOI IV.45.b) [2].
	• Action: accelerate implementation of the Intergovernmental Panel on Forests (IPF)/Intergovernmental Forum on Forests (IFF) proposals for action by countries and by the Collaborative Partnership on Forests (JPOI IV.45.g).
Corporate responsibility	• Promotion: actively promote corporate responsibility and accountability, including, through the development and implementation of international agreements and measures, international initiatives and public–private partnerships, and appropriate national regulations (JPOI V.49).
Health	• Health literacy: enhance health education with the objective of achieving improved health literacy on a global basis by 2010 (JPOI VI.54.e) [2].
	• Mortality of children: develop programmes and initiatives to reduce, by 2015, mortality rates for infants and children under five years by two-thirds, and maternal mortality rates by three-quarters, of the prevailing rate in 2000 (JPOI VI.54.f) [1].
	• HIV/AIDS: reduce HIV prevalence among young men and women aged 15 to 24 years by 25 per cent in the most affected countries by 2005 and globally by 2010, as well as combat malaria, tuberculosis and other diseases (JPOI VI.55) [1].
Sustainable development of Small Island Developing States (SIDS)	• Global Programme of Action (GPA): undertake initiatives by 2004 aimed at implementing the Global Programme of Action for the Protection of the Marine Environment from Land-based Activities to reduce, prevent and control waste and pollution and their health-related impacts (JPOI VII.58.e) [2].
	• Tourism: develop community-based initiatives on sustainable tourism by 2004 (JPOI VII.58.g) [2].
	• Energy: support the availability of adequate, affordable and environmentally sound energy services for the sustainable development of small island developing states, including through strengthening efforts on energy supply and services by 2004 (JPOI VII.59.a) [2].

Table 2.1 *Continued.*

Issue	Targets
Sustainable development for Africa	• Barbados Programme: review implementation of the Barbados Programme of Action for the Sustainable Development of Small Island Developing States in 2004 (JPOI VII.61) [2]. • Agriculture: improve sustainable agricultural productivity and food security in accordance with the Millennium Development Goals, in particular to halve by 2015 the proportion of people who suffer from hunger (JPOI VIII.67) [2]. • Food security: support African countries in developing and implementing food security strategies by 2005 (JPOI VIII.67.a) [2]. • Energy: support Africa's efforts to implement the New Plan for African Development (NEPAD) objectives on energy, which seek to secure access for at least 35 per cent of the African population within 20 years, especially in rural areas (JPOI VIII.67.j.i) [2].
Means of implementation	• Education: ensure that, by 2015, all children will be able to complete a full course of primary schooling and that girls and boys will have equal access to all levels of education relevant to national needs (JPOI VIII.62.e, X.116.a and X.117.g) [1]. • Gender equity: eliminate gender disparity in primary and secondary education by 2005 (JPOI X.120) [4]. • Education for sustainable development: recommend to the United Nations General Assembly that it consider adopting a decade of education for sustainable development, starting in 2005 (JPOI X.124.a) [2].
Institutional framework	• National strategies: take immediate steps to make progress in the formulation and elaboration of national strategies for sustainable development and begin their implementation by 2005 (JPOI XI.162) [3]. • Governance: adopt new measures to strengthen institutional arrangements for sustainable development at international, regional, national and local levels (JPOI XI.139). • Commission on Sustainable Development (CSD): enhance the role of the CSD, including through reviewing and monitoring progress in implementation of Agenda 21 and fostering coherence of implementation, initiatives and partnerships (JPOI XI.145). • Integrated approach: facilitate the integration of environmental, social and economic dimensions of sustainable development into the work programmes of the UN regional commissions (JPOI XI.160, 160.a–160.d).

Notes: JPOI = Johannesburg Plan of Implementation; [1] = reaffirmation of Millennium Development Goals (MDGs); [2] = new target; [3] = reaffirmation of 1992 Rio Earth Summit target; [4] = reaffirmation of Dakar Framework for Action on Education for All
Source: adapted from UN DESA (2002) and UN (2002)

Box 2.2 Examples of commitments at the World Summit on Sustainable Development (WSSD)

Asia Development Bank

- US$5 million grant to United Nations Human Settlements Programme (UN-Habitat) and US$500 million in fast-track credit for the Water for Asian Cities Programme.

European Union

- Water for Life initiative: partnerships for meeting the goal on water and sanitation, primarily in Central Asia and Africa;
- US$700 million Partnership Initiative on energy;
- nine major electricity companies with the UN signed up to a range of programmes to coordinate technical cooperation for sustainable energy projects in developing nations;
- US$80 million committed to the replenishment of the Global Environment Facility (GEF).

South Africa

- Eskom (Energy Utility Company): partnership to extend modern energy services to neighbouring countries.

US

- US$970 million in investments over the next three years in sanitation and water projects;
- US$43 million to be invested in energy in 2003;
- US$2.3 billion through 2003 on health (a proportion of this had previously been allocated to the Global Fund);
- US$90 million in 2003 for sustainable agricultural programmes;
- US$53 million for forests between 2002–2005.

Financial commitments

Whilst there were a number of financial announcements made during the WSSD, much of this money appears to have been recycled from commitments made at previous international meetings, such as at the UN Financing for Development conference that took place in Monterrey in early 2002. After Monterrey there were some expectations that the US would spend some of the money committed at WSSD, particularly on water and energy. The EU was more progressive in this regard, outlining a timetabled plan for how member states would aim to reach the target of 0.7 per cent of national gross domestic product (GDP) being given as Official Development Assistance (ODA) by 2010. Debt relief and debt cancellation were also weakly addressed. The ever-controversial area of global public goods also saw a direct reference removed from the text, to be replaced by the watered-down commitment to examine 'issues of global public interest'. Little by way of tangible outcomes was therefore achieved in the financial arena.

Governance outcomes

Looking more specifically at governance issues, the JPOI details broad commitments for institutional enhancement. In the introduction to Chapter XI, it states:

> *Measures to strengthen sustainable development institutional arrangements at all levels should be taken within the framework of Agenda 21 and should build on developments since UNCED, and should lead to the achievement of,* inter alia, *the following objectives:*
>
> *(a) strengthening commitments to sustainable development;*
> *(b) integration of the economic, social and environmental dimensions of sustainable development in a balanced manner;*
> *(c) strengthening of the implementation of Agenda 21, including through the mobilization of financial and technological resources, as well as capacity-building programmes, particularly for developing countries;*
> *(d) strengthening coherence, coordination and monitoring;*
> *(e) promoting the rule of law and strengthening of governmental institutions;*
> *(f) increasing effectiveness and efficiency through limiting overlap and duplication of activities of international organizations, within and outside the United Nations system, based on their mandates and comparative advantages;*
> *(g) enhancing participation and effective involvement of civil society and other relevant stakeholders in the implementation of Agenda 21, as well as promoting transparency and broad public participation;*
> *(h) strengthening capacities for sustainable development at all levels, including the local level, in particular those of developing countries;*
> *(i) strengthening international cooperation aimed at reinforcing the implementation of Agenda 21 and the outcomes of the Summit* (JPOI, 2002, para 139).

Summarizing the main themes that relate to strategic or governance aspects, the JPOI can be said to raise issues in seven areas:

1   partnerships;
2   institutional strengthening and capacity-building;
3   integrated management and ecosystem approach;
4   legal and regulatory frameworks;
5   horizontal coordination and cooperation;
6   vertical coherence;
7   good governance.

Partnerships

Recognition of the vital role of partnerships was a key achievement of the WSSD. Some 220 partnership initiatives were launched during the summit.[2] If the Rio Earth Summit gave us the idea of involving stakeholders to deliver better informed decisions, then Johannesburg recognized that stakeholders should be involved in the practical delivery of the global agreements, including through what was coined 'multi-stakeholder partnerships' involving a range of interest groups.

The JPOI indicates the degree to which partnerships were prioritized by governments in the process, indicating that:

> . . . *implementation should involve all relevant actors through partnerships, especially between governments of the North and South, on the one hand, and between governments and major groups, on the other, to achieve the widely shared goals of sustainable development . . . such partnerships are key to pursuing sustainable development in a globalizing world (JPOI, 2002, para 3).*

The JPOI explicitly endorses Partnership Initiatives 'by all relevant actors to support the outcome of the World Summit on Sustainable Development' (JPOI, para 156.b). The Commission on Sustainable Development (CSD) is identified as the key global forum to 'serve as a focal point for the discussion of partnerships that promote sustainable development, including sharing lessons learned, progress made and best practices' (see Box 2.3). Multi-stakeholder processes were also identified in the JPOI as an important approach, including for assisting agricultural management and to be applied in the UN regional economic commissions. While these were valuable statements, there is a lack of clear political frameworks by which partnership processes would be supported.

Concerns about this policy gap were raised not only by non-governmental organizations (NGOs) but also by some governments regarding the poor connection between the JPOI and 'Type II' partnership initiatives. They questioned whether the Type IIs were merely being used by governments to relinquish the burden of responsibility for implementation, placing it entirely on the shoulders of the 'partners'. A number of NGOs also indicated that they were worried about several references to public–private partnerships (PPPs) in sections on agriculture, energy, water and trade. Such groups suggested that PPPs may not be suitable for all sectors and may not lead to sustainability outcomes. They called for a more flexible and accountable approach in developing Partnership Initiatives according to their needs.

Multilateral institutions are slowly beginning to take on board the need to support the involvement of different stakeholders; but this process needs to be considerably improved. In many international processes there remains no or little link between the engagement of stakeholders in 'interactive' dialogues and the 'formal' intergovernmental negotiating process. Perhaps the most advanced model of international stakeholder engagement was demonstrated at the Bonn International Freshwater Conference in 2001. The outcomes from the Ministerial Dialogue session that directly involved stakeholders were fed into the final text, which was then agreed. The preparations for the WSSD were designed on the

---

Box 2.3 Key Johannesburg Plan of Implementation references to partnerships

- *Partnerships*: general (JPOI 3, 125, 127.d, 139.g, 156.b, 168, 169); workplace partnerships and programmes (JPOI 18.d);
- *Agriculture*: general (JPOI 40.h, 40.j); production and food security (JPOI 7.j, 7.k);
- *Water*: drinking water and adequate sanitation (JPOI 8.f, 25.b); integrated water resource management (JPOI 26.g);
- *Energy* (JPOI 9.g, 20.g);
- *Corporate environmental and social responsibility and accountability* (JPOI 18.b);
- *Transport* (JPOI 21.b);
- *Waste*: general (JPOI 22); chemicals and hazardous wastes (JPOI 23.d);
- *Oceans*: fisheries (JPOI 31.g); Global Programme of Action (GPA) (JPOI 33.a);
- *Vulnerability, risk assessment* (JPOI 37.g);
- *Tourism* (JPOI 43.a);
- *Biodiversity* (JPOI 44.f);
- *Forests* (JPOI 45, 45.f);
- *Mining, minerals and metals* (JPOI 46.a);
- *Trade*: general (JPOI 96); globalization (JPOI 49); Doha and Monterrey commitments (JPOI 99);
- *Health*: healthcare (JPOI 54.e, 54.l); health impacts of air pollution (JPOI 56.a);
- *Small Island Developing States (SIDS)*: climate change (JPOI 58.j); environmentally sound energy (JPOI 59.a);
- *New Plan for African Development (NEPAD)*: marine environment (JPOI 62.i); energy (JPOI 62.j(i));
- *Latin America and Caribbean*: South–South cooperation (JPOI 74);
- *Technology*: tech-transfer (JPOI 106.a, 106.c); science and technology (JPOI 108, 103.e); Earth observation technologies (JPOI 132.c);
- *Rio Principle 10* (JPOI 128);
- *Research and education*: research (JPOI 108); education (JPOI 124.b);
- *Developing countries*: capacity-building (JPOI 125);
- *UN Commission on Sustainable Development (CSD)* (JPOI 145, 146, 148.b);
- *World Summit on Sustainable Development (WSSD) follow-up* (JPOI 156.b);
- *Regional commissions* (JPOI 160.b, 160.d);
- *National*: public participation (JPOI 164); sustainable development councils (JPOI 165);
- *Local*: Local Agenda 21 (JPOI 167);
- *Youth* (JPOI 170).

---

basis of a bottom-up process in order to ensure that the experiences of all stakeholders at all levels were included in the review of progress and the challenges that were impeding further implementation. Multi-stakeholder dialogues were held during each of the formal preparatory meetings and during the summit itself. In addition to this, a civil society forum was held during the course of the summit. Such a participatory process should have resulted in the full inclusion of stakeholder concerns and experiences in the negotiated outcomes. And while this was the case for some issues, on many others it was not. The central problem was that multi-stakeholder dialogues fell foul of being ineffective. They were poorly structured and were held in conjunction with, rather than in advance of, the governments' formal negations. This meant that civil society recommendations were not fed into the negotiations in a timely manner and resulted in an enormous amount of frustration by these groups at the summit. The need to have stakeholder models that create 'better informed decisions' will be critical to the future credibility and reputation of the UN and other intergovernmental bodies, including the WTO, the World Bank and the International Monetary Fund (IMF).

Institutional strengthening and capacity-building

Throughout the JPOI there are commitments to help build up institutional capacity in order to support sustainable development. A special emphasis is placed in the agreement on ensuring institutional strengthening in Africa, including commitments to the New Plan for African Development (NEPAD), to build up technological capacity, as well as environmental institutions. The implementation of NEPAD is being held under close scrutiny. Of particular interest is the degree to which NEPAD ensures transparency and supports the participation of stakeholder groups in its development, implementation and monitoring processes, as well as the level of commitment by the donor community to give Africa sufficient resources to enable it to develop itself is also of import.

The JPOI also renews international support for initiatives such as the United Nations Development Programme's (UNDP's) Capacity 21 initiative. The UNDP relaunched Capacity 21 at the WSSD to become 'Capacity 2015'. It seems to be applying lessons from Capacity 21's past experiences by encouraging better linkages between national strategies for sustainable development and poverty reduction strategies. It has also made a shift of emphasis to include not only the national level but also capacity-building at the local level.

Integrated management and ecosystem approach

A key governance principle to emerge from the 1992 Rio Earth Summit is the need to use integrated management of natural resources. The JPOI makes specific commitments to support integrated management of natural resources. It states that 'Managing the natural resources base in a sustainable and integrated manner is essential for sustainable development' (JPOI para 24) and includes commitments for integrated management of coastal zones, land and water. There is also a strong commitment to biodiversity in paragraph 44.b, which calls for the adoption of the ecosystem approach, as well as for the integration of the UN Convention on Biological Diversity (CBD) principles into national economic policies and international financial institutions. However, there is no consistency to this approach in the rest of the JPOI. Indeed, the chapters deal with issues in a 'ring-

---

Box 2.4 Johannesburg Plan of Implementation references to institutional strengthening and capacity-building

- *General:* at all levels (JPOI 139); evolutionary process (JPOI 157);
- *Global Environment Facility (GEF):* national institutions (JPOI 20.n);
- *Energy:* general (JPOI 20.s); Small Island Developing States (SIDS) national bodies (JPOI 59.b);
- *Oceans:* marine and coastal biological diversity (JPOI 32.b); Protection of the Marine Environment from Land-based Activities (JPOI 33.a);
- *Disasters:* vulnerability, risk assessment and disaster management (JPOI 37.b, 37.c);
- *Health and sustainable development* (JPOI 54.k);
- *Small Island Developing States (SIDS)* (JPOI 58.d);
- *Africa:* New Plan for African Development (NEPAD) (JPOI 62.b); science and technology (JPOI 62.d); research (JPOI 62.e); environmental legislation (JPOI 62.h); Africa and disaster management (JPOI 65.a); Africa, urbanization and human settlements (JPOI 71);
- *Partnerships* (JPOI 125);
- *Developing countries:* market information (JPOI 47.c); trade (JPOI 96.a); environmental technology transfer (JPOI 105.b); transfer technology (JPOI 106.b); centres of excellence (JPOI 20.l); participation (JPOI 125); capacity 21 (JPOI 127, a, b, c, d); donor support (JPOI 117, 129);
- *Regional:* (JPOI G);
- *National:* (JPOI H); infrastructure (JPOI 163).

---

fenced' manner, which is unlikely to be conducive to adopting a more integrated approach. It also seems that governments continue to disagree about the idea of interdependence between all ecosystems – another of the problem areas of the summit. The 'WEHAB' papers (on water; energy; health; food and agriculture; and biodiversity) produced by the Secretary General for the summit provide a useful example of how the JPOI could have adopted a more integrated approach.[3]

Key processes may help to further mobilize the principle of integration, including the CBD meetings,[4] the development of the United Nations Environment Programme's (UNEP's) Global Programme of Action (GPA)[5] and progress made on implementing integrated water resource management (IWRM) plans, involving groups such as the Global Water Partnership.[6]

Legal and regulatory frameworks

There is a strong emphasis in the JPOI on national responsibilities to enforce 'clear and effective laws that support sustainable development'. Some key commitments are made in support of strengthening the legal and regulatory architecture for thematic issues. On forests, for example, governments commit to:

Box 2.5 Johannesburg Plan of Implementation references to integrated management and the ecosystems approach

- *Integrated management of natural resources:* general (JPOI 24); oceans and coasts (JPOI 30.b, 30.e, 30.g); fisheries (JPOI 31.g); agriculture (JPOI 40, 40.b); UN Convention on Biological Diversity (CBD) (JPOI 44.a); forests (JPOI 45.f); integrated water resource management (IWRM) (JPOI 26, 66, 66.b); Africa and Information Communication Technology (ICT) (JPOI 69); West Asia and IWRM (JPOI 78);
- *Ecosystem approach:* fisheries (JPOI 30.d, 32.c); biodiversity (JPOI 44.e); sustainable tourism (JPOI 70.b).

Take immediate action on domestic forest law enforcement and illegal international trade in forest products, including in forest biological resources, with the support of the international community, and provide human and institutional capacity-building related to the enforcement of national legislation in those areas (JPOI, 2002, para 45.c).

There are also calls for the ratification of various multilateral agreements, including the 1982 Agreement on Straddling and Highly Migratory Fish Stocks, the Rotterdam Convention on Prior Informed Consent (PIC) Procedures for Certain Hazardous Chemicals and Pesticides in International Trade, the Stockholm Convention on Persistent Organic Pollutants (POPs), as well as the Kyoto Protocol to the Convention on Climate Change.

During the negotiations there was also a push for a new 'international regime to promote and safeguard the fair and equitable sharing of benefits arising out of the utilization of genetic resources'. This would be incorporated within the CBD and linked to progressing the Bonn Guidelines that specifically address the issue of benefit-sharing. Progress on the climate change agenda was perhaps the most surprising, with commitments to ratify the Kyoto Protocol being presented by Canada, Mexico, China and Russia. Russia's commitment is particularly significant since it contributes 17 per cent of all developed country carbon dioxide (CO_2) emissions – it led to the enforcement of the protocol when Russia finally ratified the agreement in 2004. However, without other key players, such as the US and Australia, it still remains a concern whether a sufficient level of CO_2 reductions will be obtained to fulfil the (albeit limited) targets of Kyoto.

Other relevant multilateral processes to follow where the JPOI established new targets include the Conference of the Parities (COP) for two key conventions relating to the management of chemicals: the Rotterdam Convention on Prior Informed Consent (PIC) and the Stockholm Convention on Persistent Organics Pollutants (POPs).

However, improving the coordination across the different Multilateral Environmental Agreements (MEAs) was left largely untouched by the WSSD; thus, further

---

Box 2.6 Johannesburg Plan of Implementation references on legal and regulatory frameworks

- *Energy:* general (JPOI 9.e); international financial institutions (IFIs) (20.j);
- *Production and consumption:* (JPOI 16);
- *Chemicals:* (JPOI 23);
- *Water:* (JPOI 26.b);
- *Oceans:* Law of the Sea (JPOI 30.a); fisheries (JPOI 31.b);
- *Radioactive wastes:* (JPOI 34.b);
- *Ozone:* (JPOI 38);
- *Land and water-use rights:* (JPOI 40.i);
- *Grasslands:* (JPOI 39.g);
- *Biodiversity:* (JPOI 44);
- *Forests:* (JPOI 45.c, 45.f);
- *Corporate accountability and responsibility:* (JPOI 47.a);
- *Unilateral measures:* (JPOI 102);
- *Foreign occupation:* (JPOI 103);
- *Environmentally sound technology:* (JPOI 105.d);
- *National legislative responsibility:* (JPOI 162.a);
- *Public participation:* (JPOI 146);
- *Institutional frameworks:* (JPOI 145.a).

---

opportunities will depend upon the work of environmental bodies, particularly UNEP.

Horizontal coordination and cooperation

There remains a considerable degree of crossover, duplication and conflict over the governance of many key issues relating to sustainable development. These problems will only begin to be tackled through greater vertical and horizontal integration of dialogue and decision-making across organizations. The JPOI contains many references that call for improved horizontal coordination. The section on the United Nations Economic and Social Council (ECOSOC) also creates an opportunity for strengthening this approach, where governments have committed to 'Increase [their] role in overseeing system-wide coordination and the balanced integration of economic, social and environmental aspects of United Nations policies and programmes aimed at promoting sustainable development'. The CSD was also requested to foster greater coherence between implementation and partnership processes. The section on water (JPOI, 2002, para 29) is particularly strong, calling on governments to:

> *Promote effective coordination among the various international and intergovernmental bodies and processes working on water-related issues, both within the United Nations system and between the United Nations and international financial*

institutions, drawing on the contributions of other international institutions and civil society to inform intergovernmental decision-making.

The UN system is called to establish an effective, transparent and regular inter-agency coordination mechanism, including on issues such as oceans and coasts. A stronger role for UNEP was also endorsed at the WSSD, including a commitment to provide more effective environmental coordination for the UN system at large.

A new UN reform process was launched at the United Nations General Assembly in 2003. The Secretary General released his report (UN, 2003), which touches upon the need for better coordination within the UN, as well as streamlining the institution. In the report he notes a vast number of 15,484 meetings and some 5879 reports were produced during a two-year period (2000–2001). The Secretary General called for better coordination and alignment of activities to priorities in various UN bodies in order to reduce the heavy burden placed on countries. The conclusions of two key UN research programmes should help support this process of enhancing the UN's effectiveness and focus. The UN University's Interlinkages Initiative made some key proposals on enhancing international environmental governance[7] and the UN World Institute for Development Economics Research (WIDER) report on *Governing Globalization: Issues and Institutions* (2002) deals with the relationship between the UN economic bodies, the WTO and the international financial institutions (IFIs).[8] In addition, the next few years will be a crucial testing time to see whether the Multilateral Environmental Agreements (MEAs) and the WTO trade agreements will be able to make any progress in clarifying their relationship.

Good governance

In a sense, all of the governance outcomes from the JPOI relate to establishing norms of good governance for sustainable development. However, the JPOI also includes specific references to the values and principles that should underlie the process.

The Rio Principles from the 1992 Rio Declaration outline many of the core elements of good governance for sustainable development, and were one of the major outcomes from the Rio Earth Summit. However, ten years on it seems that governments could not resist the opportunity to try and renegotiate what had already been agreed. References to the Rio Principles were seen as one of the most contentious areas within the JPOI negotiations. In particular, resolution could not be reached on the inclusion of the Precautionary Principle, the Principle of Common but Differentiated Responsibility and the Ecosystems Approach. The problems in negotiations became so extreme that a conflict resolution called a 'contact group' was set up to deal exclusively with the Rio Principles. During the discussions, reference to adopting the precautionary principle with regard to biodiversity conservation was dropped. Attempts to water down the wording on the precautionary 'approach' were made. This carried various implications, including implications for the precautionary treatment of new biotechnologies – for example, genetically modified organisms (GMOs). On the Principle of Common

---

Box 2.7 Johannesburg Plan of Implementation references on coordination and cooperation

- *Child labour:* (JPOI 13);
- *Energy:* (JPOI 20.s, u);
- *Water:* observation and research (JPOI 28); international and intergovernmental bodies (JPOI 27); UN bodies (JPOI 29);
- *Wetlands:* (JPOI 32.e);
- *Oceans:* sustainable fisheries (JPOI 30.f, 30.g, 31.g); oceans (JPOI 30.c);
- *Climate:* Vulnerability, risk assessment and disaster management (JPOI 35.j); climate change (JPOI 36.f); air pollution (JPOI 37);
- *Earth observation:* land, atmosphere and oceans (JPOI 38.h); technologies (JPOI 132.a);
- *Narcotics:* (JPOI 40.n);
- *Sustainable agricultural production and food security:* (JPOI 40.p);
- *Mountains:* (JPOI 42.a);
- *Tourism:* (JPOI 43.a, b);
- *Biodiversity:* (JPOI 42.q);
- *Forests:* (JPOI 45.e, f, i);
- *Trade:* technical assistance (JPOI 47.e); regional agreements (JPOI 51); World Trade Organization (WTO) (JPOI 90.d, 97, 97.c); Doha and Monterrey commitments (JPOI 100.a);
- *Health:* HIV/AIDS (JPOI 48.a);
- *Capacity-building:* developing countries (JPOI 110);
- *International:* law (JPOI 104); institutions (JPOI 140.b, 151.b), UN system (JPOI 142); United Nations Economic and Social Council (ECOSOC) (JPOI 144.a, 144.c); UN functional commissions and subsidiary bodies (JPOI 144.d);
- *Regions:* general (JPOI 72); Africa (JPOI 62, 62.b); Latin America and Caribbean (JPOI 73); regional commissions (JPOI 159).

---

but Differentiated Responsibility, the developed states argued that it should only refer to differential treatment on environmental issues, not to development and trade matters. This issue resulted in creating an impasse between developed and developing countries. In the end, much of the debacle was resolved by the introduction of a more general restatement of commitment to the Rio Principles as a whole. This was undeniably a poor outcome, and did not address the need for the wider application of these principles. The negotiations on the principles offer a clear case for the accusation that a number of the outcomes of the summit were regressive.

References to human rights, another important area of good governance, are also few and far between. However, principles of accountability and transparency do appear several times in the text, particularly in relation to key sectors, such as

---

Box 2.8 Key references to good governance in the Johannesburg Plan of Implementation

- *Good governance:* general (JPOI 138); Africa (JPOI 62.a); international level (JPOI 141);
- *Rio Principles:* (JPOI 8);
- *Transparency and accountability:* consumer information (JPOI 15.e); corporate responsibility and accountability (JPOI 18, 140.f); energy (JPOI 20.o); chemicals and hazardous wastes (JPOI 23); partnerships (JPOI 26.g); oceans and coasts and UN (JPOI 30.c); mining, minerals and metals (JPOI 46.a); international trade and finance institutions (JPOI 47.b, 86.a, 86.b); industrial sector in Africa (JPOI 62.g); water supply and sanitation (JPOI 66.a); public- and private-sector financing mechanisms (JPOI 86.e); trade and domestic regulation (JPOI 99.c); issues of global public interest (JPOI 114); implementation of Agenda 21 (JPOI 139.g); reform of international financial architecture (JPOI 141); administrative and judicial institutions (JPOI 163); member and observer states, environment and human rights (JPOI 169);
- *Human rights:* general (JPOI 5); rights of workers (JPOI 10.b); standard of living (JPOI 40.a); land and water (JPOI 40.i); indigenous knowledge (JPOI 44.j); intellectual property rights (JPOI 44.r); health (JPOI 54); New Plan for African Development (NEPAD) (JPOI 62.a); right to development (JPOI 5, 56.a, 138, 169); land and resources (JPOI 67.b); medicine (JPOI 100); UN Charter (JPOI 102); social services (JPOI 102); self determination (JPOI 103, 104); environment and human rights (JPOI 169).

---

water, energy, finance and trade. At the national level, the JPOI states that good governance is essential and should be based on:

- sound environmental, social and economic policies;
- democratic institutions that are responsive to the needs of the people;
- the rule of law;
- anti-corruption measures;
- gender equality;
- an enabling environment for investment (JPOI, 2002, para 4).

In terms of accountability, the JPOI commits governments to ensuring the completion of the United Nations Convention against Corruption. The adoption of the convention was, indeed, achieved in Merida, Mexico, in December 2004.[9] In addition, the United Nations Millennium Project has sought to improve transparency on the MDGs through monitoring and reporting on national progress.[10] The project has already undertaken 12 national pilot reports on national progress in implementation.

In relation to corporate governance, voluntary initiatives remained the preferred option at the WSSD. This is far from the Framework Agreement on Transnational Corporations (TNCs) that NGOs such as Friends of the Earth were demanding. However, a new consensus appeared to emerge on the need for mandatory standards. This will potentially open the way for discussions on legally binding global standards for business in the future. Those groups campaigning for a more legally binding approach for TNCs will continue to press for it in other arenas.

A ten-year work plan for sustainable production and consumption was initiated at the WSSD, which may carry implications for business. The Global Reporting Initiative (GRI) corporate sustainability reporting guidelines were also launched at the summit. GRI has since begun expanding its work by developing guidelines for specific sectors.[11]

Vertical coherence: Building from the base

We live in an increasingly interconnected, interdependent world. The local and the global are intertwined. Local government cannot afford to be insular and inward looking. Fighting poverty, exclusion and environmental decay is a moral issue, but also one of self-interest. Ten years after Rio, it is time for action by all spheres of government, all partners. And local action, undertaken in solidarity, can move the world (Local Government Declaration to the World Summit on Sustainable Development, 2002).

The JPOI says that good governance should apply to all levels. As Kofi Annan states in his report (UN, 2003): 'good governance at the local, national and international levels is perhaps the single most important factor in promoting development and advancing the cause of peace'. A real battle took place during the WSSD to retain the reference to the important role of the sub-national levels – local and regional. A number of developing countries were entirely opposed to any such references because they were unwilling to have the international community define areas that they considered to be a national responsibility. However, local government representatives attending the summit said that the WSSD outcomes must recognize:

- the importance of good local governance in creating sustainable communities;
- the urban dimension of sustainable development and the interdependence of urban and rural areas;
- the role of local governments in developing partnerships for sustainable development, working with national governments, international agencies and civil society;
- opportunities to promote and encourage diversified action at the local level.

Some of these principles have been adopted in the JPOI. Notably, in Chapter XI on 'Strengthening institutional frameworks', paragraphs 165–167 clearly support local authorities and encourage local-level action for accelerating implementation. Governments agreed to 'Enhance the role and capacity of local authorities as well

> ## Box 2.9 Key references to local action in the Johannesburg Plan of Implementation
>
> - *Poverty eradication:* national programmes (JPOI 7.c) and slum programmes (JPOI 11.e);
> - *Disaster prevention:* community-based management (JPOI 36.e); African assistance (JPOI 65.a);
> - *Sustainable agriculture:* land and water resources (JPOI 40.b, d);
> - *Desertification:* droughts and desertification (JPOI 41.b, e);
> - *Eco-tourism:* sustainable tourism, education and training programmes (JPOI 43, 43.b, 70.c);
> - *Capacity-building:* globalization, sustainable development programmes (JPOI 127.b, 139.h, 153).

as stakeholders in implementing Agenda 21 and the outcomes of the summit and in strengthening the continuing support for Local Agenda 21 programmes' (JPOI, 2002, para 167).

Other sections of the JPOI include strong recommendations for local action (see Box 2.9).

At the WSSD local authorities gathered to present a new phase of local engagement in sustainable development, calling it Local Action 21. The aim will be to develop specific action-focused strategies that will expand and accelerate implementation in more than 6000 communities that have already undertaken Local Agenda 21 processes across the globe. In a declaration to the WSSD they made a number of commitments to take this forward (see Box 2.10).

After the WSSD, Konrad Otto-Zimmermann, Secretary General of the International Council for Local Environmental Initiatives (ICLEI), wrote an article about what the move from the political agenda to action would look like. He stated, 'First, it will mean assisting communities to go beyond general sustainable development planning and address specific factors that prevent a great number of them from becoming sustainable: issues such as poverty; injustice, exclusion and conflict; unhealthy environment; and insecurity' (see www.iclei.org). The answer to tackling these issues he said was through 'pro-actively creating sustainable communities and cities'. He called for a greater link between local and global goals and he proposed that Local Action 21 should introduce and establish instruments of municipal management to ensure implementation, effective monitoring and continual improvement.

CSD 11: A programme for implementation

Set up in 1993 following the Rio Earth Summit, the Commission on Sustainable Development (CSD) is mandated with the task of carrying forward the

---

Box 2.10 Local Government Declaration to the World Summit on Sustainable Development

Commitments by local governments

We reaffirm our strong commitment to Agenda 21, and further commit ourselves ... [o]ver the next decade, to build upon the successes of Local Agenda 21 and accelerate implementation through Local Action 21 campaigns and programmes that create sustainable communities and cities while protecting global common goods (JPOI, 2002, para 6).

Requests to national governments

We ask our national governments ... [t]o launch and support national campaigns for local sustainable development planning and the protection of global common goods so as to support Local Action 21 (JPOI, 2002, para 8).

Johannesburg commitments, formally signed off at the United Nations General Assembly meeting in November 2002.

The 11th session of the CSD (CSD 11) in 2003 was the first substantive meeting of the CSD after the WSSD. Chaired by Vallie Moosa, Minister for the Environment and Tourism, South Africa, the primary objective of the meeting was to discuss and make decisions on the organizational reform and future work programme of the Commission, as mandated in the JPOI. The meeting successfully resulted in the adoption of the Resolution for the Future Programme, Organization and Methods of Work of the Commission on Sustainable Development.

The Resolution makes a number of specific commitments. While linking into other international commitments, such as achieving the Millennium Development Goals (MDGs), governments agreed that the principle focus of the CSD's work should be to contribute to 'advancing implementation of Agenda 21, the Programme for the Further Implementation of Agenda 21 [agreed at Rio+5] and the JPOI at all levels'. The decision states that the CSD's work programme will address:

- constraints and obstacles in the process of implementation;
- thematic cluster of issues for each two-year action-orientated 'implementation cycle' (see Table 2.2).

In essence, the Resolution outlines a multi-year programme of work built around a series of Implementation Cycles. These two-year cycles are focused on a predetermined cluster of issues. Included within the Resolution are decisions on the modalities for reporting on progress; guidance for partnerships and reporting on them; the role of the regional level; the involvement of major groups; and enhancement of UN system-wide coordination. A resounding message from the

CSD session was the need for greater consistency and coherence in policy-making, implementation and monitoring of major UN conferences. The JPOI provided a foundation for many of the decisions taken during the meeting.

Organizational reform

It is the function of the CSD to review and expedite the implementation of Agenda 21, the Programme for the Further Implementation of Agenda 21 and the Johannesburg Plan of Implementation through mobilization of stakeholders at all levels. In a clear change from the past ten years, the CSD adopted a multi-year programme of work featuring two-year implementation cycles. This consists of a Review Year and a Policy Year.

Year 1, the Review Year, will assess the overall implementation of sustainable development agreements, with a focused evaluation of, and report on, progress under the thematic cluster of issues for each particular year (see Table 2.2). This aims to improve understanding of challenges, obstacles and opportunities to implementation in these areas, with a view to informing policy discussions in the second year. Regional Implementation Meetings, which the Regional Economic Commissions were invited to organize, were recommended to take place during each Review Year – prior to the international Review Session. The involvement of the regional levels is an important one, providing evidence of the CSD's commitment to adopting a more bottom-up approach to policy and decision-making. This important step allows regions to identify solutions to obstacles and challenges, and to embrace new and emerging issues and opportunities specific to their region. Further innovation is shown in the decision to include partnership elements, including organizing a regular forum for the sharing of experience, best practice and capacity-building, as well as Partnership Fairs and Learning Centres during the governmental sessions.

Year 2, the Policy Year, serves as the policy- and decision-making year, culminating in an international Policy Session – an intergovernmental meeting that would conclude the implementation cycle. Each Policy Session will seek to take decisions to assist the further implementation of the issues being considered in that cycle. Although the Policy Sessions will predominantly be for negotiating decisions, they will also aim to support the initiation of new partnerships and initiatives.

Future programme of work

Members of the CSD were initially divided as to how the programme of work should develop. Essentially, two polarized schools of thought existed: at one pole countries supported the review of only one issue per Implementation Cycle and, at the other, countries called for broad thematic clusters of issues to be dealt with. The final outcome of compromise led to the adoption of a select thematic cluster of issues being addressed during each Implementation Cycle. At CSD 11, the thematic clusters were set for the next seven cycles. Although this is useful in allowing predictability and, therefore, preparedness, the consequences of fixing the work programme for the next 14 years should not be taken lightly. Consideration

Table 2.2 *Multi-year Programme of Work of the UN Commission on Sustainable Development (CSD)*

Cycle	Thematic cluster	Cross-cutting issues
2004/2005	• Water • Sanitation • Human settlements	Poverty eradication; changing unsustainable patterns of consumption and production; protection and management of the natural resource base of economic and social development; sustainable development in a globalizing world; health and sustainable development; sustainable development of SIDs; sustainable development for Africa; other regional initiatives; means of implementation; institutions' frameworks for sustainable development; gender equality; and education.
2006/2007	• Energy for sustainable development • Industrial development • Air pollution/atmosphere • Climate change	Poverty eradication; changing unsustainable patterns of consumption and production; protection and management of the natural resource base of economic and social development; sustainable development in a globalizing world; health and sustainable development; sustainable development of SIDs; sustainable development for Africa; other regional initiatives; means of implementation; institutions frameworks for sustainable development; gender equality; and education.
2008/2009	• Agriculture • Rural development • Land • Drought • Desertification • Africa	Poverty eradication; changing unsustainable patterns of consumption and production; protection and management of the natural resource base of economic and social development; sustainable development in a globalizing world; health and sustainable development; sustainable development of SIDs; sustainable development for Africa; other regional initiatives; means of implementation; institutions frameworks for sustainable development; gender equality; and education.
2010/2011*	• Transport • Chemicals • Waste management • Mining • Ten-year framework for programmes on sustainable consumption and production. patterns	Poverty eradication; changing unsustainable patterns of consumption and production; protection and management of the natural resource base of economic and social development; sustainable development in a globalizing world; health and sustainable development; sustainable development of SIDs; sustainable development for Africa; other regional initiatives; means of implementation; institutions frameworks for sustainable development; gender equality; and education

Table 2.2 *Continued.*

Cycle	Thematic cluster	Cross-cutting issues
2012/2013*	• Forest • Biodiversity • Biotechnology • Tourism • Mountains	Poverty eradication; changing unsustainable patterns of consumption and production; protection and management of the natural resource base of economic and social development; sustainable development in a globalizing world; health and sustainable development; sustainable development of SIDs; sustainable development for Africa; other regional initiatives; means of implementation; institutions frameworks for sustainable development; gender equality; and education
2014/2015*	• Oceans and seas • Marine resources • Small Island Developing States (SIDS) • Disaster management and vulnerability	Poverty eradication; changing unsustainable patterns of consumption and production; protection and management of the natural resource base of economic and social development; sustainable development in a globalizing world; health and sustainable development; sustainable development of SIDs; sustainable development for Africa; other regional initiatives; means of implementation; institutions frameworks for sustainable development; gender equality; and education.
2016/2017	Overall appraisal of implementation of Agenda 21, the Programme for the Further Implementation of Agenda 21 and the Johannesburg Plan of Implementation (JPOI)	

Note: *This thematic cluster will remain part of the Multi-year Programme of Work as scheduled unless otherwise agreed by the CSD (applies for clusters 4, 5 and 6) will need to be given to the time frame, which in some instances is inappropriate. For example, the JPOI biodiversity target is due to be addressed at the CSD after the target date has passed.

It is the mandate of the CSD to strike a balance between the three pillars of sustainable development. In theory, this has been achieved through the identification of cross-cutting issues, as detailed under Chapter IX of the JPOI 'Means of Implementation' (see Table 2.2). Further issues such as Small Island Developing States (SIDs), Africa, education, sustainable production and consumption, and gender equity have also been highlighted. Further thought will have to be given on how to tie in the cross-cutting issues to the thematic areas that are addressed in one cycle, while ensuring that the process does not become too unwieldy. Strong guidance will be required from the Secretariat on this issue.

Partnerships

As noted earlier in this chapter, the JPOI commitment to support partnership activities was seen by many as a progressive step by the UN. However, this was overshadowed by strong concerns that the inclusion of 'Type II' partnership initiatives would provide a mechanism for governments to avoid making their own commitments to take action. In an attempt to mitigate this disquiet, it was clearly stipulated in the CSD 11 Resolution that Partnership Initiatives should be complementary to, but are not a substitute for, government commitments. Further to this, guidelines for partnerships were developed, taking into consideration the Bali Guiding Principles for partnerships that had been developed during the WSSD negotiations.[12]

While the CSD remains the focal point for discussing and registering partnerships, the CSD Secretariat no longer holds responsibility for assessing their credibility, as they did during the summit process. The burden of responsibility now falls to the partnerships themselves to report, preferably biannually and on a voluntary basis, on the progress made. It was an important move that the partnerships will be assessed on their practical contribution to implementation, and to ensure greater transparency and accountability. However, the NGO community has expressed ongoing concerns that this is essentially a very weak mechanism for holding partnerships to account, and that the onus once again will fall on them to provide a watchdog role over Partnership Initiatives – a role which many do not feel they should be expected, or even have the capacity, to fulfill. Away from these valid concerns, it is hoped that voluntary reporting will provide a useful tool for self-monitoring.

In terms of funding partnerships, it was agreed that UN funds, programmes and agencies should not divert funds from mandated programmes to support the partnerships. Furthermore, while it was recognized that the partnerships need to be based on predictable and sustained resources, especially for developing counties, no specific commitments or recommendations were made in this regard.

The Secretariat is required to produce a summary report on partnerships at the end of each Review Year. These considerations will aim to help inform policy decisions during the following session. This process will hopefully facilitate more responsive policy development, resulting in recommendations that support and promote partnerships and initiatives at all levels, ultimately increasing implementation on the ground.

The involvement of major groups

The CSD was set up to facilitate the involvement of different representatives of civil society in discussions on sustainable development within the UN, and for the past ten years it has been heralded as the most advanced and effective mechanism for achieving multi-stakeholder participation in intergovernmental processes. Improvements are, nevertheless, required to improve the way in which stakeholders are able to engage with decision-making processes within the CSD, and the UN more generally.

Despite the apparent political will to involve major groups, stakeholders and civil society in a more participatory manner, anxieties remains over the definition and use of these terms. The recent outcomes of the Cardoso Panel of eminent persons, nominated by the UN Secretary General to make recommendations on the future role of civil society in the UN system, may help to clarify these concepts, and help to further promote the effective involvement of stakeholder in decision-making processes across the UN.[13]

Reporting

Governments agreed to encourage further work on the effective use of indicators for reporting at the national level. They supported establishing an effective system of reporting to allow for review, evaluation and monitoring of progress towards implementation, sharing lessons learned and best practice, and identifying actions taken, as well as opportunities, obstacles and constraints. National reporting remains voluntary; but it was agreed that governments should include information on the status of national strategies for sustainable development.

Governments called on the CSD Secretariat, with other UN organizations, to streamline reporting requirements with a view to highlighting broad trends, constraints, challenges and emerging issues. They also asked for technical assistance to help countries produce their national reports, including providing national reporting guidelines and questionnaires.

An international collaborative approach

Governments agreed to enhance collaboration in all areas, including encouraging the UN agencies, programmes and funds, the Global Environment Facility (GEF), and international and regional financial and trade institutions to participate actively with and inform the CSD of their activities. This is in order to:

- promote stronger links between implementation at national to international levels;
- strengthen coherence and collaboration between organizations;
- identify gaps in implementation;

- increase efficient use of resources for implementation;
- promote UN system-wide inter-agency cooperation and coordination, taking into account UN reform and utilizing the United Nations Chief Executive Board for Coordination (CEB).

The UN Secretary General was asked to include in his CEB report proposals outlining an integrated and comprehensive response by the UN system towards sustainable development.

While the move to adopt a coherent and integrated approach is welcomed, and appears to be supported by the reform of the CSD, ongoing facilitation of this process will be required in order to ensure that the system-wide coordination that the CSD is working towards is achieved. A growing concern is the way in which the CSD interacts with bodies such as the WTO, who is invited to participate in discussions. This issue must be resolved in order to ensure consistency in policy-making, and to guarantee that sustainable development agreements do not become subservient to decisions made elsewhere.

Ongoing concerns

References to the local and sub-national level (regional governments) were conspicuous by their absence in the CSD 11 Resolution. This is a real shortcoming of the CSD, and one which undermines the fundamental role that these levels have in implementing international commitments. This concern extends to the weak references in relation to the involvement of stakeholders. If the CSD is to achieve its objective of encouraging and adopting a fully participatory approach to sustainable development, official recognition must be given to these valuable spheres of governance and to stakeholders not referred to in the list of nine major groups.

In theory, the future organization of work of the CSD looks to be a reasonably robust model, with sufficient flexibility to allow the involvement of governments and stakeholders at appropriate times. However, despite this relatively positive view, substantial concern remains over the practicalities of the future work programme. The adoption of a bottom-up approach is a good thing, as is the flexibility of the work programme; however, this does leave an overlooked area in terms of the capacity of relevant actors to contribute in the process. A real challenge exists for stakeholders and developing country governments to provide information and participate in a timely and productive manner, ensuring that they really are an effective voice in the relevant decision-making processes.

The 11th session of the CSD completed its tasks in agreeing a reform of the organizational structure and programme of work for the CSD, principally with the agreements of the Resolution to strengthen and reaffirm the mandate of the CSD. The process was successful in illustrating that multilateralism remains a valuable mechanism for achieving international agreements. It is hoped that with its new modalities in place, the CSD will no longer fall into the trap of being little more than a talk-shop or a breeding ground for junior negotiators.

The political will to revitalize the CSD clearly exists amongst governments and stakeholders alike, and if the perennial problems of inadequate funding, lack of integrated thinking and the attendance of appropriate ministers can be overcome, then it could become the powerful body it was set out to be ten years ago. The first CSD Implementation Cycle (2004–2005) has been an important test of this new system, putting the theory into practice. It is hoped the working of the CSD can only improve over time.

Looking ahead

There are some major fault lines running through current governance systems that may make it very difficult to carry out strategic follow-up and implementation of sustainable development. Much of this tracks back to the balancing act of reconciling the sovereignty and needs of the nation state with the recognition of increasingly global interdependence and responsibility. UK Prime Minister Tony Blair, in his statement to the Johannesburg summit, said 'We know the problems and we know the solution is sustainable development'; but without the real political will to face up to some of these more challenging and fundamental underlying issues sustainable development is likely to remain a distant dream.

Most immediately, the next few CSD cycles will be held under the international microscope. The international community is depending upon the revised CSD process to reinvigorate confidence that the process can deliver real outcomes. Crucially, the CSD should include activities aimed at strengthening governance frameworks for sustainable development at all levels.

The story is not all doom and gloom. The shift at Johannesburg towards a more balanced and joined-up view of environmental, social and economic arenas is significant. This will need to be supported by a move away from tackling priority issues, such as trade, climate change or human rights, in isolation. It will need to bring in wider representation from across different government departments and spheres of government, as well as to establish mechanisms that ensure the effective involvement of different sectors of society within the CSD process. If some of these things start to happen, then we might begin to move from merely a vision of global interdependence to establishing practical mechanisms and allocation of resources to get on with the job of implementation.

Notes

1   According to Agenda 21 there are nine major groups: non-governmental organizations, trade unions, indigenous people, women, business and industry, science and technology, local authorities, youth, and farmers.

2   Further information about the WSSD partnership initiatives is available at www.un.org/esa/sustdev/partnerships/partnerships.htm.

3   Further information about the WEHAB papers is available at www.johannes burgsummit.org/html/documents/wehab_papers.html.

4   Further information about the UN Convention on Biological Diversity is available at www.biodiv.org/doc/.
5   Further information about the Global Progamme of Action is available at www.gpa.unep.org/.
6   Further information about the Global Water Partnership is available at www.gwpforum.org/servlet/PSP.
7   Further information about the UN University's Interlinkages Initiative is available at www.unu.edu/inter-linkages.
8   Further information about the WIDER report on *Governing Globalization: Issues and Institutions* is available at www.wider.unu.edu/research/1998-1999-5.1.publications. htm.
9   Further information about the UN Convention against Corruption is available at www.unodc.org/unodc/en/corruption.html#UN.
10   Further information about the Millennium Project is available at www. unmillenniumproject.org/html/about.shtm.
11   Further information about the Global Reporting Initiative is available at www.globalreporting.org/guidelines.
12   Further information about the Bali Guidelines is available at www.un.org/esa/sustdev/ partnerships/guiding_principles7june2002.pdf .
13   Further information about the report of the Cardoso Panel is available at www.un.org/ reform/panel.htm.

References

UN (United Nations) (2002) *Johannesburg World Summit on Sustainable Development Plan of Implementation*. From the Report of the WSSD, 26 August to 4 September 2002. A/ Conf.199/20, available at www.un.org/jsummit/html/documents/summit_docs/ 131302_wssd_report_reissued.pdf

UN (United Nations) (2003) *Secretary General's Report on Strengthening the United Nations: An Agenda for the Future*, available at http://daccess-ods.un.org/doc/UNDOC/GEN/N02/ 583/26/PDF/N0258326.pdf?OpenElement

UN DESA (United Nations Department for Social and Economic Affairs) (2002) *Key Outcomes of the Summit*, available at www.un.org/jsummit/html/documents/summit_docs/ 2009_keyoutcomes_commitments.doc

WIDER (2002) *Governing Globalization: Issues and Institutions*. Edited by Deepak Nayyar for WIDER series on Studies in Development Economics, Oxford University Press

Part 1

The Three Pillars of Sustainability

3

Environment: The Path of Global Environmental Governance – Form and Function in Historical Perspective

Maria Ivanova

Introduction

Global governance has emerged as a term as intensely contested and ill understood as globalization. The concept of governance and especially *global* governance is regarded by some as a euphemism for world government[1] or even as a conspiracy by the North to impose its rules on the South.[2] And while some analysts deny the very existence of global governance, maintaining that state sovereignty is firmly implanted in contemporary political life and the primary driver of world affairs (Gilpin, 2002), others criticize the concept of global governance as too complacent about what is at stake and a deterrent of progress towards a higher form of international organization (Latham, 1999; Yunker, 2004). No world government is in sight; but sovereignty has been voluntarily curtailed when the issues at hand have demanded collaborative, collective solutions. Peace and security, communicable diseases, financial stability, trade, knowledge and the global commons are all areas where the complexity and multidimensionality of problems require coherent policies at the global level. States have empowered 'anchor institutions' within these domains, including the United Nations (UN) Security Council, the World Health Organization (WHO), the International Monetary Fund (IMF), the World Trade Organization (WTO), the World Intellectual Property Organization, and the United Nations Environment Programme (UNEP), to ensure effective collective action (International Task Force on Global Public Goods, 2004). However, this multilateralism now appears under threat as the world's democracies are at odds over the economic, environmental and social agenda; the North–South conflict threatens to undermine the stability of the trading system; and the Western alliance on which much of the current institutional order was built is compromised (Bernstein and Ivanova, forthcoming).

This chapter identifies and analyses the major constraints and barriers in the environmental governance system, keeping in mind the general tensions that face the global governance architecture. Environmental issues such as climate change, ocean pollution, fisheries depletion, and deforestation emerged as international political concerns only during the last three decades. Yet they exemplify both the complexity and interconnectedness of the contemporary world and the difficulty of coordinating solutions among multiple national and transnational entities. The current international environmental system is weak, fragmented, poor in resources and lacking in authority (French, 1992; Conca, 2000; Esty and Ivanova, 2002; UN University, 2002a). These deficiencies weigh ever more heavily as states recognize their inability to address critical problems on a national basis and turn to international organizations for facilitation of collective response. This chapter traces the historical development of the current arrangements and explains the choice of organizational form, outlines the key gaps in environmental governance, examines the core functions of an 'anchor' institution, and proposes institutional options to ensure better coherence and effectiveness.

Global governance: Defining the context

Governance is about the choices we make and the way in which we carry them out. The very need for governance arises from the interactions of members of a social group – be it a tribe, kingdom or a state (Figueres and Ivanova, 2002). Upon realization of interdependence, the need for some form of collective management develops in order to avoid conflicts and attain common goals. Governance is therefore a tool to facilitate coordination of the collective activities of individuals in a group. Yet, it is *not* synonymous with government (Rosenau and Czempiel, 1992; Young, 1999, 2000; Keohane and Nye, 2000). Government acts with authority and creates formal obligations; but private corporations, non-governmental organizations (NGOs) and their respective associations are all active participants in and creators of governance. An effective governance system is 'one that channels behaviour in such a way as to eliminate or substantially to ameliorate the problem that led to its creation' (Young, 1994). When the problems concern the entire planet, governance becomes particularly important and difficult:

> *Earth has no CEO. No board of directors. No management team charged with extracting resources responsibly or maintaining the living factories – the forests, farms, oceans, grasslands, and rivers – that underlie our wealth. No business plan for a sustainable future. . . In fact, dealing with Planet Earth is a collective and largely uncoordinated affair'* (WRI et al, 2003).

The need for coherent governance arrangements transpired in the call for sustainable development governance at the World Summit on Sustainable Development (WSSD) in 2002. The term denotes the institutional framework connecting the governance systems for economics, environment and social issues. International economic institutions form the strongest of the three structures with a regime centered on the international financial and trade organizations, including the World Bank, the IMF and the WTO. The social pillar of sustainable development, while weaker, is represented by well-regarded institutions such as the International Labour Organization (ILO) and the United Nations High Commissioner for Human Rights (UNHCHR) and is equipped with compelling dispute-resolution mechanisms in the face of the European Court of Human Rights, the Inter-American Commission on Human Rights and the African Charter on Human and People's Rights. The governance structures for the environment are by far the weakest and most fragmented (Speth, 2002, 2003).

International environmental responsibilities are spread across multiple organizations, including the United Nations Environment Programme (UNEP) and close to a dozen other UN bodies, such as the Commission on Sustainable Development (CSD), the World Meteorological Organization (WMO), the International Oceanographic Commission (IOC), the United Nations Educational, Scientific and Cultural Organization (UNESCO) and others. Adding to this fragmentation are the independent secretariats to the numerous environmental conventions. UNEP estimates that there are now over 200 multilateral environmental treaties, a number of which have their own independent secretariats (UNEP, 2001a). At first glance, the organizational proliferation in the environmental field might even seem encouraging and in line with the argument of mainstreaming environment into the mandates of all relevant organizations. However, the practical result has been a series of jurisdictional overlaps, gaps and 'treaty congestion' (Brown Weiss, 1995), leading to operational and implementation inefficiencies, inconsistencies and overload of the national administrations.

While the linkages between the economic, social and environmental aspects of development have been explicitly recognized, the overall architecture of the international governance system does not reflect this conception (UN University, 2002b). Currently, the responsibility for establishing and maintaining coordination among international organizations lies primarily within these agencies themselves and the logic of power determines the flow of information and pattern of cooperation. Moreover, disjointed priorities within national governments lead to conflicting viewpoints in different international forums. A coherent and just architecture of sustainable development governance would only be attainable if the three composite governance pillars were equally strong and self-standing. The rest of this chapter will analyse the constraints and opportunities within the system of environmental governance with an eye toward options for reform.

Organizational architecture for environment: A walk through history

The contemporary governance architecture for international environmental issues originated with the establishment of the United Nations Environment Programme

(UNEP) as a result of the 1972 Stockholm Conference. The conference convened 113 governments, 14 UN specialized agencies, several UN programmes and departments, and numerous NGOs, elevating environmental issues from a local and national concern to the international and global level. Governments recognized 'the need for a common outlook and for common principles to inspire and guide the peoples of the world in the preservation and enhancement of the human environment' (UN, 1972). The following 30 years witnessed a flurry of environmental activities. Sixty per cent of the multilateral environmental treaties have been established since Stockholm (UNEP, 2001a). An even larger percentage of national environmental ministries have been set up since 1972. Yet environmental progress has been fitful at best. In the words of one prominent contributor to global environmental governance, it is 'an experiment that has largely failed' (Speth, 2004).

Why has the system failed? Why have environmental institutions grown in number and diminished in authority? What are the levers that could be pulled to correct the course? Undoubtedly, the problems at hand are difficult – hard to see, spread over space and stretched out in time. The political base to support environmental issues also tends to be weak and scattered as short-term economic considerations and sovereignty concerns override any potential political dividend. Furthermore, the response has been flawed – the underlying causes of environmental deterioration have remained ignored, the institutions created have been weak and inadequate, and consensus-based law-making has led to impotent treaties (Speth, 2004).

Frequently, the contention is put forth that the system was deliberately designed to be ineffective due to the deep underlying currents of supposedly large economic costs and perceived threats to national self-government. Rarely have any analysts, however, looked to history in detail for insights on why and how the architecture for environmental governance was established and evolved. This section tells the story of UNEP's establishment as the core international environmental organization and highlights two important issues: individual leadership and collective vision. Many of the events in global environmental governance that we currently take for granted as the inevitable course of history were the product of individual acts of leadership. In addition, the collective decision on the governance architecture for the environment was not informed by deliberate desire to incapacitate the system. Rather, the evolution of the institutions was a product of historical forces and developments with predictable, yet largely unforeseen, effects.

Leadership matters

Environmental concerns were gaining increasing attention and traction during the 1960s. Young activists rallied behind the environmental cause as a symbol for their fight against the capitalist establishment, wasteful use of natural resources and indiscriminate employment of modern technology. The environmental movement also gave them an outlet for protest against national borders. Conservatives, somewhat surprisingly, were also supporters of environmental concerns as they professed a more traditional and less wasteful lifestyle. Disasters such as the 1967 Torrey Canyon massive oil spill further sharpened public concern and attracted attention to reports about the impending death of the oceans, the creeping cross-border pollution from smokestacks in other jurisdictions, the impending depletion of natural resources and food sources, and the threats of nuclear testing. The issues were thus ripe for international attention, although governments continued to deny any occurrence of environmentally irresponsible behaviour and any adverse impact on human and ecosystem health (Åström, 2003).[3]

In 1967, the environment was firmly placed onto the international and global political agenda as a result of the efforts of a few individuals. Inga Thorssen, Swedish negotiator and diplomat at the United Nations, set out to derail the UN plans to convene an international conference on the peaceful use of atomic energy, the fourth in a row. An ardent supporter of disarmament, she believed that expensive UN conferences on nuclear energy had to be stopped as they benefited mostly the North's nuclear industry. Under her influence, the Swedish delegation decided, without instructions from Stockholm, to challenge the proposal when it was tabled at the General Assembly (Bäckstrand, 1971; Åström, 2003). Thus, on 13 December 1967, Börje Billner of the Swedish delegation put forth a proposal to hold a conference on the human environment in order to 'facilitate coordination and to focus the interest of member countries on the extremely complex problems related to the human environment'. In the spring of 1968, the next step was taken. After multiple consultations with other delegations and with American environmental experts, the Swedish government was convinced by its delegation in New York to launch a formal initiative.

The matter was raised at the 45th session of the United Nations Economic and Social Council (ECOSOC) through a convincing memorandum outlining the purpose of the conference to help governments and the public in countries around the world understand the seriousness of environmental problems. The environmental debate at the time was vigorous and well informed about concrete issues such as water and air pollution, acid rain, erosion, and possible climate change. The interconnectedness between these problems, however, was not yet fully comprehended. Moreover, the economic, social and political consequences were unclear to the public as well as to policy-makers. The memorandum thus emphasized the need for a forum where governments and international organizations could debate the issues and come to a collective decision about concrete action (Åström, 2003).

In the subsequent Resolution 1346 (XLV), ECOSOC underlined the urgent need for intensified action at the national and the international level to 'limit and, where possible, to eliminate the impairment of the human environment'. The General Assembly decided (Resolution 2398 (XXIII)) to convene a United Nations Conference on the Human Environment in 1972 and accepted the proposal of the Swedish government to host the event. The main purpose of the conference was 'to serve as a practical means to encourage, and to provide guidelines for, action by governments and international organizations designed to protect and improve the human environment and to remedy and prevent its impairment, by means of international cooperation, bearing in mind the particular importance of enabling the developing countries to forestall the occurrence of such problems' (GA Resolution 2581 (XIV)). Thus, the stage was set for environmental issues to command not only attention but also respect through their elevation to the international political agenda.

The UN Secretariat, however, possessed neither the scientific nor the administrative capacity to deal with what came to be known as 'the Swedish matter.' Philippe de Seynes, Under-secretary General for economic and social affairs, frequently solicited expertise and advice from the Swedish delegation. The agenda was thus shaped by a number of individuals with great knowledge and passion for the environmental cause, as well as with an understanding of the intricacies of the international political and economic context. It was recognized early on that during the period of post-colonialism, developing countries might be opposed to what could be perceived as a Northern agenda. It took great energy and commitment to convince delegations in New York that environmental issues could adversely impact economic development through lowering groundwater levels, soil erosion, increasing desertification, depleted fisheries and other similar problems. It was not, however, until Maurice Strong took on the leadership as Secretary General of the conference and made it a priority to personally communicate and meet with each and every government that the plan to boycott the 'green imperialism conference' was scrapped and developing country governments committed to attend and actively participate in the deliberations.

In fact, the four-year preparatory process was an intensive and serious undertaking, open to input from a much larger constituency than traditional intergovernmental processes. Even in preparing his report to the General Assembly covering the main problems of the conference, the secretary general consulted with member states of the United Nations and members of the specialized agencies, as well as with various NGOs. Thus, in contrast with other global governance regimes, environmental governance has been open and inclusive since its inception. This openness to inputs from UN agencies already active in the environmental arena to a great extent shaped the architectural structure of the environmental governance system.

Much attention focused on the institutional arrangements likely to result from the Stockholm conference. An intergovernmental working group on the subject was established, a number of workshops were convened, and the issue was discussed in detail by the Third Committee of the Conference, the Administrative Coordination Committee and at the Preparatory Committee meetings in Geneva and New York in 1971. The Preparatory Committee of the Conference elaborated a set of general criteria early in the process to guide the work of the secretariat in the formulation of organizational options. The emphasis was placed strongly on the need for 'form to follow function' – a maxim that is oft repeated in the contemporary debate on the organizational architecture for the environment. This vision was, in fact, the foundation upon which the environmental governance system was built.

The 1972 functional vision for environmental governance

Discussions about the expectations of the Stockholm conference centered on the premise that 'the work in the field of environment needed a common outlook and direction' (Rydbeck, 1972). The United Nations system was facing a 'stimulating challenge' (Rydbeck, 1972) to deal effectively with the interdisciplinary nature of environmental problems and adapt to growing understanding of the issues at hand. To this end, new governance mechanisms were required. As proposed by the Swedish government:

> ... *a central coordinating mechanism in the United Nations to provide political and conceptual leadership in the United Nations system, to contemplate inter alia methods of avoiding or reducing global environmental risks, methods of working out joint norms, where there is agreement that such are needed, and methods of avoiding or settling conflicts between states on environmental matters. Such a mechanism should be given enough authority and resources to ensure effective coordination of ongoing and planned activities* (Rydbeck, 1972).

Four main functions were elaborated during the preparatory process discussions as critical in the environmental domain at the international level and as the foundation upon which a new institutional mechanism would be built (A/CONF.48/11):

1 *knowledge acquisition and assessment*: including monitoring[4] of environmental quality, evaluation of the collected data, and forecasting of trends; scientific research; and information exchange with governments and other international organizations;
2 *environmental quality management*: including setting goals and standards through a consultative, multilateral process; crafting of international agreements; and devising guidelines and policies for their implementation;
3 *international supporting actions* (or what we now term capacity-building and development): including technical assistance, education and training, and public information;
4 *prevention and settlement of disputes*: including procedures for the resolution of conflicts arising between environmental priorities and other issues.

Existing international organizations were active in the discussions and argued forcefully that they were already performing many key functions as they had 'constitutional responsibilities in large areas of the human environment' (A/CONF.48/12). Some of their activities in the environmental field included collection, interpretation, analysis and dissemination of information; monitoring and surveillance; research on environmental change; development of scientific criteria and guidelines for environmental quality; development of policy guidelines; establishment of national environmental institutions, legislation and standards; establishment of regional and international agreements; development and transfer of technology; education, training and public information; cooperation on technical aspects; and funding. It was recognized, however, that these functions were performed in isolation from each other and that there was an urgent need for streamlining and coordination. Moreover, governments acknowledged that there were 'important issues which are not, at present, covered or are not covered adequately' and that appropriate institutional mechanisms were necessary to address these gaps.

The form envisioned to respond to the four core functions was 'an intergovernmental committee within the United Nations itself, serviced by a small, high-level secretariat with access to the scientific and technical community' (Rydbeck, 1972). To be able to fulfill its mandate effectively, the intergovernmental body was to be of limited size, yet based on equitable geographical distribution, comprised of senior officials with environmental responsibilities and appropriate scientific advisers. The institutional location of the new body was based on the 'special nature of the environmental problems and the need to ensure maximum flexibility in the utilization of available resources' and was therefore envisioned as 'a distinct new part of the United Nations Secretariat' while working in 'close and intimate cooperation with the Department of Economic and Social Affairs . . . and with the specialized agencies and related organizations' (Rydbeck, 1972).

United Nations Environment Programme or Organization

Governments left Stockholm having signed the Stockholm Declaration, where they agreed that global environmental issues should be addressed by the UN system and identified 'an urgent need for a permanent institutional arrangement within the United Nations system for the protection and improvement of the environment'. In December 1972, the General Assembly adopted Resolution 2977 creating the United Nations Environmental Programme (UNEP) with a governing council comprised of 58 members; a 'small' secretariat to serve as a focal point for environmental action and coordination in the UN system; a voluntary environment fund to support environmental programmes; and an environmental coordination board to ensure cooperation and coordination among all UN bodies addressing environmental issues.

UNEP's status as a 'programme' placed it within the UN properly and required that it report to the General Assembly through the Economic and Social Council (ECOSOC). The UN system is made up of six principal organs, 15 specialized agencies, and several programmes and bodies. In the UN hierarchy, programmes have the least independence and authority. Specialized agencies are separate, autonomous intergovernmental organizations with governing bodies independent of the UN Secretariat and the General Assembly.[5] Besides their role in elaborating common vision, rules, and standards, they also perform many operational activities within the particular sector that they govern. UNEP was, indeed, accorded a relatively modest status through the institutional arrangement; but it is important to clarify the reasons behind this decision.

While governments were not eager to create a supranational environmental regulator, they had not set out to incapacitate the environmental agenda by creating a weak and impotent organization to serve at its core. There is no evidence to support claims that the system was rigged to be ineffective and inefficient. The official record, in fact, indicates that governments saw environmental issues as 'an integrative part of UN politics [that] should be [accorded] a higher priority amongst other issue areas subject to the attention of the United Nations'. Even recently declassified confidential materials of the UK government show that while there was interest in restricting the scope of the Stockholm Conference and reducing the number of proposals for action infringing upon its domestic decision-making processes, the UK did not set out to create a weak environmental organization. Rather, it accepted that the time had come for new institutional arrangements. In the words of an official from the UK Department of the Environment, a 'new and expensive international organization must be avoided; but a small effective central coordinating mechanism . . . would not be welcome but is probably inevitable' (cited in Hamer, 2002).

There was a general feeling among governments, even the most vocal proponents of a new intergovernmental entity, that there was 'no need for the creation of a new big agency in the field of environment' (Rydbeck, 1972). In fact, the establishment of a specialized agency for the environment was deemed counterproductive since that would make the environment another 'sector' and thus marginalize it. As Maurice Strong put it, the core functions could 'only be performed at the international level by a body which is not tied to any individual sectoral or operational responsibilities and is able to take an objective overall view of the technical and policy implications arising from a variety of multidisciplinary factors' (A/CONF.48/11). Furthermore, there was a strong sense of disillusionment with the unwieldy bureaucracy of the UN specialized agencies. A new architectural design was clearly necessary. Recognizing the complex nature of environmental issues, governments sought to create a lean, flexible and agile entity that could pull together the relevant expertise housed in the various agencies and deploy it effectively. The new entity was expected to grow into its mandate as it proved its effectiveness (A/CONF.48/11) and be 'essentially flexible and evolutionary so as to permit adaptation to changing needs and circumstances' (A/CONF.48/11/Add.1).

UNEP's institutional path

'Today, UNEP suffers from a loss of focus, strategic vision and influence. Instead of doing a limited number of things effectively, its work plan is disjointed and lacks clear priorities.' With these words Eileen Claussen, Under-secretary of State, summed up the view of the US in 1997 (Journal of the G77, 1997). Similar criticisms of UNEP have come to dominate the literature on global environmental governance (Imber, 1993). UNEP's weaknesses are often attributed to its mandate, which is seen by some as too broad and even impossible (von Moltke, 2001b) and as too narrow by others (Esty and Ivanova, 2002).

Closer examination of UNEP's original mandate elaborated in General Assembly Resolution 2997 and its evolution over the years reveals that it is clear and has stayed relatively focused on the core areas of scientific assessment, coordination, catalysing action, and environmental law and policy development. For its first two decades, UNEP was well regarded. It established an impressive record of accomplishment in raising global awareness of environmental challenges. It spawned the creation of numerous international environmental agreements and assisted developing countries in establishing national ministries of environment, as well as supporting scientific and legal infrastructures. By 1992, UNEP 'had established a reputation for conducting its small programmes in an efficient manner. Donor confidence was high, especially amongst the more skeptical American and British governments which regarded UNEP (by UN standards at least) as a paragon of focused activities and tight budgetary restraint' (Vogler and Imber, 1996).

However, the organization's ability to perform parts of its mandate, especially the coordination and catalytic functions, was constrained from the beginning due to three factors:

1   the limited resources available to contribute to other organizations' activities;
2   the physical distance and remoteness of the organization, along with the poor communications; and
3   the diminished authority of the organization as it gradually lost some of its capacity and expertise.

The catalytic and coordination functions, however, were made especially difficult during the early 1990s and beyond with the increase in the number of actors in environmental governance and the proliferation of alternative institutional arrangements. A key problem has been the emergence of new bodies with mandates overlapping UNEP's responsibilities and often with resources much larger than those at UNEP's disposal. For example, the Global Environment Facility (GEF) was created in 1990 to help developing countries finance initiatives to address specific environmental issues (the role envisioned for the environment fund in 1972). With a budget of over US$1 billion, the GEF quickly eclipsed UNEP.

UNEP was further marginalized by the preparatory process for the 1992 Rio Earth Summit. Somewhat surprisingly, it was not given the lead role in the preparatory process for the 20-year review of the Stockholm Conference. Rather, the process was directed by the General Assembly where the support for development rather than environmental concerns was much stronger. The result for global environmental governance was a compromise that showed signs of strain and contradiction. The creation of the Commission on Sustainable Development (CSD) indicated the lack of confidence in UNEP's ability to address the issue of sustainable development and caused further fragmentation of the already cluttered institutional architecture. Within a few years after the United Nations Conference on Environment and Development (UNCED), or the Earth Summit:

> . . . the lack of clarity of the role of UNEP . . . had affected both programme planning and implementation . . . there had not been the managerial or political will to make hard choices, vis-à-vis the priorities of the agency. The end result was a reduction in discernible results of UNEP's work, which had led to reduced donor confidence, lower extra budgetary contributions and further programme reductions (UN, 2000).

Envisioned as a key link among specialized agencies with environmental portfolios, UNEP instead became only one forum among many. And as it helped to bring to life new conventions, new organizational structures sprang up in Geneva, Bonn,

Montreal and elsewhere to house their management functions and secretariats. Each UNEP-hosted Multilateral Environmental Agreement (MEA) has developed its own secretariat with locations around the world. Of the seven MEAs administered by UNEP, four secretariats are located in Geneva (the Convention on International Trade in Endangered Species of Wild Fauna and Flora, or CITES; the Basel Convention on the Transboundary Movements of Hazardous Wastes; the Rotterdam Convention on Prior Informed Consent Procedures for Certain Hazardous Chemicals and Pesticides in International Trade; and the Stockholm Convention on Persistent Organic Pollutants); one in Montreal (the Convention on Biological Diversity, or CBD); one in Bonn (the Convention on Conservation of Migratory Species of Wild Animals); and only the ozone secretariat overseeing the Vienna Convention and the Montreal Protocol is based in Nairobi (however, the multilateral fund for the Montreal Protocol is based in Montreal and the implementation part of the ozone secretariat is housed at UNEP's Paris office). This fragmentation presents a serious operational challenge – UNEP staff need to travel on average approximately 6077 kilometres from Nairobi to UNEP-hosted convention secretariats. In contrast, other international organizations, including the International Maritime Organization (IMO), the International Labour Organization (ILO), and the UN Economic Commission for Europe, provide an institutional home for the conventions that have emerged under their aegis.

Almost 15 years after Rio, the promise of sustainable development for the global environment remains largely unfulfilled, while the practice of environmental governance has evolved to fit with the changing demands of a hyper-liberal global political economy, rather than vice versa (Bernstein, 2001; Bernstein and Ivanova, forthcoming). This development has not resulted in increased institutional capacity or resources, especially for UNEP. Quite the contrary, contributions to the environment fund have, in fact, decreased in real terms since the 1970s and 1980s and have dropped 36 per cent from their peak during 1992–1993. Additional sources of funding – trust funds and earmarked contributions – initially created to supplement programme activities supported by the environment fund, now finance two-thirds of UNEP's activities. While these provide UNEP with much needed resources, they come at a cost. UNEP has very little discretion over how this money is spent and the activities supported are often peripheral to UNEP's own work plan. The alternative sources of financing have contributed to a shift away from the originally envisioned normative functions and towards more operational activities (DeBock and Fergusson, 2004).

UNEP did not succeed in establishing itself as the authoritative voice or centre of gravity in international environmental policy as originally envisioned in 1972 due to a number of reasons, many beyond its control. Geographically isolated from other relevant UN operations, lacking adequate long-distance communication and transportation infrastructure, and with few opportunities to interact face to face with counterparts in other agencies and treaty secretariats, UNEP was gradually marginalized. The lack of a strong and authoritative institutional voice for the environment at the global level reinforced institutional and organizational propagation, a 'crazy quilt pattern of environmental governance [that] is too complicated and is getting worse each year' (Charnovitz, 2002). While UNEP has contributed significantly to the creation of environmental law and institutions, the disconnect between environmental needs and environmental performance in the current international system is striking. The development of international environmental policy at the global level has been highly haphazard and has left some notable gaps.

The jurisdictional gap in global environmental governance

Negative trends persist across a number of environmental indicators.[6] The spatial scale of the state, however, is inadequate in dealing with the scales of such environmental change. The state is simultaneously too small and too big to address environmental concerns effectively (Paterson, 1999). For all the rhetoric, agreements and promises of action over the past 30 years, actual institutions, processes and resources have fallen woefully short of addressing the problems for which they were established (Speth, 2003). In contrast to other global governance regimes, the environment lacks clarity at the global level since it has no real 'anchor institution' (International Task Force on Global Public Goods, 2004). No one body has been able to emerge as a leader to actively champion environmental issues, ensuring their integration within economic and social decisions.

The lack of a mechanism for dispute settlement is a glaring gap within the global environmental governance system. Even though it figured prominently as one of four key functions for an international environmental body identified in 1972, more than 30 years later, it is still non-existent. Instead, environmental disputes (most often with trade agreements) are delegated to the WTO.[7] While some analysts argue that imbuing the WTO with environmental norms is necessary (Gaines, 2002), it is not a substitute for a functioning international environmental system.

Thirty-three MEAs with trade implications have been identified.[8] Some of them have only rudimentary dispute settlement procedures and others lack them altogether (for example, the International Convention on the Regulation of Whaling). Several MEAs (for example, the Basel Convention) contain elaborate provisions; but they have never been used. Several problems arise from the disparity in dispute settlement capacities between the environment and trade regimes. The WTO's relatively short decision-making period and its enforcement power guarantee that any dispute brought before both an MEA and the WTO will likely be decided first and decisively by the WTO. The WTO rules have also had a 'chilling' effect on drafting new MEAs with potential trade implications as they penalize environmental behaviour if it compromises liberalized trade. In addition, alternative mechanisms for dispute resolution and the resulting 'forum shopping' have created substantial confusion – both for countries in establishing policy and for business wondering which set of rules are binding (Krist, 2002).

Information inconsistencies

Availability of reliable information is critical to policy-making at both the national and the international level. Clear identification of threats, changes and trends on a global scale is essential for global-scale decision-making. A suite of international organizations, scientific research centres, national governments and environmental convention secretariats are responsible for data collection and scientific assessment. Several initiatives are already in place, such as UNEP's Environment and Natural Resources Information Network, the *Global Environment Outlook* (GEO) reports, the thematic portals at UNEP.net and the recently launched Millennium Ecosystem Assessment. However, significant data gaps remain both at the local and global level. There is little coordination among data collection efforts, and comparability across jurisdictions is poor (WEF, 2002).

Compliance monitoring and reporting for multilateral environmental agreements are similarly unsystematic. The current governance framework with independent convention secretariats scattered around the world prevents the streamlining of reporting requirements and monitoring methodologies and techniques. Moreover, international environmental agreements have, until recently, contained few substantive mechanisms for monitoring and evaluation. Although environmental agreements usually require parties to report their compliance to the respective treaty secretariat, few guidelines exist on how to prepare the reports. The convention secretariats often lack the authority and resources to monitor agreements through verification of reported information or through independent assessments. The analysis and publication of collected data is also severely limited. With the proliferation of agreements, countries have found it increasingly difficult to meet their reporting obligations under the various conventions, and nations' self-reported data are often incomplete, unreliable and inconsistent (GAO, 1999). UNEP has, in fact, begun to consider the potential of streamlining reporting requirements across similar conventions.

Diversity and disparities

Differences in knowledge accumulation, data availability and participation capacities, as well as seemingly differing interests and motivations, all contribute to a widening gap between the abilities of the North and the South to respond to environmental concerns. Some argue that, as a result, environmental issues in the South have been less visible on the global environmental agenda (Karlsson, 2002). What is also disconcerting is that global issues with profound implications for the South continue to be shrugged off as primarily Northern concerns. Climate change, for example, is certain to have a much larger and more adverse impact on developing countries both due to geography (tropical regions are likely to become warmer and small island states may be submerged) and to the limited adaptation capacity (Figueres and Ivanova, 2002; Kurukulasuriya and Rosenthal, 2003; Msangi et al, 2004).

Furthermore, participation of developing countries in decision-making at the international level has been greatly hampered by the scattering of environmental activities across many international organizations. The costs associated with attending intergovernmental sessions to negotiate international environmental agreements and treaties are high, both in terms of direct economic expenses and opportunity costs of days away from the already understaffed environmental ministries.[9] Countries with limited diplomatic and financial resources have thus been forced to choose which conferences to attend, or whether to attend them at all (Kelly, 1997). Developing countries stand to gain most from a coherent international environmental system. According to Frank Biermann, a more coherent governance structure embodied in a World Environment Organization (WEO) would further the interests of developing countries because it would provide them, first, a high-level forum to unite their individual bargaining power against the major industrialized countries. Second, a WEO would assist Southern efforts to garner international support for environmental programmes in regions and sectors that are increasingly bypassed by economic globalization. Third, a WEO would create a locus to politically institutionalize the influence of non-governmental lobbyists in a way that increases the balance of opinions and perspectives (Biermann, 2000).

An issue of particular importance to developing countries since the inception of the environmental system involves who will pay for global-scale environmental problem-solving. Despite unprecedented levels of global wealth, the long-standing pledge for contributions of 0.7 per cent of gross domestic product (GDP) to development assistance has practically been rejected as contributions have instead fallen to 0.2–0.1 per cent of GDP in many countries (Koch-Weser, 2002). The current financing mechanisms are inadequate, incoherent and scattered among multiple institutions and conventions. For example, the GEF, UNEP, the World Bank, and separate treaty-based funds such as the Montreal Protocol Finance Mechanism are all involved in environmental activities of a global scale, but coordination among their efforts is minimal. A more carefully constructed financial system for sustainable development – harnessing the power of civil society and the private sector alongside national governments and international organizations – coupled with mechanisms to support technology transfers would help to alleviate North–South tensions. Yet, such a system cannot be created without the championship of developing countries for greater coherence of the various institutional mechanisms. It is these nations that stand to gain most from improved coordination, greater transparency and more coherent policies of the international organizations with environmental portfolios.

The question of values and ethics becomes particularly important when talking about global concerns and the differences between the developed and the developing world. The current governance system empowers the powerful. A more transparent and inclusive governance structure that respects the diversity of views across the world will benefit the South. Public policy and issue networks create 'virtual public space' that is easier to enter than existing physical forums. A set of modern outreach and participation mechanisms could also decrease the distance between decentralized constituencies and global decision-makers – making it easier to insert into the policy process the broad array of values, perceptions and perspectives that are now often overlooked or incompletely considered, and facilitating public understanding of global issues and relevant political decisions (Esty and Ivanova, 2003).

Implementation gap

The World Summit on Sustainable Development (WSSD) held in Johannesburg in 2002 recognized the implementation deficit in global environmental governance. Informally termed the Summit on Implementation, it sought to promote concrete action to bridge the gap between promises and action. However, what became apparent was the lack of a framework within which such action could be taken. The system of rules and principles guiding behaviour and facilitating collaboration is incoherent, incomprehensible and even incomplete. The new approaches advanced in Johannesburg such as public–private partnerships while appearing to be the pinnacle of sustainable development – combining resources, skills and commitment from various stakeholders – offer little promise for solving the deeply structural problems of global governance. In fact, in the three years since the WSSD, the notion of partnerships for sustainable development has received no attention and has been eclipsed by the Millennium Development Goals (MDGs).

As the analysis so far suggests, there are a number of institutional and structural barriers to effective environmental governance both at the national and global level. Table 3.1 summarizes examples from different issue areas that illustrate these challenges. Efforts to close the policy gaps identified in this chapter are also under way. Table 3.2 presents examples of best practices in various areas. While certainly of great significance, these initiatives would have to be embedded within a much larger effort at reforming and revitalizing the global environmental governance architecture.

Policy implications and organizational design

The system of global environmental governance is strained by the magnitude of the problems, the inadequacy of the existing institutions to respond at the appropriate scale, and the continuing pressure to adapt to the global marketplace. The legitimacy, effectiveness and equity of the system have all been compromised and many analysts have focused their attention on the form and functions of appropriate governance architecture for the environment at the global level (Vogler and Imber, 1996; von Moltke, 2001b; Esty and Ivanova, 2002; Speth, 2003, 2004; Desai, 2004; Haas, 2004; Kanie and Haas, 2004; Sanwal, 2004).

Three broad alternatives for global environmental governance reform have received attention in the literature. A fourth one is also elaborated, which takes into account the opportunities and constraints identified and offers the possibility of closing the governance gaps analysed above. Such an approach might, indeed, form the institutional basis of a renewed compromise in environmental governance (Bernstein and Ivanova, forthcoming).

Refinement of the status quo

Some commentators (von Moltke, 2001b; Najam, 2003) believe that the most feasible way of improving global environmental results is to revitalize the existing regime centered on UNEP. They argue that the current system suffers from a lack

Table 3.1 *Institutional barriers to effective governance:*
Examples from global problems

Fisheries[1]	Global governance of fisheries has failed to recognize ecosystem needs, and decision-makers have, instead, imposed policies based on political boundaries. As a result, states are left to their own devices in designing joint management strategies and international laws have not provided a framework for achieving such agreements. No methods have been developed thus far to exclude non-participatory state vessels in areas managed under rules designated by regional fisheries management organizations. In addition, other sectoral policies have been created without taking into account those governing fisheries. For example, agricultural run-off has not been monitored with fisheries management in mind.
Food security[2]	Little coordination exists amongst the variety of international organizations and mandates related to food security. For example, the International Undertaking on Plant Genetic Resources of the Food and Agriculture Organization (FAO) and FAO's International Network of Ex-situ Collections call for a multilateral system to trade germplasm freely, a policy in direct conflict with the Convention on Biological Diversity (CBD's) recognition of genetic resources as the sovereign property of states. In addition, independent scientific bodies are rarely included in decision-making when food security issues are being addressed by multiple institutions and convention secretariats.
Water[3]	Perhaps more than any other sector, water is intimately linked with most areas of human development. In the context of the WEHAB discussion (water, energy, health, food and agriculture and biodiversity) during the World Summit on Sustainable Development (WSSD), water supply and quality management lies firmly in the centre. More than 20 United Nations bodies currently manage water issues, leading to an increasingly fragmented system. Yet, more than 40 per cent of the global population depends upon ecosystem services of river basins shared by at least three countries demanding a coherent governance structure able to ensure ample supply, efficient allocation and adequate quality.

Notes: [1] *Governance for a Sustainable Future. II: Fishing for the Future. Report of the Commission on Fisheries Resources,* www.earthsummit2002.org/es/issues/Governance/whatgov2.pdf
[2] *Governance for a Sustainable Future. III: Managing Biodiversity for Food Security. Report of the Commission on Genetic Diversity in Relation to Food Crops,* www.earthsummit2002.org/es/issues/Governance/whatgov3.pdf
[3] *Governance for a Sustainable Future. IV: Working with Water. Report of the Commission on Water,* www.earthsummit2002.org/es/issues/Governance/whatgov4.pdf

Table 3.2 *Examples of best practices in environmental governance*

Global	**Millennium Ecosystem Assessment** Establishes a network for hundreds of experts worldwide and provides current scientific analysis and assessment about human and ecosystem interaction. Presents policy options to decision-makers. *www.millenniumassessment. org/en/index.htm*	**United Nations Environment Programme's (UNEP's) Finance Initiative** In collaboration with over 275 financial institutions – such as commercial banks, fund managers, investment banks, insurance and re-insurance companies, multilateral development banks and venture capital funds – promotes environmental management strategies. *www.unepfi.net/*
Regional	**Aarhus Convention** Links human rights with the environment by involving all stakeholders in sustainable development goals. Develops new process for public participation in implementation strategies and negotiations. *www.unece.org/env/pp/*	**Access Initiative** Using the Aarhus Convention as a foundation, this initiative establishes common access to information benchmarks; develops a common methodology for national-level assessments; and engages public interest groups to use chosen indicators for government performance evaluation. *www.accessinitiative.org/index.htm*
National/ local	**Citizens' Charter of Praja Foundation, India** Re-establishes accountability, transparency and participation in public governance of city services, including waterworks, solid waste management, storm water drainage, etc. This initiative created a citizen's charter and training courses for municipal officials to carry out the charter's stipulations. The charter, posted on Praja's web-site and cited in newspaper articles, has helped to educate citizens about their rights and duties. The charter has signi-ficantly advanced democracy and participation in public utility services. *www.praja.org/chartermain.htm*	**International Council for Local Environmental Initiatives (ICLEI) Information Clearinghouse** Provides information on local environmental initiatives through newsletters, case study series and technical manuals. *www.iclei.org/infoch.htm#best practice*

of political will and not from any inherent flaws. It simply has never been given a chance to work. As shown by the historical analysis above, however, the current system was not purposefully hamstrung. Reform proposals centered on such premises include elevating UNEP's status within the UN system from a programme to a specialized agency, strengthening its funding, and increasing its responsibility for managing the proliferation of multilateral environmental agreements.

Any significant effort to consolidate global-scale environmental responsibilities is considered politically impossible and may even jeopardize the effectiveness of the system. However, there is increased recognition that 'there is rampant duplication, and actors sometimes work at cross purposes', and that 'common and clear goals are conspicuous by their absence and lines of command and control are always murky'. A key proposal is 'clustering' of the various pieces of the existing environmental regime in order to improve policy coherence, tighten potential cross-issue linkages and avoid the duplication of effort that comes from full decentralization (UNEP, 2001a, 2001b; von Moltke, 2001a, 2001b; Oberthür 2002). Bolder proposals of 'improved organizational coordination, managing treaty proliferation, enabling dispute resolution and sustainable development governance' have been put forth. These analyses, however, fail to identify both why these changes would make a decisive difference and the mechanisms through which political will can be generated and harnessed.

UNEP has been engaged in reform efforts since 1997, but with little effect. The International Environmental Governance (IEG) Initiative, launched in 2001, resulted in a weak declaration with a large number of priorities and little in terms of a plan of action. The two potentially most significant reforms predate that initiative: the creation of the Environmental Management Group (EMG) and a new Global Ministerial Environmental Forum, both approved by the United Nations General Assembly in 1999. The EMG is a mechanism for enhancing inter-agency cooperation and coordination – one of the core elements of UNEP's 1972 mandate. It convenes UN agencies, convention secretariats, the Bretton Woods institutions, and the WTO in Geneva under the chairmanship of the UNEP executive director to:

> . . . *promote inter-linkages, encourage timely and relevant exchange of data and information on specific issues and compatibility of different approaches to finding solutions to those common problems, contribute to the synergy and complementarity among and between activities of its members in the field of environment and human settlements and, hence, act in a complementary manner and add value to the existing UN system-wide inter-agency cooperation* (EMG, 1999).

Few concrete results can be shown to date, however, and the effectiveness of this mechanism is difficult to judge. The Global Ministerial Environment Forum was designed to raise UNEP's profile by including a ministerial-level meeting of Governing Council members at its bi-annual meetings, and meeting in a Governing Council special session in off years. However, its mandate is co-terminus with UNEP's, and the resolution creating it explicitly recognizes 'the need to maintain the role of the Commission on Sustainable Development as the main forum for high-level policy debate on sustainable development' (UNGA, 1999).

Refocus efforts to the national level

A second group of analysts argues that energies put into changing the international architecture are misplaced. The priority should be to strengthen domestic environmental capacity (Juma, 2000). This position reflects a false dichotomy. Whereas strengthening national and local capacity is required for effective governance, the issue at the global level is whether the institutional architecture will support and reinforce such efforts. This is especially the case for developing countries. International institutions often set the agenda and provide normative leverage for initiating national legislation and action. They also support implementation through direct financial contributions and capacity development. Currently, the normative climate and material incentives favour economic development at the expense of environmental stewardship, rather than their integration at the national as well as international level. In the absence of reform of international economic institutions or the creation of more authoritative environmental institutions, improvement will depend upon system-wide reform within existing institutions, including the WTO and regional trade agreements such as the North American Free Trade Agreement (NAFTA) (Bernstein and Ivanova, forthcoming).

While this is not out of the question, there is little evidence that any such reform will take place. Rather, one runs the real risk of subordination of environmental concerns to trade issues. In the absence of a strong environmental architecture, potential conflicts will naturally migrate to the economic and trade structures, where they will be posed as challenges to free trade rather than to the environment. For example, Rio Principle 12, based on the trade norm of non-discrimination, reinforces a binary view of all trade-related measures as either liberalizing or protectionist by imposing the burden of proof on national environmental regulations to show that they are not discriminatory when it states that 'trade policy measures for environmental purposes should not constitute a means of arbitrary or unjustifiable discrimination or a disguised restriction on international trade' (UNGA, 1992). Nowhere does it say that non-discrimination or open markets should not constitute an unjustifiable restriction on environmental protection or ecosystem health. This normative environment makes trade-offs difficult between efficiency, economic growth, corporate freedom and environmental protection, and thus risks justifying inaction if tough regulatory choices, which imply trade-offs with market values, are necessary to get the desired ecological effects (Bernstein and Ivanova, forthcoming).

Fundamental structural reform

Proposals for major structural reform derive from a conclusion that the existing global-scale environmental architecture is deeply dysfunctional and structurally flawed, making a fresh start easier than reform along the margins. A growing number of politicians (Ruggiero, 1998; Chirac, 2001; Gorbachev, 2001; Panitchpakdi, 2001), academics (Esty, 1994, 2000; Biermann, 2000; Runge, 2001; Whalley and Zissimos, 2001, 2002) and others (Zedillo Commission, 2001; Charnovitz, 2002) support this view. Beyond the difficulties of trying to fix a failed structure, those arguing for this approach often note that the existing regime was designed for a pre-globalization era before the full spectrum of worldwide environmental problems was understood and the depth of current economic integration was achieved. Moreover, globalization has changed the political landscape away from inter-governmentalism towards fragmented authority and the ascendancy of markets, conditions that reveal the limitations of national regulation and the need for social regulation of the global marketplace.

The case for a major overhaul of the environmental regime is centered on several premises:

- the 'public goods' logic requiring that collective action be organized at the scale of the problem to be addressed (Olson, 1965);
- the potential of a new body to overcome the fragmentation of the current structure, obtain synergies in addressing problems, and take advantage of opportunities for better issue prioritization, budget rationalization and bureaucratic coordination;
- the need for an organization to serve as a counterpoint and a counterweight to the WTO, the World Bank and other international economic institutions, especially given the judicial powers of the WTO; and
- the need for an authoritative international environmental body with a first-rate staff, a reputation for analytical rigor and the capacity to take on tasks such as dispute resolution (Esty and Ivanova, 2002).

The political prospects for wholesale reform in the short to medium term, however, appear slim. A 2003 French proposal to the United Nations General Assembly for a new United Nations Environment Organization (UNEO) has generated renewed interest in the strengthening and reform of UNEP, although it has not yet succeeded in bringing about the political momentum required to implement that change. States cannot even agree whether the UNEP Governing Council should include universal membership, in part because some, especially developing countries, view any such move as an attempt by stealth to turn UNEP into a UN specialized agency, which could evolve into a World Environment Organization (IISD, 2004). Furthermore, there is little tolerance for establishing a more coherent authority over the numerous multilateral environmental agreements.

New governance approach: A global environment mechanism

A fourth option for institutional change is Esty and Ivanova's (2002) proposal for a Global Environmental Mechanism (GEM), further developed in Bernstein and Ivanova (forthcoming). It centres on a structure that can deliver the *functions* needed at the global level. Whereas this option avoids the pitfalls and poor prospects of a new World Environment Organization, it recognizes that shoring up a failing governance structure will not suffice given path dependencies in UNEP's operation and location, as well as its lack of authority to engage the broader global governance system. This option offers the best hope for a renewed compromise that successfully integrates liberalism and environmentalism. The argument depends upon making the case that such a structure can facilitate the necessary dialogue within the liberal order and existing institutions, neither of which show signs of disappearing any time soon.

Institutionally, a GEM attempts to capture the middle ground of governing by acknowledging the diversity and dynamism of environmental problems and the need for specialized responses. No single bureaucratic structure can build an internal organization with the requisite knowledge and expertise to address the wide-ranging, dynamic and interconnected problems that we now face (Esty and Ivanova, 2002). The issues demanding immediate attention arise on various geographic scales, requiring a multi-tier response structure (Ostrom, 1990; Esty, 1999; Karlsson, 2000; Vogler, 2000). They demand capacities in multiple areas, including ecological sciences, public health, risk assessment, cost-benefit analysis, performance measurement and policy evaluation, as well as a sound ethical foundation. Today's global environmental governance challenge thus requires a more virtual structure built on a multi-institutional regime capable of drawing in a wide array of underlying disciplines through governments, NGOs and global public-policy networks.

The core governance functions required under these conditions to a great extent mirror the ones identified in 1972 and include:

- provision of adequate information and analysis to characterize problems, track trends and identify interests, as well as monitoring and reporting on performance;
- creation of a 'policy space' for environmental negotiation and bargaining; and
- sustained build-up of capacity for addressing issues of agreed-upon concern and significance.

Consequently, a GEM would comprise:

- a global information clearinghouse with mechanisms for data collection, assessment, monitoring and analysis to reveal the nature of environmental problems;
- a global technology clearinghouse with mechanisms for technology transfer and identification and dissemination of best practices to help build capacities where needed; and
- a negotiation forum to elucidate values, bring forth ethics and justice concerns, and facilitate agreements that improve environmental quality and reconcile the interests of different parties.

Rather than formal bureaucratic structures, these elements are more likely to take the form of networks that would build on the expertise of existing institutions, only creating new mechanisms where key functions are non-existent or inadequate. Nonetheless, an office akin to the United Nations High Commissioner for Human Rights (UNHCHR) could add needed moral authority and agenda-setting capacity (Haas, 2004). This office might, for example, evolve out of the new Environmental Management Group in Geneva.

The information clearinghouse would contribute to the creation of a common vision and encourage long-term thinking by providing timely, relevant and reliable data on environmental issues, risks and trends on the global scale. Information on how similar problems are solved in various national contexts can aid national-level administrations in adopting best practices and learning. Comparative performance analysis across countries could provide greater transparency and encourage positive competition. The technology clearinghouse would focus on problems of capacity and develop incentives to motivate the private sector to disseminate technological advances optimally. An effective environmental technology clearinghouse would contain information on best practices around the world and facilitate technology development and continuous learning.

The real test for such a GEM, however, would be its ability to facilitate reform of existing institutions to sufficiently address environmental concerns. In this regard, the negotiation forum component of this proposal is absolutely essential, linked to something akin to a high commissioner's office. Together, they can facilitate a high-level political forum to try to catalyse the necessary dialogue within existing institutions, such as the WTO's Committee on Trade and Environment, the Commission on Sustainable Development (CSD), the Global Compact and even non-state governance schemes, as well as to provide a forum for multilateral and bilateral bargaining. The new Environmental Management Group is already a step in this direction, and might be enhanced if states were to agree to let it evolve a more political role. In addition to what EMG already does, this office would facilitate learning and coordination across the full range of environmental governance institutions, as well as provide a high-profile office to promote environmental norms and develop new ones, promote national environmental infrastructure and stimulate action on the environment. While more modest than a WEO, such an office would significantly raise the profile of environmental issues and provide a focal point to move the agenda forward where negotiations within existing institutions have been stalemated (Bernstein and Ivanova, forthcoming).

Conclusion

The debate on form and function has not lost relevance in the 30 years since the Stockholm deliberations. UNEP was created to deliver the key functions of information provision, coordination of the environmental activities of the UN system, development of environmental policy and law, and catalysing action within governments, specialized agencies and private actors. While it has contributed tremendously to the development of international environmental law over the last 30 years, and its mandate is sufficient for a normative agency, this does not appear to be sufficient to protect the global environment. A key question that deserves academic and political attention is whether UNEP's mandate and organizational capacity are sufficient for it to serve as the 'leading global environmental authority that sets the global environmental agenda, that promotes the coherent implementation of the environmental dimension of sustainable development within the United Nations system and that serves as an authoritative advocate for the global environment' (UN, 1997).

The conceptual framework laid out in this chapter emphasizes that values, interests and power are all important factors in delivering global environmental solutions; that knowledge is essential; that institutions and partnerships are required at the international level; and that effective involvement of national and local entities is critical. Knowledge, awareness and political will regarding international issues and global concerns change over time. Public awareness and political decisions move issues from the fringes to central stage, while advances in technology create new possibilities and the results of scientific research change our understanding of global phenomena. Thus, a flexible, agile, multilayered governance structure drawing in a number of global issue networks will be critical to solving an ever-changing and evolving problem set.

Notes

1   Neo-conservative websites, for example, warn that global governance is a deceptive tactic formulated by elites to impede upon self-government and national independence by building a new world order: 'Global governance is world government – despite the UN's claims to the contrary' (www.worldnetdaily.com/news/article.asp?ARTICLE_ID=28865). Some charge that issues such as global warming, ozone depletion and ecosystem destruction are being falsified to justify the need for global governance (www.wealth4freedom.com/truth/5/globalgov.htm).

2   Martin Khor (1995), for example, has stated that 'globalization is what we in the third world have for several centuries called colonization' (cited in Scholte, 2000).

3   For example, the Japanese government continued to deny that any environmental disasters had taken place within its borders as a result of unregulated discharge of lead, cadmium, and polychlorinated biphenyl (PCB), while tens of thousands of people had died a painful death. Subsequently, the sickness developed by acute methyl mercury poisoning received the name of the Japanese town where the chemical factory was located – Minamata disease. The accumulated methyl mercury mainly attacks the central nervous system and in acute cases can lead to sudden insanity, unconsciousness and death. The methyl mercury pollution posed not only a direct health hazard, but also decimated fishing – a critical income source – and deprived people of their will to live. Patients also had to fight arbitrary prejudice and discrimination against them for having a 'mysterious' or 'contagious' disease, as well as unfounded accusations that they were malingering. Such friction gradually destroyed the social fabric of the town (www.asianresearch.org/articles/2324.html).

4   Monitoring is used as:

> ... the collection of 'base-line' environmental data and of information on changes in the quality of media which, directly or indirectly, may significantly affect the health or well-being of man. It does not connote the policing or surveillance of compliance with regulations or standards, though information obtained by monitoring will be a valuable indication of the effectiveness of control measures (A/CONF.48/11).

5   Some of the specialized agencies include the United Nations Food and Agriculture Organization (FAO), the World Health Organization (WHO), the World Meteorological Organization (WMO), the International Bank for Reconstruction and Development (World Bank), the International Maritime Organization (IMO), the United Nations

Educational, Scientific and Cultural Organization (UNESCO) and the United Nations Industrial Development Organization (UNIDO).

6   For example, tropical forests are cleared at the rate of 1 acre (0.4 hectares) per second. The rate of extinction of birds and mammals is estimated to be 100 to 1000 times the rate of natural species loss. Half of the available freshwater is being consumed. Seventy per cent of fisheries are exploited to capacity or are under stress (Speth, 2002; WRI, 2000; World Watch Institute, 2001). These facts, however, do not go unchallenged. Some analysts posit that the environmental record is not nearly as bad as portrayed by 'doomsayers' and that the achievements in terms of quality of life improvement are substantial (Lomborg, 2001).

7   *The WTO has a sophisticated dispute settlement procedure – arguably the most developed of any international institution. As Gabrielle Marceau of the WTO Legal Affairs Division writes, under this procedure, 'any WTO member that considers that any of its WTO benefits have been nullified or impaired has an absolute right to trigger the WTO dispute settlement mechanism and request consultations and the establishment of a panel' (Marceau and González-Calatayud, 2001, p85). The WTO process leads to the adoption of a WTO panel report or a WTO appellate body report within 12 months, and the implementation of the panel's recommendations in 18 months from the time the dispute was formally registered. This process seeks to remove barriers or policies found incompatible with WTO rules. If this cannot be done, the second best solution is for the injured party to be compensated by the offending party. If this does not occur, then the WTO allows for trade retaliation as a last resort. The WTO process is basically legalistic, and a complaining member can insist on a decision. The WTO does not have the option to postpone consideration of the case or to decline to take up the dispute (Krist, 2002).*

8   Among these are the Convention on Biological Diversity (CBD), the Convention on International Trade in Endangered Species of Wild Fauna and Flora (CITES), the Convention for the Protection of the Ozone Layer (Montreal Protocol), the United Nations Framework Convention on Climate Change (UNFCCC) and Convention on the Control of Transboundary Movements of Hazardous Wastes and their Disposal (Basel Convention).

9   Edith Brown Weiss (1995) points out that:

        A normal negotiation may require four or five intergovernmental negotiating sessions of one to two weeks each during a period of 18 months to two years. The Climate Convention negotiations required six sessions of two weeks each in less than 16 months. Despite this very full and expensive schedule of negotiations, the Climate Convention negotiations were only one of more than a half dozen global or regional environmental agreement negotiations occurring more or less at the same time.

References

Åström, S. (2003) *Ögonblick: Från Ett Halvsekel I Ud-Tjänst. [Moment: From Half a Century of Foreign Affairs Duty]*. Lind & Co, Stockholm

Bäckstrand, G. (1971) 'Samtal På Den Statliga Kommiten För Vetenskap Och Teknik (Gknt)' ['Conversation at the State Committee for Science and Technology, Moscow between

the Soviet Union (Ananichev) and Sweden (Bäckstrand and Swartz)']. Utrikesdeparte-
mentet, Politiska Avdelningen, Fjärde byrån, Swedish Foreign Ministry archives,
Stockholm

Bernstein, S. (2001) *The Compromise of Liberal Environmentalism*. Columbia University
Press, New York

Bernstein, S. and Ivanova, M. (forthcoming) 'Institutional fragmentation and normative
compromise in global environmental governance: What prospect for re-embedding?' in
S. Bernstein and L. W. Pauly (eds) *Global Governance: Towards a New Grand Compromise?*
SUNY Press, Albany, NY

Biermann, F. (2000) 'The case for a World Environment Organization'. *Environment*, vol
42, no 9, p22

Brown Weiss, E. (1995) 'International environmental law: Contemporary issues and the
emergence of a new world order'. *Geo Law Journal*, vol 81, p675

Charnovitz, S. (2002) 'A World Environment Organization'. *Columbia Journal of
Environmental Law*, vol 27, no 2, pp323–362

Chirac, J. (2001) 'Jacques Chirac s'empare de l'écologie'. *Le Monde*, 5 May 2001

Conca, K. (2000) 'The WTO and the undermining of global environmental governance'.
Review of International Political Economy, vol 7, no 3, pp484–494

DeBock, L and Fergusson, J. (2004) 'UNEP's Financial Performance'. Yale School of
Forestry and Environmental Studies, Course research paper, Connecticut

Desai, U. (2004) *Environmental Politics and Policy in Industrialized Countries*. MIT Press,
Cambridge, MA

EMG (Environmental Management Group). (1999) 'Terms of reference' available at http://
/mirror.unep.org/pdf/EMG%20TOR.pdf

Esty, D. (1994) 'The case for a Global Environmental Organization', in P. Kenen (ed)
Managing the World Economy: Fifty Years After Bretton Woods. Institute for International
Economics, Washington, DC

Esty, D. (1999) 'Toward optimal environmental governance'. *New York University Law
Review*, vol 74, no 6, pp1495–1574

Esty, D. (2000) 'The value of creating a Global Environmental Organization'. *Environment
Matters*, vol 6, no 12, pp13–15

Esty, D. and Ivanova, M. (2002) 'Revitalizing global environmental governance: A function-
driven approach', in D. C. Esty and M. H. Ivanova (eds) *Global Environmental
Governance: Options and Opportunities*. Yale School of Forestry & Environmental Studies,
Connecticut

Esty, D. and Ivanova, M. (2003) 'Toward a Global Environmental Mechanism', in J. G.
Speth (ed) *Worlds Apart: Globalization and the Environment*. Island Press, Washington,
DC

Figueres, C, and Ivanova. M. (2002) 'Climate change: National interests or a global regime?'
in D. C. Esty and M. H. Ivanova (eds) *Global Environmental Governance: Options and
Opportunities*. Yale School of Forestry & Environmental Studies, Connecticut

French, H. (1992) 'Strengthening global environmental governance', in L. Brown (ed)
State of the World 1992, Norton and Co, New York

Gaines, S. E. (2002) 'International trade, environmental protection and development as a
sustainable development triangle'. *RECIEL (Review of European Community and
International Environmental Law)*, vol 11, no 3, pp259–274

GAO (US General Accounting Office) (1999) *International Environment: Literature on the
Effectiveness of International Environmental Agreements*. US GAO, Washington, DC

Gilpin, R. (2002) *The Challenge of Global Capitalism: The World Economy in the 21st Century*.
Princeton University Press, Princeton, NJ

Gorbachev, M. (2001) 'The American and Russian people don't want a new confrontation'.
Newsweek, 27 April 2001

Haas, P. (2004) 'Global environmental governance in terms of vertical linkages', in N. Kanie and P. Haas *Emerging Forces in Environmental Governance*, United Nations University Press, Tokyo

Hamer, M. (2002) 'How developed nations plotted to undermine global pollution controls'. *New Scientist*, 5 January 2002

IISD (International Institute for Sustainable Development) (2004) 'Summary of the eighth Special Session of the United Nations Environment Programme's Governing Council/ Global Ministerial Environment Forum, 29–31 March 2004'. *Earth Negotiations Bulletin*, vol 16, no 35, 2 April 2004, available at http://www.iisd.ca/vol16/enb1635e.html

Imber, M. (1993) 'Too many cooks? The post-Rio reform of the United Nations'. *International Affairs*, vol 69 no 1, pp55–70

International Task Force on Global Public Goods (2004) 'International cooperation in the national interest: A cross-cutting approach to enhancing the provision of global goods with specific focus on global commons'. Working paper prepared by the Secretariat of the International Task Force on Global Public Goods, 28 October 2004, available at http://www.gpgtaskforce.org/show_file.aspx?file_id=28

Journal of the G77 (1997) 'Third world countries cry foul over UNEP'. Nairobi chapter, available at http://www.g77.org/Journal/marapr97/13.htm

Juma, C. (2000) 'The perils of centralizing global environmental governance'. *Environment Matters*, vol 6, no 12, pp13–15

Kanie, N. and Haas, P.(2004) *Emerging Forces in Environmental Governance*. United Nations University Press, Tokyo

Karlsson, S. (2000) *Multilayered Governance: Pesticides in the South – Environmental Concerns in a Globalized World*. Department of Water and Environmental Studies, Linkoping University, Linkoping

Karlsson, S. (2002) 'The North–South knowledge divide: Consequences for global environmental governance', in D. C. Esty and M. H. Ivanova (eds) *Global Environmental Governance: Options and Opportunities*. Yale School of Forestry & Environmental Studies, Connecticut

Kelly, M. (1997) 'Overcoming obstacles to the effective implementation of international environmental agreements'. *Georgetown International Environmental Law Review*, vol 9, no 2, pp447–488

Keohane, R. and Nye, J. (2000) 'Introduction', in J. S. Nye and J. D. Donahue (eds) *Governance in a Globalizing World*. Brookings Institution Press, Washington, DC

Khor, M. (1995) 'Address to the International Forum on Globalization'. New York City, November

Koch-Weser, M. v. B. (2002) 'Sustaining global environmental governance: Innovation in sustainable development finance', in D. C. Esty and M. H. Ivanova (eds) *Global Environmental Governance: Options and Opportunities*. Yale School of Forestry & Environmental Studies, Connecticut

Krist, W. (2002) *The WTO and MEAs – Time for a Good Neighbor Policy: A Policy Brief from the Trade and Environment Forum*. Woodrow Wilson International Center for Scholars, Washington, DC

Kurukulasuriya, P. and Rosenthal, S. (2003) 'Climate change and agriculture: A review of impacts and adaptations'. Paper no 91 in Climate Change series, Department of the Environment, The World Bank, Washington, DC

Latham, R. (1999) 'Politics in a floating world: Toward a critique of global governance', in M. Hewson and T. J. Sinclair (eds), *Approaches to Global Governance Theory*. State University of New York Press, Albany, NY, pp. 23–53

Lomborg, B. (2001) *The Skeptical Environmentalist: Measuring the Real State of the World*. Cambridge University Press, Cambridge

Marceau, G. and Gonzalez-Calatayud, A. (2001) 'The Relationship Between the Dispute Settlement Mechanisms of MEAs and Those of the WTO', *Trade and the Environment, the WTO and MEAs*, Heinrich Boll Foundation, Washington, DC, pp71–90

Msangi et al (2004) *A Global Perspective on Climate Change Impacts on Developing Country Agriculture: Towards a Synthesis and Research Agenda for the Challenge Program on Water and Food*. CGIAR Challenge Program on Water and Food, Theme 5: Global and National Food and Water Systems

Najam, A. (2003) 'The case against a new international environmental organization'. Global Governance, vol 9, no 3, September 2003, pp367–384

Oberthür, S. (2002) *Clustering of Multilateral Environmental Agreements: Potentials and Limitations*. United Nations University, Institute of Advanced Studies, Tokyo

Olson, M., Jr. (1965) *The Logic of Collective Action*. Harvard University Press, Cambridge, MA

Ostrom, E. (1990) *Governing the Commons: The Evolution of Institutions for Collective Action*. Cambridge University Press, Cambridge

Panitchpakdi, H.E., Supachai (2001) 'Keynote address: The evolving multilateral trade System in the New Millennium'. *George Washington International Law Review*, vol 33, no 3, pp419–449

Paterson, M. (1999) 'Interpreting trends in global environment governance'. *International Affairs*, vol 75, no 4, p793

Rosenau, J. N. and Czempiel, E. O. (1992) *Governance without Government: Order and Change in World Politics*. Cambridge University Press, Cambridge

Ruggiero, R. (1998) 'A global system for the next fifty years'. Address to the Royal Institute of International Affairs, Royal Institute of International Affairs, London

Runge, C. F. (2001) 'A Global Environment Organization (GEO) and the world trading system'. *Journal of World Trade*, vol 35, no 4, pp399–426

Rydbeck, O. (1972) Statement by Ambassador Olof Rydbeck in the Preparatory Committee for the United Nations Conference on the Human Environment at its fourth session in New York on Monday, 6 March 1972. Permanent Mission of Sweden to the United Nations (on file with author)

Sanwal, M. (2004) 'Trends in global environmental governance: The emergence of a mutual supportiveness approach to achieve sustainable development', *Global Environmental Politics*, vol 4, no 4, November 2004, pp16–22

Scholte, J. A. (2000) *Globalization: A Critical Introduction*. Palgrave, New York

Speth, J. G. (2002) 'A new Green regime: Attacking the root causes of global environmental deterioration'. Environment, vol 44, no 7, pp16–25

Speth, J. G. (ed) (2003) *Worlds Apart: Globalization and the Environment*. Island Press, Washington, DC

Speth, J. G. (2004) *Red Sky at Morning: America and the Crisis of the Global Environment*. Yale University Press, New Haven, CT

UN (United Nations) (1972) 'Report of the United Nations conference on the human environment'. UN, Stockholm. Available at http://www.unep.org/Documents/Default.asp?DocumentID=97

UN (1997) *Nairobi Declaration on the Role and Mandate of UNEP*. UN, Nairobi

UN (2000) 'Follow-up to the 1996 review of the programme and administrative practices of the United Nations Environment Programme', note by the Secretary-General, UN General Assembly Fifty-fourth session. Agenda items 118 and 127. Available at www.un.org/Depts/oios/reports/a54_817.htm

UN University (2002a) *International Environmental Governance: The Question of Reform – Key Issues and Proposals*. United Nations University Institute for Advanced Studies, Tokyo

UN University (2002b) *Sustainable Development Governance: The Question of Reform: Key Issues and Proposals*. United Nations University Institute for Advanced Studies, Tokyo

UNEP (United Nations Environment Programme) (2001a) *International Environmental Governance: Multilateral Environmental Agreements* (MEAs). UNEP, Bonn

UNEP (2001b) *Improving International Environmental Governance among Multilateral Environmental Agreements: Negotiable Terms for Further Discussion* – A Policy Paper. UNEP, Bonn

UNEP (2001c) *International Environmental Governance: Report of the Executive Director.* UNEP, Nairobi

UNGA (United Nations General Assembly) (1992) 'Report of the United Nations Conference on Environment and Development (Rio de Janeiro, 3–14 June 1992)'. A/CONF.151/26 (vol 1), General Assembly, 122 August 1992. Available at http://www.un.org/documents/ga/conf151/aconf15126-1.htm

UNGA (1999) 'Implementation of and follow-up to the outcome of the United Nations Conference on Environment and Development and the nineteenth special session of the General Assembly'. A/RES/53/188, 12 February 1999, fifty-third session Agenda item 94 (a). Resolution adopted by the General Assembly on the report of the Second Committee (A/53/609/Add.1). Available at http://daccessdds.un.org/doc/UNDOC/GEN/N99/768/25/PDF/N9976825.pdf?OpenElement

Vogler, J. (2000) *The Global Commons: Environmental and Technological Governance.* J. Wiley and Sons, Chichester

Vogler, J. and Imber, M. (1996) *The Environment and International Relations.* Routledge, London

von Moltke, K. (2001a) *Whither MEAs? The Role of International Environmental Management in the Trade and the Environment Agenda.* International Institute for Sustainable Development, Winnipeg, Canada

von Moltke, K. (2001b) *On Clustering International Environmental Agreements.* International Institute for Sustainable Development, Winnipeg, Canada

WEF (World Economic Forum) (2002) *Environmental Performance Measurement: The Global Report 2001–2002.* WEF, Geneva, Switzerland

Whalley, J. and Zissimos, B. (2001) 'What could a World Environmental Organization do?' *Global Environmental Politics,* vol 1, no 1, pp29–34

Whalley, J. and Zissimos, B. (2002) 'Making environmental deals: The economic case for a World Environment Organization', in D. C. Esty and M. H. Ivanova (eds) *Global Environmental Governance: Options and Opportunities.* Yale School of Forestry & Environmental Studies, Connecticut

WorldWatch Institute (ed) (2001) *Vital Signs 2001: The Environmental Trends that Are Shaping Our Future.* W. W. Norton and Co, New York

WRI (World Resources Institute) (2000) *World Resources 2000–2001: People and Ecosystems.* Oxford University Press, New York

WRI, UNDP, UNEP and World Bank (World Resources Institute, United Nations Development Programme, United Nations Environment Programme and the World Bank) (2003) *World Resources: 2002–2004.* World Resources Institute, Washington, DC

Young, O. R. (1994) *International Governance: Protecting the Environment in a Stateless Society.* Cornell University Press, Ithaca, NY

Young, O. R. (1999) *Governance in World Affairs.* Cornell University Press, Ithaca, NY

Young, O. R. (2000) *Global Governance: Drawing Insights from the Environmental Experience.* MIT Press, Cambridge, MA

Yunker, J. (2004) 'Effective global governance without effective global government: A contemporary myth'. *World Futures: The Journal of General Evolution,* vol 60, no 7, October/November 2004

Zedillo Commission (2001) *Report of the High-level Panel on Financing for Development.* New United Nations, New York

4

Economy: The Economic Problem of Sustainable Governance[1]

Andrew Simms

Introduction

More than a decade after the 1992 Earth Summit in Rio, attempts to govern the global environment and manage the world economy are hopelessly disconnected. The economy is set on a path of orthodox growth powered by fossil fuels, while the environment is being progressively destabilized by the consequence of that growth – global warming. Yet, both economic and environmental governance are supposed to accomplish the same thing – namely, a world in which all people can enjoy well being and quality of life. This chapter demonstrates this by using the example of how the international community's failure to agree a realistic solution to climate change stands to undermine, if not wreck, the world's best efforts to improve people's economic well-being. It then looks at what should be done about it.

The economic problem

Europeans and Americans dream of Jamaican beach holidays. Of those who actually get there, met off the plane by steel bands and coached directly to all-inclusive resorts, none get to meet Elsie. She was the reason I was there.

Elsie was a grandmother several times over. On her knee a baby called Growth screamed. Elsie's daughter had denied she was pregnant, complaining instead that she merely had a 'growth'. The baby would get a proper name one day; but for then, Growth stuck. Ask Elsie how many grandchildren she had and she laughed and said: 'A whole lot of them.' Elsie said she was 61 years old; but, although it seemed unkind to even think it, she looked a lot older. She survived by making and selling small amounts of charcoal and working at a cleaning job once a week.

In her house — a wooden shack with two beds where she lived with three generations of her family – there was no running water or electricity. For privacy their yard was protected by sheets of rusting metal fence. A couple of other houses stood nearby. The way in which the lanes around her house were divided up into yards gave rise to the infamous 'yardy' tag given to organized Jamaican gangsters.

Thin wires wriggled down from overhead power cables to many of the other yards, each containing two or three huts-come-houses. Stealing electricity was common, but potentially lethal among the flimsy wooden buildings. House fires were common, another cost of social marginalization. Only official home owners got legal access to services such as electricity. Most of Elsie's neighbours were squatters in the eyes of the law even if they had lived there for decades.

Baby Growth was not the poorest of the poor in Jamaica when I went there to gather evidence at the height of the Jubilee 2000 debt campaign. But in a country drained by foreign debts, divided by enormous inequality and imploding with violence, if Growth lived up to her name it would have been a triumph against all odds.

To get to Elsie's place you drove down a tarmac road that cut through the zinc fencing and dust lanes of Bennetlands, one of Kingston's downtown 'communities'. Compared to many other roads in the area it was a good one. But it was also the sort of road that the local middle classes feared to drive down after dark.

On a bend in the road that the project took its name from, the poorly funded S-Corner clinic provided a range of basic services to the local community: a health clinic, school classes, access to drinking water and, in the absence of a proper public sewage system, help with sanitation. They even ran a modest nutritional scheme encouraging people to grow their own food to eat and sell. But before the clinic could even begin to carry out its heroic tasks, it had another problem.

The community whom S-Corner served was not just poor and lacking amenities, it was rife with violence. The clinic could only function by first brokering peace treaties between local warring factions. It was doctor, teacher, plumber, engineer and peace keeper all at the same time. Strikingly, also, the clinic wasn't the result of well-meaning charities parachuting 'good works' into the area. It grew out of local people who moved into an abandoned building and organized things for themselves, negotiated with the building's owners and got the clinic going.

But rather than working to support such courageous local people, global governance, in the shape of the World Bank and the International Monetary Fund (IMF), worked implicitly against them.

According to Angella Stultz-Crawle, the Jamaican woman who ran the clinic, under pressure from the IMF, money available for social programmes in Jamaica had halved. S-Corner was already picking up the tab for people who had fallen through the threadbare government safety net; but they too only had half the funds they needed. She wrote to the government's Ministry of Health asking for more support and got a letter in reply that read, 'We are so sorry, we wish we could help; but as you know we have to be paying debts and we don't have [the funds] and, therefore, that is why we cannot help. We empathize with your situation, but we cannot do much more than what we are doing.'

Here, in microcosm, was what J. M. Keynes described with deceptive simplicity as 'the economic problem': the struggle to meet basic human needs and lift people out of the struggle for subsistence. Jamaica was far from the poorest of countries. But even there, towards the end of the last millennium, were symptoms of the world's collective failure to organize its affairs to solve the economic problem. They were symptoms repeated thousands of times in dozens of countries, often regardless of the fact that, with political will, the necessary resources were not very far away.

At the time I was in Bennetlands, for every US$1 the government spent, nearly half, 46 cents, went on debt service. Unemployment was high. HIV infection rates were doubling every two years. It was getting harder and harder for the country to earn a living from its principal exports, such as sugar and bananas, due to a long-term downward pressure on prices, in spite of the fact that the island was rich in natural resources and should have had no problem.

Angela saw the consequences of skewed spending priorities every day at first hand:

> *There's the reduction in health programmes, reduction in education, in roads, in lights. Just walking around you see people living in dirt yards, scrap board houses. It is repaying. Everyday you hear the government come out and say: 'Oh, we have met our IMF deadlines, we have paid', and everyone claps. These people don't know anything. Had it not been for local people's resistance to these things, their own innovativeness, they would have been totally devastated.*

The conference express

A song called 'Things can only get better' became a temporary national anthem in the UK during 1997. It was adopted by the Labour party in an election campaign that led to the end of nearly two decades of Conservative Party rule. But an assumption of steady, if faltering, human progress has long been at the heart of Western civilization.

In the wider world, the final few decades of the last millennium saw the emergence of a unique international consensus among governments (even though frequently disingenuous). An end to global poverty was to become the focus of nations working together and through their appointed agencies, such as the World Bank. At least since the controversial appointment of the US government official Robert McNamara as President of the World Bank in 1968, commitment to poverty eradication has been a necessary matching accessory to most gatherings of heads of state. The problems of countries such as Jamaica, and others even poorer in Latin America, Africa and Asia, were supposed to be consigned to history.

But by the beginning of the final decade of the last millennium, things were still not going well. The Cold War and the legacy of the Soviet and US superpowers fighting proxy wars in poor countries had left the world in an unstable and conflict-ridden mess. Far from poor countries enjoying a 'peace premium' after the collapse of the Soviet Union, their loss of geopolitical importance had the opposite effect.

During this time the rhetoric of the 'war on terror' was still far off. With all the money supposedly freed up from military spending that was no longer necessary in a world with only one superpower left, aid was supposed to go up. But it didn't; aid shrank throughout the following decade. A commercial debt crisis that hit Latin America during the 1980s also gave way to a public debt crisis in Africa and elsewhere in the 1990s. Something drastic needed to happen in the build-up to the new millennium.

The United Nations, unfrozen by the end of the Cold War, seeing its opportunity took a big, deep breath and, beginning with the Earth Summit in Brazil in 1992, turned the 1990s into a railroad with stops every few minutes for another major international conference of unquestionable importance.

Along the line that stretched around the world's great cities, from Beijing to Copenhagen, there were stations where civil servants and activists gathered by the thousands to talk about the planet's prospects for drinkable water; equality between men and women; social development; human rights; urban living conditions; having enough to eat; cancelling the debts of poor countries; and finding money to pay for it all.

The final challenge fell to a gathering in the city of Monterrey in 2002, just before the tenth anniversary of the original Earth Summit. It was problematic and indicative. Diplomats use language with great subtlety. For months nobody could decide what to call the gathering: whether it was a conference, a summit or just a meeting would convey different levels of political commitment to the outcome. In the event, it proved largely irrelevant as only a dribble of new resources were pledged anyway.

Issues thrown up in special conferences organized by the United Nations spilled over into the regular meetings of the Group of 8 (G8), a club of the world's self-appointed most powerful and important countries, and other get-togethers of the World Bank, the IMF and the World Trade Organization (WTO).

Had all the money spent on business-class travel, hotel and restaurant bills instead been put into a separate fund and wisely allocated, it is just possible that the problems may have been solved anyway. But as J. K. Galbraith famously observed of senior bankers and politicians in the US at the time of the Wall Street crash during the late 1920s, it is important for important men to convene important meetings about important issues to show that they are important, and to reassure the public that something is being done. But, then, as now, the most substantial thing to happen was usually the meeting itself, not anything that came out of it.

However, many of the conclusions from ten years of well-meant conference-hopping were gathered together into a mini-manifesto to improve the lot of the world's poor. Eventually known as the Millennium Development Goals (MDGs) they became the focus for aid agencies and pretty much everyone involved at the international level in tackling poverty. Plans were drawn up, aid programmes were reshaped and more global civil servants clocked up even more air miles flying around the world to spread the good news.

An important footnote for anyone interested in how the world has staggered towards running itself is the very different treatment given to social and environmental issues, on the one hand, and economic issues, on the other. The former are generally seen as 'soft' policy best kept in its natural setting of community groups and non-governmental organizations (NGOs), while the latter, economic issues, are 'hard' policy and are to be managed by the real powers of government, finance and big business. Agreements to uphold social and environmental goals are typically voluntary and there is no real penalty if a country decides not to play ball. If, however, a country does not live up to a trade deal or to the letter of its arrangements with the international financial institutions (IFIs), it will very quickly find itself in the global dock. In this arena nothing is left to chance.

Trade sanctions and black-listing by the international bankers await countries who try to go their own way where the global economy is concerned. The global environment, on the other hand, is deemed worthy of only voluntary *ad hoc* attempts to look after it.

What is striking is how the most noble and moral ambitions of the international community, which are condensed into environmental agreements, and campaigns to cancel developing world debt and to raise people out of want and suffering, tend to emerge from people and community groups agitating outside government, at the grassroots level.

As Kofi Annan said at the UN's Millennium Forum in May 2000:

> *Barely had the pepper fog settled over the Seattle protests before NGOs were branded as confrontational or even contrarian, disruptive or even destructive, anti-technology or even anti-progress. Those labels overlook the pioneering role of NGOs on a range of vital issues, from human rights to the environment, from development to disarmament. We in the United Nations know that it was [they] who set the pace on many issues.*[2]

Ironically, these are also the groups criticized in the mainstream for pointing out how economic globalization has failed the poor and the environment.

On the other hand, the international economic agreements that have so far demonstrably failed people in poverty, such as those overseen by the WTO and others such as the North American Free Trade Agreement (NAFTA), emerged out of close collusion between big business, big finance and government. At the infamous meeting of the WTO in Seattle in 1999, the US organizers had a large help desk for the world's media. Any journalist who had an enquiry could go to them. There they had a reference book with contacts offering people to comment on any issue that emerged. Very late one night, when the negotiations were deadlocked and the press room was empty, I took the book from behind the desk and leafed through. There were pages and pages of contacts for every imaginable big business and trade association, from US chicken farmers to car-makers. Human rights organizations, unions and environmental groups were nowhere to be found.

The great reversal

But not only do efforts to tackle poverty suffer a lack of teeth. They suffer, perhaps, the greatest oversight of our time. Because all of these earnest and self-important attempts to get our international act together, one thing was significantly overlooked: global warming. And, as someone joked about the Labour Party's favourite song of 1997, it might not be long before a new version is needed: 'Things can only get bitter'.

The failure to properly account for the impacts of climate change makes a mockery of more than a decade of political efforts. Agreeing bold new goals for nations to collectively pursue (a consensus that is the essence of global governance) was a great achievement. But as these challenges to the goals show, without a realistic plan to stop climate change they may be a complete waste of time.

Goal 1: Lifting people out of poverty

There is a target to halve between 1990 and 2015 the proportion of people living in poverty – defined as those whose income is less than US$1 per day. There are lots of problems with this way of measuring poverty. Quality of life can, for example, be very good in a community who looks poor because it does not use cash for many of its transactions, preferring instead other forms of barter and exchange. And quality of life can be very bad in more cash-rich societies who have less community spirit and more crime, loneliness and degraded environments.

However, in order to address the system using its preferred counting method, global warming makes the sums go horribly wrong. Disasters stemming from the climate tend to target the poor and keep them that way. Most so-called natural disasters tend to be climate related and most of the people affected by them live in poor countries. Single extreme weather events can devastate whole economies. Hurricane Mitch hit Central America in 1998. In a few days it destroyed three-quarters of the annual earnings of Honduras, and set the country back decades in terms of progress, according to its prime minister. Farming was wrecked and virtually all of the country's crucial banana plantations were flattened. According to the United Nations Environment Programme (UNEP), economic losses due to 'natural' disasters are doubling every ten years. Insurance companies need to plan ahead. What they are seeing looks disastrous.

Andrew Dlugolecki, a former director of the global insurance giant CGNU, plotted the rising trend of economic losses from disasters, most of them climate driven, against likely global economic growth over the coming decades. He came to the astonishing conclusion that some time around the middle of the 2060s – that is, during the lifetimes of people alive today – economic losses will outstrip global income. In other words, the world economy will have been bankrupted by 'natural' disasters. And, Dlugolecki's projections were conservative because they did not allow for the possibility of accelerated, or runaway, climate change, which many in the research community consider highly likely.

A 1 metre sea-level rise, possible within the next century or so, would, for example, displace 80 per cent of Guyana's population and impose costs equivalent to ten times the country's annual earnings. A more modest 50 centimetre sea-level rise would, ironically, bankrupt oil-rich Venezuela. The country could simply not afford to either protect its coastline or replace everything that got washed away.

Goal 2: Making sure people have enough to eat

By 2015, again, the intention is to halve the tally of around 800 million people in the world who do not have enough to eat. Now, it's true that the world produces more than enough food for everyone to be well fed. The fact that they are not is testimony to governments' penchant for economic ideas that look good on paper, rather than ideas that work in practice. Where the lives of poor people are concerned, the winds of *laissez-faire* markets still blow strong. The poor are still expected to fit in with markets rather than the other way around. But redistribution is a bit like gardening; it requires intervention. Unless, that is, you don't mind your garden being overrun with a couple of multinational corporate super weeds that get lucky and take over the vegetable patch and herb garden and strangle your favourite plants. Unfortunately, radical pro-poor market reform, which would involve, for example, giving people a fair share of the land, is nowhere globally on the cards. And climate change stands to make the task of getting dinner on the table a whole lot harder.

Generally speaking, global warming means that wet areas will get wetter, and dry areas will get drier. This is particularly a problem for places such as Africa. During the great floods in Mozambique in 2000, the worst for 150 years, the lowlands of the Limpopo River were inundated for three months. Sometimes flooding can be a good thing. If short term, it can benefit crops such as rice. But Mozambique's floods lasted so long that the United Nations Food and Agriculture Organization (FAO) said there had been a 'complete wipe-out of plant genetic resources'. Everything was destroyed: seeds, food stores and all the crops in the field.

Ironically, historical records show that total annual rainfall across Africa has been declining since 1968. When the rains come not at all, or all at once, the problem is either the devil of drought or the deep blue sea of flood. Over the past 25 years the Sahel has experienced the most 'sustained decline in rainfall recorded anywhere in the world within the period of instrumental measurements'. The great famines of the 1970s and 1980s had many political causes, as well. But as the land becomes drier, smaller and smaller political sparks can start the fires of famine. During 2002, 12 million people in Southern Africa faced hunger and disease due to a crisis driven by two years of drought.

Most farming in sub-Saharan Africa is fed directly by rain. It accounts for over two-thirds of jobs and more than one third of the region's earnings. Farmers in the region have, over time, proved incredibly resilient to environmental changes. But global warming stands to push them over the edge.

Crop yields are projected to fall by one fifth in a region where 200 million already go hungry. In the UK, people spend the equivalent of 12 cents of every US$1 on food. In sub-Saharan Africa, the figure is between 60 to 80 cents. Climate change could create the worst of all worlds. Local food prices are driven up due to scarcity. Expensive imports are then bought with declining revenue from the sale of Africa's cash crop exports, which are grown instead of food for local consumption.

Goal 3: Getting children into school

Another goal is to make sure that every child goes to primary school. What threat could climate change pose to this impressive aim? When Hurricane Mitch struck Central America, one quarter of the countries schools were flattened. Wherever extreme weather events and rising sea levels threaten centres of population, they also threaten education. Then, of course, there are the hidden threats. Hunger, disease and forced migration all make schooling difficult, if not impossible. Global warming promises more problems with all three. A hungry or sick child makes a poor pupil. A child on the move is difficult to teach.

Around one half of the world's population live in coastal areas threatened with upheaval due to sea-level rise – for example, along the coasts of Bangladesh and Vietnam. Bangladesh fears that in coming years it could see 20 million people displaced due to global warming. During the mid 1990s, it was estimated by Norman Myers of Oxford University that there were already 25 million environmental refugees in the world, and that the figure could increase due to climate change to around 150 million by the middle of this century. As farms fail in a warming world, famine could create 50 million environmental refugees in Africa alone by 2060.

Today, people who are forced to flee for environmental reasons get none of the protection given to people fleeing political persecution or wars. They are seen as second-class refugees. A drought devastated Afghanistan for three years from 1998, leading 80,000 people to flee to neighbouring Pakistan. But the Pakistani authorities argued that because they were fleeing a 'natural' disaster they did not deserve refugee status. This meant that they were not entitled to help from the relevant UN agencies. Those who fled were effectively starved back across the border. It's hard to imagine giving all children a decent, basic education if millions of them are running from the effects of a disturbed climate. At the same time, international law fails to give governments at home or abroad an obligation for their care, protection and education.

Goal 4: Giving women a better deal

This goal promotes equality between men and women, and seeks to give girls as good a deal at school as boys get. But, under the status quo, climate change is likely to make life more difficult. Whatever is bad for poor communities will be bad for women. Stuck with 'traditional female roles' – in other words, doing all the work on the farm and in the household – women will bear the greater burdens that global warming dumps on the poor.

As greater pressure is placed on already stretched government budgets by the costs of climate change, the poorest members of the community, who already have least access to health and education services (women) will become poorer and more marginalized.

Goal 5: Sorting out the health problem

Here is a sweeping set of targets that is vulnerable to climate change. These targets seek to cut by two-thirds the number of children who die before their fifth birthday, to reduce by three-quarters the number of women who die as a result of childbirth, and to stop and reverse the spread of major killers such as HIV/AIDS, malaria and other diseases.

But as the former chair of the Intergovernmental Panel on Climate Change (IPCC) Robert Watson, said: 'Projected changes in climate could lead to an increase in the number of people at risk of malaria of the order of tens of millions annually.' Locations where mosquitoes and tsetse flies can thrive will change, introducing the diseases they carry, such as malaria, dengue and yellow fevers, to new populations. Epidemiologist Andrew Dobson of Princeton University was quoted in *Science* magazine as saying: 'Climate change is disrupting natural ecosystems in a way that is making life better for infectious diseases. The accumulation of evidence has us extremely worried. We share diseases with some of these species. The risk for humans is going up.'

Many dangers cross over from other problems that are a result of global warming. For example, we've already seen the threat to people's ability to feed themselves. Hungry, malnourished people are also more susceptible to disease. Poor people, too, are also more vulnerable to disease. The difference of infection and survival rates concerning HIV/AIDS between rich and poor countries also demonstrates the significant degree to which the illness is a disease of poverty.

Drought, too, pushes people to drink from ever-more polluted water sources. Climate change could be setting in train a domino effect that topples the weakest members of global society.

Floods and storm surges contaminate drinking water supplies. Floods driven by the El Nino phenomena along the East African coastline brought cholera in 1997 and 1998. There was also an outbreak of rift valley fever that jumped the species boundary from cattle. Warming temperatures also mean that some diseases that would normally die off in the cold of winter may now proliferate more aggressively: 'It's not only going to be a warmer world, it's going to be a sicker world.'

The problems are not isolated to poor countries. In 2003 a sudden heatwave that coincided with national holidays in France led to around 15,000 deaths above the seasonal average. Rising heat-related deaths will particularly affect the world's burgeoning mega-cities, which already create 'hotspots' warmer than the natural background temperature because the way in which they are built up interrupts the natural exchange of heat between the ground and the atmosphere.

Goal 6: Clean drinking water, sorting out city slums and 'sustainable development'

In a rather throw-away fashion, and without really thinking through the consequences, this goal calls on countries to 'integrate the principles of sustainable development' within country policies. It also aims to halve the proportion of people who do not have reliable safe drinking water by the year 2015, and to improve the lot of 100 million slum dwellers, somewhat arbitrarily, by the year 2020.

To begin with, and as a fundamental test case, the first point would require all countries to play their part in a global plan that stood a realistic chance of stopping climate change. Such a plan is the foundation stone of anything that can call itself sustainable development. And yet, as described later on, it is very far from the international target that the world has today, set by the Kyoto Protocol.

The aim of increasing access to safe drinking water is also fatally compromised by global warming. Around 1.3 billion people are estimated to lack enough safe water to drink. With growing economies and rising populations, that figure is expected to double by 2025. Worryingly, worldwide water consumption rose twice as fast as population over the duration of the last century. Scenarios for climate change suggest that, in spite of more extreme storms and rainfall in some areas, in many arid and semi-arid regions of the world water supplies will decrease drastically. Asia's great rivers, such as the Tigris, Euphrates, Indus and Brahmaputra, are expected to experience a one quarter drop in flow. At the same time, more and more people are expected to cram into Asia's mega-cities, putting even more pressure on existing water supplies. India's capital Delhi may exhaust freshwater reserves by 2015 and two-thirds of China's cities already face serious shortages.

Most of the world's mega-cities are coastal and are uniquely vulnerable to climate change and sea-level rise. Across Asia, urban populations are rising between four and five times faster than rural ones. The pressure on quality of life in big cities is already unbearable for millions even without global warming. Pumping groundwater at unsustainable rates can also worsen the problem by causing subsidence. As desalination plants become more necessary for drinking water and slum dwellers need to move away from particularly vulnerable areas, the costs imposed on developing countries become still more of a burden.

Two other problems and how they are related to environmental governance . . .

Trade

The World Trade Organization (WTO) exists, primarily, to promote international trade for its own sake. The fact that it has, to date, failed the world's poorest countries does not prevent ardent free trade advocates from claiming that trade liberalization will, *per se*, benefit those most in need. As mentioned above the WTO, like the IMF, is an institution of global governance that does have economic sanctions available to enforce its rules on member countries. The same is not currently true for multilateral environmental agreements, the institutions that shepherd them and their signatories. For example, pending innovative legal actions, there is nothing to force the US into compliance with the Kyoto Protocol, which although it did not ratify, it had signed, along with the precursor agreement, the United Nations Framework Convention on Climate Change (UNFCCC). This means that a *de facto* hierarchy exists in the international system, with environmental and social agreements falling further down the power ladder than economic agreements.

To draw a rough parallel with national government in the UK, it would be as if only the departments of trade and industry and the Treasury were in the Cabinet, with environment, health, employment and social security left outside and not represented when the big decisions were made. This creates real problems when difficult issues arise.

For example, international trade has increased astonishingly during recent decades. One day's trade at the turn of the millennium approximately equalled a whole year's commerce 50 years earlier. Trade as a share of total world economic output also increased steadily over the same time frame. Air freight increased fastest of all. From the existence of virtually no airfreight 50 years ago, in 1998 the equivalent of 1 tonne of goods was flown 100 billion kilometres.

But staggering gaps exist between the governance of economic and environmental issues. The greenhouse gas emissions that stem from international trade from so-called bunker fuels – the fuels that power the transport of goods in international air and marine freight – are not included in the modest targets of the Kyoto Protocol to cut emissions. They enjoy, literally, a free ride.

Furthermore, if countries want to develop their own energy security by investing in lean, low carbon domestic industries, they could fall foul of the Article 5 of the WTO Agreement on Subsidies and Countervailing Measures. Similarly, attempts to introduce energy efficiency standards to meet climate change goals could similarly be challenged under the WTO Agreement on Technical Barriers to Trade. Under this regime, countries are not allowed to discriminate between traded goods on the basis of the way in which they have been made, even if one is produced in a wasteful and environmentally damaging fashion and another is not. Eco-labelling, even when voluntary, has also typically been viewed with suspicion as an attempt to introduce non-economic criteria into trade.

Debt

Somehow the world arrived at a situation where 'debtor' is a term synonymous with economically weak developing world countries, while 'creditor' referred to the superficially shiny efficiency of the rich industrialized nations. These terms are more than merely economically descriptive. They carry weight and moral judgements. Debtor equals feckless, dependent and largely incapable. Creditor means supportive, generous, trustworthy and solid. But, in terms of the global environment, the words have taken on these meanings in direct contradiction of reality.

The US, for example, a spider at the centre of the web of the international financial community, often behaves with the piety of an old high street bank manager. At the same time, however, it is simultaneously the world's biggest economic and environmental debtor. Debt is about power, politics and how you play the system. But now the system could be about to break down.

Conventional developing world foreign debt dominated the international development debate in the second half of the 1990s. Millions signed petitions. Thousands attended demonstrations. Dozens of reports were written. As a result of the biggest international mobilization since the anti-apartheid movement, officials made a U-turn in policy. They decided that the debts of the poorest countries were, indeed, unsustainable and designed a labyrinthine mechanism to deal with it.

In July 2001, Jubilee Research, a successor to the Jubilee 2000 coalition campaign, published a report called *Flogging a Dead Process* (see www.jubilee2000uk. org/media/170701Flogging_process.htm). The report described how all 23 countries, from an original list of 41 that had qualified for the so-called Highly Indebted Poor Countries initiative (HIPC), were returning to having 'unsustainable debt burdens'. In spite of winning some limited debt relief for a handful of countries to be spent on health and education, and building an international campaign movement, a harsh judgement would say that everyone's best efforts had failed. The poorest countries in the world were back to square one.

Perhaps the problem was that the outstanding poor country foreign debt, mostly African, standing at around US$350 billion, was simply not big enough to pose a worry to the powerful and to demand action.

Governing the global environmental commons

Then something happened that started to turn the world upside down. A connection was made and, looked at afresh, creditors became debtors and vice versa.

All that it takes is a different accounting system. If, instead of using abstract international finance as a guide, we look at natural resource accounts, things appear differently and the challenge of environmental governance comes into focus. If we measure the degree to which countries are over- or under-consuming fossil fuels against a reasonable measure of sustainable consumption, a picture emerges in which financial creditors become environmental debtors and, likewise, financial debtors become environmental creditors.

In governance terms it is illuminating to compare and contrast the attempts of the international community to develop agreements that deal with these twin crises: the HIPC initiative and the Kyoto Protocol.

Who pays the price?

- *Carbon debt:* the poorest people in the poorest countries suffer overwhelmingly the worst impacts of climate change. By 2025 nearly half of people living in developing countries will be vulnerable to 'hydro-meteorological disasters', otherwise known as floods and storms.
- *HIPC debt:* the populations of the poorest countries pay for the debt through their taxes and through the loss of investment in schools and hospitals.

Who is responsible for the debts?

- *Carbon debt:* historically, the industrialized countries of the rich world are almost entirely responsible for climate change.

- *HIPC debt:* the debts that weigh heavily on the shoulders of poor people are invariably the consequence of collusion between elites, North and South. Nevertheless, the scale of outstanding un-payable debt for poor countries is oddly similar to the amount they lost in declining terms of trade during a single decade from the early 1980s.

Who controls the process?

- *Carbon debt:* rich countries drive the Kyoto Protocol and decide for themselves how much they should do to control climate change.
- *HIPC debt:* rich countries and their appointed representatives in the financial institutions drive the HIPC initiative and decide how much poor countries should pay.

Are the targets adequate?

- *Carbon debt:* the Kyoto Protocol proposes an average 5.2 per cent cut in carbon dioxide (CO_2) emissions for rich countries against 1995 levels. The scientific consensus is that cuts of 60 to 80 per cent are necessary. Some, such as the head of UNEP, go further, calling for cuts of 90 per cent or more. The UK's Secretary of State, Margaret Beckett, stated that current US policy could leave their emissions 25 per cent higher in 2010, compared to the 7 per cent cut that the US agreed to in Kyoto.
- *HIPC debt:* notionally, HIPC will write off around one third of the debts of 23 qualifying countries. Jubilee Research at the New Economics Foundation (NEF) estimates that 39 of 42 countries need 100 per cent cancellation, plus a doubling in aid to reach the Millennium Development Goals.

How is 'stabilization' achieved?

- *Carbon debt:* no official proposal in the international negotiations comes close to stabilizing climate change.
- *HIPC debt:* a macro-economic plan that imposes measures for economic stabilization is a precondition to qualifying for conventional debt relief.

Is adjustment demanded?

- *Carbon debt:* US citizens lead one of the most fossil-fuel intensive lifestyles in the world. Yet, the US administration dismisses as unacceptable any demand to change the American way of life in response to climate change.
- *HIPC debt:* Agreeing to fundamental economic adjustment is a precondition to qualifying for conventional debt relief.

Who designs the stabilization and adjustment?

- *Carbon debt:* for what little there is, the rich countries design the stabilization and adjustment.
- *HIPC debt:* again, rich countries design the stabilization.

Is it legal?

- *Carbon debt:* industrialized countries are setting up carbon trading regimes to help implement the Kyoto Protocol. However, you cannot trade what you do not own. Consequently, before there is an agreed global basis for allocating emissions entitlements, any emissions trading is effectively trading in stolen goods.
- *HIPC debt:* the Group of 8 industrialized countries control 49 per cent of votes on the board of the IMF, and voting allocations are related to the size of financial contributions. In most electoral democracies, paying for votes would be considered a criminal offence.

Given the economic problem of global governance neatly demonstrated by the poor country debt crisis, and the environmental problem of global governance comprehensively illustrated by climate change, what should be done?

Environmental governance has to be a process of reconciling the ecological debts of the rich and, in the process, halting the life-threatening, development-destroying phenomenon of climate change. It has to generate the resources and free up the environmental space necessary to meet people's basic needs and enhance the well-being of populations trapped in hardship.

Something positive may emerge from poor countries' negative experience of market-led economic adjustment programmes over the last few decades. The principles may now be used to design sustainable economies for the original architects of adjustment – the rich countries.

Conventional adjustment is a two-stage process. Stabilization comes first, followed by a fundamental re-gearing of the economy. How might this apply to tackling ecological debt and establishing environmentally sustainable economies?

The first task would be to remove major distortions. Standard economic measurements do not include social and environmental costs. This means two things. The economy free rides on the way in which families care for workers and the way in which natural resources are used up, like spending a one-off family inheritance. The second effect is a hugely over-valued economy – like a company's accounts that only show income, not expenditure.

Full-cost accounting would create the proper feedback of information to the economy, helping return balance to the nation's economic accounts for more prudential economic planning. Adjustment will be a much longer, negotiated process. Adjustment implies two key approaches: first, a broad range of reforms to develop greater economic democracy; and, second, that all economic planning is set within known environmental limits – primarily, in this case, climatic tolerance.

Essentially, these changes are about restoring the balance of environmental payments – something that results from the trade between human economic activity and the natural environment. But before a balance can be achieved the ecological deficit, manifest in the damaging accumulation of CO_2 in the atmosphere, must be eliminated.

The adjustment process will need to be set within parameters and an orderly framework – something that is very different from the Kyoto Protocol. The leading complementary and alternative approach is called contraction and convergence.

It is never likely that everyone in the world will use identical amounts of fossil fuels. However, it is highly likely that any deal to manage the global commons of the atmosphere will have to be based on the principle that, in a carbon-constrained world, everyone should have equal entitlements to their share of the atmosphere's ability to safely absorb pollution.

Such an agreement implies that those people and nations who take the economic benefits by emitting more than their fair share will somehow have to pay compensation to the 'under-emitters' by purchasing their spare entitlements. Otherwise, they run up a huge ecological debt.[3] The necessary process is to cap total emissions, progressively reduce them and share, equally, entitlements to emit.

If a target is set for an acceptable concentration of greenhouse gases in the atmosphere, and an 'emissions budget' set to meet it, it becomes possible to work out for every year from now until the target is met what everybody's logical and equal share is of the atmosphere's ability to soak up our waste emissions.

To do this a formula is used so that, in an agreed timeframe, entitlements to emit are pre-distributed in a pattern of international convergence so that, globally, shares become equal per capita. This unavoidable procedure – if chaos is to be avoided – was described and given the term 'contraction and convergence' by the London-based Global Commons Institute.[4]

In essence, the world has a carbon cake strictly limited in size. Beyond certain dimensions it becomes rapidly poisonous for everyone, and the only way to begin negotiations on how to cut the cake is to start with the principle that we all have equal access rights. What we do with them is another matter.

Conclusion

Economic problems cannot be solved without putting a halt to global warming. At the same time, no solution to global warming will be politically acceptable or morally defensible without a framework that provides the environmental space necessary to improve the lot of the global majority living in the Southern hemisphere.

It may be that there will be global economic upheaval due to the use of fossil fuels even before the affects of global warming become any worse. Developing countries may well be hit first by a growing divergence between demand for, and production of, oil. At this point, due by consensus within the industry to occur at some point in the coming decade, economic life will become much more hazardous and expensive for oil-importing countries. The great oil shocks of the 1970s may pale by comparison. To prevent conflict and upheaval this problem, too, will need a constitutional settlement for which the international machinery does not yet exist.

Sustainable governance means learning to live within our natural resource budget, and in such a way that solves the economic problem for all. Global warming creates a very simple test for economics. From now on every economic policy and practical project will have to be examined as to whether it is climate proof and climate friendly.

Box 4.1 How contraction and convergence (C&C) works to reconcile the ecological debt of climate change[5]

All countries collectively agree a target for a stable atmospheric concentration of carbon dioxide in the atmosphere. A 'global emissions budget' is then calculated, derived from the target atmospheric concentration figure. The target is reviewed annually so that it can be revised with new scientific findings. Once the 'contraction budget' has been decided, the next question is how to distribute the entitlements within it between countries. Under contraction and convergence, the allocations of emissions entitlements between countries would converge by a specific date.

By that year, entitlements would be allocated in proportion to national population as it was in a specified baseline year. Full emissions trading is a design feature of the concept. Contraction and convergence (C&C) would reduce the complexity of climate negotiations to two simple variables that would need to be agreed: the target atmospheric concentration of carbon dioxide (CO_2) and the date at which entitlements would converge at equal per-capita allocations.

The approach offers the best chance of solving a great, and immensely destructive, international paradox. Developing world countries stand to be hit first and worst by global warming. The Millennium Development Goals (MDGs) will all be undermined, if not wrecked, by global warming. Yet, developing world countries have been reluctant to play along with the climate negotiations as conducted to date. They see no reason why (if rich countries have had a free ride on the Earth's finite fossil fuel resources for the whole of their development) that they should jeopardize their own economies through accepting any perceived restraints on their activity. But contraction and convergence deals with this seemingly inescapable trap.

Developing countries have consistently refused to take part in a framework that pre-allocates the property rights to a finite carbon budget in a manifestly inequitable way – so-called 'grandfathering' – in which the starting point is one where countries 'inherit' their historical emission levels. This approach creates, in effect, a carbon aristocracy.

By specifying a set date for convergence at equal per-capita rights, the C&C approach would give developing countries surplus emission allocations that they could then sell to countries that need extra permits – most of them developed. The revenue flow from the sale of surplus permits would give developing countries an income flow from climate change policy, which would encourage participation, and would also create an added incentive to invest in clean technologies.

Developing world countries also stand to benefit more the sooner that such an agreement is made. As time passes, the cuts needed to prevent runaway global warming become bigger and tradable emissions become fewer. In the intervening period, rich over-polluting countries are abusing the global commons of the atmosphere without having to pay.

C&C and the US

Interestingly, Contraction and Convergence (C&C) would also fit with the stated position of the otherwise recalcitrant US. In his statements on climate change, President Bush set out specific criteria for what sort of treaty the US would be willing to sign up to. These include a truly global deal, with emission targets (or, from another perspective, entitlements) for developing countries and the need for a science-based approach. C&C, with its global participation design and formal greenhouse gas concentration target, is exactly such an approach. C&C is also fully consistent with the famous 1997 Byrd Hagel US Senate resolution that stipulated that the US would not sign up to any treaty that did not include developing countries.

This has enormous and, from a development perspective, very positive consequences since it can liberate resources to finance development. However, as action to combat global warming is delayed, emissions grow and populations rise, and the sustainable size of a carbon cake slice will get smaller and smaller. In other words, the sooner we act the better.

Notes

1　This material in this chapter is largely taken from the book *Ecological Debt: The Health of the Planet and the Wealth of Nations*, published by Pluto Press (Sims, 2005). The six sections on the Millennium Development Goals draw from the report *The End of Development*, which was a joint project between Andrew Simms and Jonathan Walter, editor of the *World Disasters Report*, and published jointly by the New Economics Foundation and the Bangladesh Centre for Advanced Studies. The report is available from www.neweconomics.org.

2　United Nations Secretary General Kofi Annan (2000) 'Address to the Millennium Forum', New York, 22 May 2000

3　NEF (New Economics Foundation) (2002) *Balancing the Other Budget: Proposals for Solving the Greater Debt Crisis*, NEF, London. Available at http://www.neweconomics.org/gen/z_sys_PublicationDetail.aspx?PID=111

4　For a detailed explanation of contraction and convergence, see the Global Commons Institute's website at www.gci.org.uk.

5　Adapted from Evans, A. (2002) *Fresh Air? Options for the Future Architecture of International Climate Change Policy*, NEF, London

5

Society: Participation and Engagement

Maria Figueroa Küpçü[1]

Introduction

The global threats of our age include terror, deadly weapons, genocide, infectious disease, poverty, environmental degradation, and organized crime. They will not wait for states to sort out their differences (Kofi Annan, UN Secretary General, 2004).[2]

The 21st century has witnessed unprecedented increases in the participatory nature of governance. Technological breakthroughs and economic integration have accelerated a process of globalization that has shaped new political and social dynamics. For the first time in history, a majority of the world's people live in democratic regimes (UNDP, 2002).[3]

Today, citizens expect greater say in the decisions that impact upon their communities. Participation for results has become central to successfully implementing the internationally agreed sustainable development commitments.

Global consensus has advanced a significant body of soft law on sustainable development over the past three decades. Each progressive United Nations global conference (notably, Stockholm in 1972 to Rio in 1992, and Johannesburg in 2002) has refined the definition of sustainable development to better integrate environmental issues with the poverty alleviation, good governance and economic justice agendas. At the vanguard are calls for governments to recognize the fundamental linkage between human rights and sustainable development.

The reality on the ground, however, has not reflected the progress at the global level. Even the 2015 Millennium Development Goals (MDGs) risk becoming broken promises if governments do not increase the scope and scale of their implementation efforts. The participation of non-state actors, therefore, has become an essential component of success, and people's participation in good governance[4] for sustainable development – from policy design to decision-making and implementation – is leading to better long-term outcomes.

This chapter explores the social dimension of governance for sustainable development, and how participation and engagement are being fostered in key institutions to aid the design and implementation of sustainable development policy. It outlines the architecture within which these players work and the techniques they use to interact. The chapter also examines obstacles to participation as the world community strives to create and implement policies in which sustainable development is a key value.

Improving the social dimension of good governance

From governing by hierarchy to governing by networks

In increasingly complex societies, nations are evolving from 'governing by hierarchy' to 'governing by network' (Goldsmith and Eggers, 2004). Hierarchical government bureaucracy, the predominant organizational model of the 20th century, favoured highly uniform and routine processes to deliver public value. The complex character of 21st-century problems, however, is poorly suited to this rigid structure. New models of governance are emerging that are capable of greater flexibility, speed and adaptability.

As governments look for ways to deal with the challenges of globalization, their role is changing from one of direct service provider to one in which they must 'engage and manage external partners' (Goldsmith and Eggers, 2004). Governing by network relies on the ability to leverage cross-sector partnerships to implement innovative funding and management relationships. It sees participation of key interest groups from civil society and business as essential to creating lasting public value. It believes that involving new actors in decision-making improves the ultimate outcome by creating shared responsibility, improving transparency, and better targeting services to community needs (Jones, 2003).

The process of working with new partners offers tremendous potential and enormous challenges. Cross-sector relationships must bridge vastly different organizational cultures, find common objectives and create trust. How to manage such complex webs of relationships without getting tangled? Over the past two decades a new vocabulary has developed to describe the techniques and mechanisms that shape this interaction.

Major groups and stakeholders

> *In a world being swept by globalization in the economic sphere, and democratization in the social and political spheres, multi-stakeholder is a necessary condition for sustainability* (Cielito Habito, Philippines Minister of the Environment and Commission on Sustainable Development chair, April 1998).

In 1914 there were 1083 international non-governmental organizations (NGOs), some of which were active in global policy-making. By 2000, there were more than 37,000, one fifth of these formed during the 1990s (UNDP, 2002). The explosion of global civil society has pressured governments to become more transparent, accountable and responsive. It has also required channels for constructive expression. The emergence of a 'stakeholder space' is a significant phenomenon of the past decade (Dodds, 2004).

The term 'stakeholder'[5] came into active use in UN documents during the late 1990s to reflect the diversity of groups participating in global policy-making and implementation (Hemmati et al, 2002). At the global level, NGOs had traditionally been represented as informal advisers to governments. But the visibility and activism of NGOs in the process leading to the 1992 United Nations Conference on Environment and Development (UNCED) in Rio resulted in the formal recognition of nine specific 'major groups'[6] within the conference's negotiated outcome: Agenda 21. This set a precedent for the role of specific groups of non-state actors in global policy-making and implementation.

The outcome of UNCED also created an impulse for 'peer review' and coordination among civil society groups. With a stake in decision-making, new groups began to take the initiative to make operational Agenda 21 commitments. Local authorities, for example, now had independent standing in a system that had previously subordinated them to national-level interests. The International Union of Local Authorities (IULA) undertook to launch a Local Agenda 21 campaign, thereby filling an important gap in the chain of local to global linkages.[7] Only nine major groups are still formally recognized; but the process has galvanized other groups to lobby for access and participation, among them sub-national governments, educators and media representatives.

As the influence of stakeholders has increased, there has been greater scrutiny about who they are, who or what they represent, and how they govern themselves. Governments worry about the legality of non-elected representatives whose increasingly sophisticated lobbying has influenced policy and financial decisions. Developed country stakeholders consistently outnumber those from developing countries, generating criticism of 'Northern'-dominated environmental agendas. Governments and stakeholders continually struggle to create a helpful distinction among the great variety of groups involved – those better suited to academic analysis, policy-making or implementation. The balance between 'participative' and 'representative' democracy is continually tested as governments try to take note of 'interests' and not 'individuals'.

Stakeholders have become more active at the global level through a variety of formal and informal mechanisms. Some remain at the discretion of national governments, such as some countries' practice of including non-state representatives to take part in official government delegations. Others are the initiative of stakeholders themselves as in the case of NGO-organized parallel events that accompany summits and negotiations.

The Habitat II Conference, held in Istanbul in 1996, was the first to formalize stakeholder involvement in the global policy-making process. Major group representatives were allowed to suggest text amendments and to present their views directly to governments in panel presentations of the 'Second Committee'. Though a promising structural innovation, the presentations of the Second Committee had virtually no impact as they were held at the same time as official negotiations.

Nevertheless, Habitat II set important precedents by bringing stakeholders out of the corridors and into the conference rooms of global summits. By 1997, the United Nations General Assembly had recognized the right of stakeholder representatives of the nine major groups to address thc General Assembly, the same status given to a head of state (Dodds, 2004).

Multi-stakeholder dialogues

Multi-stakeholder processes (MSPs) have gained momentum during recent years as governments seek ways of involving stakeholders that are compatible with their pre-existing institutional arrangements and strong norms. These processes take numerous forms, including informal consultations, thematic panel presentations, side events, working groups, high-level discussions and 'multi-stakeholder dialogue' (MSD):

> *In a dialogue of stakeholders, representatives not only state their views, but listen to each others' views for the purpose of developing mutual understanding, including each others' value-base, interests, goals and concerns. Dialogue requires the willing participation of all participants; even one person whose primary orientation is towards getting her or his way can destroy the dialogue* (Hemmati et al, 2002).

The Commission on Sustainable Development (CSD),[8] the UN's coordinating structure for sustainable development policy and implementation, has been an innovator in this technique. Dialogues have been a regular part of its proceedings since 1998 when the first dialogue was held on the theme of industry. The preparatory process of organizing a dialogue is a multi-stakeholder process itself. The CSD Secretariat convenes key stakeholders. Position papers on pre-agreed issues are prepared and circulated in advance to help frame the dialogue agenda. The outcome of the dialogue with governments informs the official deliberations, with analysis, recommendation and the perspective of stakeholders.

The CSD dialogue model has been successfully replicated in other fora. The Organisation for Economic Co-operation and Development (OECD) has held dialogues with trade union representatives to address contentious topics such as biotechnology. The Global Compact Initiative, launched at the World Economic Forum in 1999, was designed to advance corporate citizenship through MSP by bringing together companies, UN agencies and civil society to address issues of human rights, labour, environment and anti-corruption.

While MSDs have become a regular feature of policy preparatory processes, many factors influence their success and impact. MSDs require political will to conduct them and to value their outcomes. To be done well, they require time, human and financial resources. This is especially challenging when multilateral negotiations come under their inevitable pressures. Successful dialogues work with clear objectives and thematic focus, advance planning, pre-established ground rules, trained facilitation and resources to assist follow-up efforts (Ferenz, 2002).

But to be more than talk, MSD outcomes must flow into official policy process. The dialogues of the Bonn 2001 Global Freshwater Conference took an important step in this regard. These MSDs were coordinated by trained facilitators as opposed to the conference secretariat. Focusing the topics of the dialogues reinforced governments' focus on issues of equity and pro-poor distribution of water resources. The timing of sessions, immediately before related ministerial sessions, helped to focus attention on stakeholder views in the official negotiations.[9] Most importantly, the chair of the dialogues was able to draw out MSD recommendations for a response by governments.

Global public policy networks

Global public policy networks (GPPNs), an outgrowth of MSDs, are voluntary arrangements formed to develop policy recommendations on transnational issues, where national governments lack sufficient knowledge or capacity to do so. GPPNs have addressed issues such as debt relief (led by Jubilee 2000), landmines (led by the International Campaign to Ban Landmines) and the construction of large dams (led by the World Commission on Dams). Those dealing with environmental and health issues are more prevalent than any other kind of public–private network (Streck, 2002):

> *A typical network (if there is such a thing) combines the voluntary energy and legitimacy of the civil society sector with the financial muscle and interest of business and the enforcement and rule-making power and coordination and capacity-building skills of states and international organizations. . . Spanning socio-economic, political and cultural gaps, networks manage relationships that might otherwise degenerate into counterproductive confrontations* (Reinicke and Deng, 2000).

GPPNs often develop in situations of deadlock where there is inadequate information or consensus to move forward (Streck, 2002). They have been helpful in adding issues to the global agenda, creating standards that governments can adopt by consensus, and in fostering public awareness.

GPPNs can also boost institutional effectiveness by serving as a pilot phase arrangement that, if successful, develops into part of the global governance architecture. The Global Environment Facility (GEF) is one such example. GEF was formed as a joint venture of the United Nations Development Programme (UNDP), the United Nations Environment Programme (UNEP) and the World Bank in 1991. It pools these partners' resources and funds only the incremental costs of environmental projects dealing with global warming, biodiversity, international waters, ozone depletion and persistent organic pollutants (WEHAB working paper on energy, 2002). In so doing, GEF successfully leveraged US$1billion into US$6billion for developing country projects. Following its pilot phase, GEF's methodology was severely criticized by NGOs whose views were excluded in the original design of the project. Reforms led to a better melding of traditional governance features of UN and Bretton Woods systems, with a significant role for NGOs. While the GEF is still dominated by the partners that created it, it has sufficiently integrated stakeholders to gain greater legitimacy and impact among its beneficiaries (Streck, 2002).

Because they are voluntary arrangements, leadership is a key element in creating and sustaining GPPN. GPPNs have not formed, for example, on critical but controversial issues, such as genetically modified foods – despite the need for global policy recommendations on such issues. More needs to be learned about how to create incentives for GPPNs to form and how to transform successful GPPNs into lasting parts of governance architecture.

Partnerships

One of our major challenges is making sustainable development go to scale, to make something that has worked in a dozen places work in a thousand places (Nitin Desai, WSSD Secretary General, September 2002).

Like GPPN, public–private 'partnerships' (PPP) have gained prominence as way of mobilizing new resources for sustainable development. International organizations and governments actively and enthusiastically promote partnerships as ways of tapping business' funds and research and development (R&D) or of engaging civil society's networks and expertise. Secretary General Annan said that the World Summit on Sustainable Development (WSSD) took 'a major leap forward' by recognizing partnerships as a major outcome of the summit.[10] This development is a breakthrough for an institution that only decades ago was deeply sceptical of the private sector's global ambitions.

The potential of partnerships is certainly alluring. Over 220 WSSD partnerships[11] were identified before the summit, totalling at least US$235 million in resources.[12] Lead partners in these ventures include multinational corporations, such as British Petroleum, Novartis and J. Walter Thompson.

Since WSSD, other UN agencies have begun incorporating partnerships in their efforts. In 2004, the United Nations Conference on Trade and Development (UNCTAD) XI, introduced an agenda item on multi-stakeholder partnerships for the first time. Instead of encouraging all types of partnerships, UNCTAD XI focused on partnership development in four priority areas –- information and communication technologies for development; commodities; investment; and capacity-building and training (including academic institutions) – to help reinforce its mission (UNCTAD, 2004).

Reaction among NGOs and the private sector has been mixed. Many civil society groups have voiced concern about governments off-loading their responsibility to the promise of partnerships. They also worry about the inherent power imbalances between sectors. Will greater private-sector involvement weaken multilateralism? Are partnerships accountable to the beneficiaries they are designed to help? Will governments become too dependent on private-sector funding to criticize their partners? As one expert observed:

How much of a voice does the World Health Organization have in setting priorities for world health with its budget of approximately US$1 billion, when the Global Alliance on Vaccines Initiative (GAVI) has US$1 billion just for vaccines and the Bill and Melinda Gates Foundation is spending well over US$6 billion on infectious diseases (HAI Europe, 2000)?

NGOs warn that partnerships require careful monitoring to understand their true impact.

Corporations also have viewed partnerships cautiously. Some corporations have welcomed the opportunity to reinforce their global reputations and extend their markets. But there is also careful scrutiny on how these affect the financial bottom line. Partnership can be a costly and time-consuming effort.

One of the first challenges is truly defining partnerships for sustainable development. Cooperative arrangements can vary greatly in terms of goals, structure, timeline and power relationships (HAI Europe, 2000). Calling them all 'partnerships' is misleading as it hides the true nature of these arrangements. In the health field, for example, these arrangements can also be labelled 'corporate sponsorship', 'lobby activities' or 'publicly subsidized research collaborations' (HAI Europe, 2000)

As voluntary initiatives, partnerships are not bound to engage or represent the constituencies they affect. Lacking participatory processes, can partnerships truly be pro-poor? Partners also set the standards of disclosure and transparency for their governance processes. Since there is no 'code of conduct' that binds partnerships, do these follow the criteria of good governance?

Especially worrisome are the distorting effects that partnerships can have when they become dependent upon private-sector resources or disconnected from global policy norms. Médecins Sans Frontières' (MSF's) experience with drug donations is illustrative. MSF had solicited drug donations from companies in order to help critically ill people quickly and cost effectively. Eventually, however, it found that this practice distorted rational drug use and even slowed the development of generic production (HAI Europe, 200).

To whom are public–private partnerships accountable? Many of the WSSD partnerships are still in the start-up phase and function on loose definitions of roles and responsibilities. Ultimately, who is responsible if the partnership sours or begins to work counter-productively? Many NGOs have expressed concern that corporations will have gained the benefits of 'blue-washing' their images before they achieve any of the long-term sustainable development outcomes promised.

Spontaneously generated, it is clear that partnerships are not 'balanced'. As of December 2004, 297 partnerships were registered in the UNDESA partnership database.[13] Despite the urgent need for capacity-building at the national level, only 4 per cent of the partnerships launched after WSSD are national in scope.[14] Geographic representation is also lopsided. Of the 61 registered regional partnerships, 42 per cent focus on Asia and the Pacific, 37 per cent on Africa, while only 8 per cent focus on Latin America and the Caribbean, 8 per cent on Europe and North America and 5 per cent on West Asia. In addition, most partnerships are focused on education, technology transfer and ways of strengthening the institutional framework for sustainable development. Few tackle themes such as gender equality or desertification, which are critical to achieving WSSD outcomes. Partnerships' current funding also illustrates the challenge. While most WSSD partnerships are still fundraising, most of those that are funded are supported by international organizations, not by the private sector.[15]

The first International Forum on Partnerships for Sustainable Development, held in Rome in 2004, distilled lessons from partnership experiences to date. Partnerships can succeed when they set achievable goals, defined roles and a shared commitment to communication. They are weakened by many factors, including a limited capacity at the local level to operationalize the objectives; underdeveloped legislation; weak involvement of the private sector; competing pressure to show fast results though sustainable development is a long-term process; lack of leadership from Southern partners; and lack of linkage between partnerships and global processes.[16]

It is clear that partnerships must be evaluated to evolve. The Cardoso Panel, appointed by Secretary General Annan to evaluate the UN's experience with civil society, and NGOs have recommended establishing an 'office of constituency engagement and partnerships' to help bring together the experiences of partnerships across the UN system.[17] This recommendation has been echoed by many in the NGO community who believe that distilling the lessons of those arrangements can create long-lasting sustainable development.

Global-level governance

The global level has been especially innovative in experiments with stakeholder participation. Perhaps this is due to the transnational character of global-level problems or the absence of a central global government. Here the challenge is supporting results at the regional, national and local levels.

The WSSD joined major strands of the environment and development policy agendas. The Johannesburg Plan of Implementation (JPOI) reiterates commitments made since 1992 on sustainable development and incorporates the Secretary General's WEHAB (water, energy, health, food and agriculture, and biodiversity) initiative.[18] At the same time, the WSSD commits itself to the poverty alleviation agenda and the UN Millennium Development Goals (MDGs). These two policy strands have come together in the new work programme of the CSD.

Preparing the WEHAB initiative brought together UN system agencies and institutional coordinating mechanisms to identify policy obstacles and priorities for action. This process created better inter-agency dialogue and exposed important structural gaps. For example, as 'water' and 'energy' lacked an institutional home at the global level, improving coordination on these was declared a high priority.

WEHAB also set the stage for the CSD's new work programme, which has the potential to improve stakeholder participation in governance and policy development (Table 5.1). This multi-year work programme is a significant management innovation at the UN. Its design creates the opportunity for a systematic review progress on sustainable development targets. Now that agenda issues have been clustered, prioritized and segmented, the quality of government and stakeholder inputs is expected to be more focused and action oriented.[19]

However, an ongoing criticism of CSD multi-stakeholder dialogues has been the weak linkage of dialogue recommendations to binding outcomes of inter-governmental processes. The Secretary General, in his report to WSSD's PrepCom

Table 5.1 *Key agencies highlighted in WEHAB papers by specific theme*

WEHAB	Lead agency	Key collaborative agencies/groups
Water		UN system: Food and Agriculture Organization (FAO); UN Department of Economic and Social Affairs (UNDESA); UN Development Programme (UNDP); UN Environment Programme (UNEP); UN Educational, Scientific and Cultural Organization (UNESCO); UN Human Settlements Programme (UN-Habitat); UN International Children's Fund (UNICEF); UN Development Fund for Women (UNIFEM); UN Industrial Development Organization (UNIDO); World Health Organization (WHO); World Meteorological Organization (WMO) International Network on Water, Environment and Health (INWEH) of United Nations University (UNU) regional commissions
Energy		UN system: FAO; Global Environment Facility (GEF);[20] International Atomic Energy Agency (IAEA); UNEP; UNESCO; UNIDO; UNIFEM; WHO; WMO; UNDP; World Bank; UNDESA regional commissions
Health and environment	WHO	UN system: FAO; IAEA; International Fund for Agricultural Development (IFAD); International Labour Organization (ILO); Joint UN Programme on HIV/AIDS (UNAIDS); UNDP; UNEP; UN Population Fund (UNFPA); UNICEF; UNIFEM; World Bank regional commissions
Agriculture	FAO in coordination with UN Administrative Coordination Committee (ACC) Network on Rural Development and Food Security[21]	UN system: IFAD; UNDP; UNEP; UNIFEM; World Food Programme (WFP); World Bank Consultative Group on International Agricultural Research (CGIAR); Convention on Biological Diversity (CBD) regional commissions
Biodiversity	CBD	UN system: FAO; UN Conference on Trade and Development (UNCTAD); UNDP; UNESCO; UNEP; World Bank; GEF CGIAR; Convention on International Trade in Endangered Species of Wild Fauna and Flora (CITES); Convention on the Conservation of Migratory Species of Wild Animals (CMS)

Source: WEHAB working papers, 2002

II, identified two major shortcomings of stakeholder participation in the process: inadequate participation of women and developing country representatives (ECOSOC, 2002, para 169), and the fact that 'stakeholder participation is rarely allowed in actual decision-making' (ECOSOC, 2002, para 170).[22]

NGOs such as Stakeholder Forum have called for giving the chairs of MSD the authority to draw out key outcomes and to bring these into the intergovernmental process. As in the case of the 2001 Bonn Freshwater Conference, this would ensure that stakeholder views had policy bite, not just rhetorical bluster.

Regional-level governance

At the regional level, the primary challenge has been supporting country-level efforts to comply with and integrate policy. Regional initiatives have come under increasing pressure by civil society, business and international organizations to implement participatory processes. Yet, national governments, especially those with weak governance structures, are often unwilling to make MSPs a priority. Regional-level efforts help to overcome this reluctance with institutional arrangements and funds.

Following WSSD, the United Nation's five regional commissions[23] organized 'implementation meetings' to bring together regional funds, finance and trade institutions, as well as stakeholders in order to determine how regional processes could support the outcomes of the WSSD. These advanced initiatives, such as the New Partnership for Africa's Development (NEPAD), the Initiative of Latin America and the Caribbean on Sustainable Development and the Phnom Penh Regional Platform on Sustainable Development for Asia and the Pacific.[24] While the regional efforts vary in their ability to engage stakeholders, NEPAD illustrates an interesting experience of adaptation.

NEPAD, adopted by governments at the Organization for African Unity (OAU) at the Lusaka Summit in 2001, is a commitment by African governments to integrate sustainable development commitments within national development processes. NEPAD priorities coincide with the MDG commitments, thus creating a consistent analytical framework and measurement process by which governments can track progress on both initiatives. Achieving these commitments is seen as integral to generating economic growth in the region.

African governments seem to be demonstrating the political will for NEPAD to succeed by the institutional arrangements that they have made. In many countries, the initiative is given cabinet-level attention. In Algeria, for example, the NEPAD focal point is the minister responsible for African and Maghreb affairs, a high-level post within the Ministry of Foreign Affairs, reporting directly to the president and council of ministers. In Nigeria, work is coordinated by a senior special assistant to the president. High-level commitment to the NEPAD framework has affected horizontal and vertical coordination within the government bureaucracy. African governments' stated commitment to 'good governance' has been further strengthened by NEPAD's innovative African Peer Review Mechanism. This is a government-to-government learning process through which countries volunteer to have their progress reviewed by a panel of independent eminent persons.

While NEPAD has been an important governmental initiative, it has been criticized by African NGOs for inadequate stakeholder participation. Many called NEPAD an illegitimate outcome because it did not involve stakeholders in the original design process. It also did not give stakeholders a role in implementation. Though many countries launched 'outreach initiatives' to popularize NEPAD's goals among the public, these met with limited success.

In response, the first NEPAD multi-stakeholder dialogue was held in 2003 to assess the initiative's first three years. Heads of state from South Africa, Nigeria, Senegal and Algeria came together with several hundred stakeholder representatives. Two dialogues were organized on the basis of broad background papers to review the 'conditions for sustainable development' and specific sectoral progress. While primarily an occasion for speeches, the effort to address stakeholder views through multi-stakeholder dialogue has helped to support similar country-level initiatives to engage groups such as trade unions, workers and government-owned businesses.

National-level governance

At the national level, governments are often too challenged just creating interdepartmental synergies to focus resources on effective stakeholder processes. Where MSPs do exist, the challenge is institutionalizing their links to official policy processes.

Agenda 21 called for national strategies for sustainable development (NSSD), which 'build upon and harmonize the various sectoral economic, social and environmental policies and plans that are operating in the country' by 2002 (UNDESA, 2004). NSSD are the primary mechanisms by which countries report their progress to the CSD.

A 2003 review of NSSD gathered initial evidence that progress implementing NSSD was proceeding very slowly. Based on country reports received at that time, the assessment indicated that only 23 of 191 countries were actively implementing an NSSD. In Western Asia, Africa and Asia and the Pacific, a total of 7 out of 110 countries had developed NSSD (UNDESA, 2004). The WSSD renewed the commitment of Agenda 21 that all countries should adopt an NSSD, this time by 2005.

Agenda 21 and the WSSD also recommended that countries establish national committees (or councils) for sustainable development (NCSDs) to coordinate the implementation of sustainable development commitments. Since 1992, a number of countries have created NCSDs that involve stakeholders in the design, evaluation and implementation of NSSD.

NCSDs have typically been established as advisory bodies. Without legal authority, NCSD recommendations risks being ignored if they are not closely linked to governmental processes and institutions. Comhar is the Irish government's National Sustainable Development Partnership. This 25-member committee is appointed by the minister for the environment and local government and gathers representatives from five areas: the state/public sector; economic sectors; environmental NGOs; social/community NGOs; and the professional/academic sector. Comhar's recommendations flow into the work of the Irish Ministry of Environment, though they have also supported others, such as the Irish Department of Finance.

NCSDs often create processes that follow new norms within traditional governmental systems. The Philippine Council for Sustainable Development (PCSD) was established to develop and coordinate the Philippine Agenda 21 (PA21) strategy. The round table body includes government departments, NGOs, business and trade unions. It has established a network of local councils to involve grassroots perspectives. PCSD is one of the few Filipino government bodies that work on the basis of consensus. The forum is a place for debate and expression by various sectors that has helped inform the national policy dialogue and popularize sustainable development goals.

The creation of NCSDs typically prompts intra-governmental coordination; however, this has not always resulted in increased stakeholder involvement. The Czech Republic launched broad public consultation on a proposed NSSD between 1998–2001, which resulted in such sharp disagreements that the process had to be put on hold. The process was taken up again under the Governmental Council for Sustainable Development, which unites the former Commission for International Relations and the Advisory Board of the Deputy Minister for Ecological Policy. While different stakeholders are involved, the focus of the body is decidedly governmental and academic.[25]

Coordination among sub-national governments, while in its infancy, requires a note here as another mechanism for strengthening stakeholder participation at the national level. The WSSD was the first time that sub-national governments, such as those representing Tuscany or West Java, coalesced as a group in global policy-making for sustainable development. The Network of Regional Governments for Sustainable Development (NRG4SD) has identified common principles and a shared commitment to pursuing sustainable development at the sub-national level. Through this mechanism, sub-national governments and associations share knowledge and coordinate initiatives, thus playing a critical role as links between local efforts and national objectives.

Local-level governance

In the past the World Bank institutes have been dealing with government, people like you. . .Yet, no impact. They're now dealing directly with the people. . .We would like you to hear the people you are governing . . .and how they suggest a way out of our numerous problems (citizen in Imo, Nigeria, at CENA dialogue; World Bank, 2004a).

'The sad story is that we are a community of dependents. . .This kind of dependency is what this kind of discussion is to help us break' (government official in Kano, Nigeria, at CENA dialogue; World Bank, 2004a).

Participation at the local level requires developing capacity and integrating MSP within sub-national, regional and national processes.

An increasingly popular local development approach, especially among social funds, has been direct community support:

> *Decentralized sectoral approaches rely on functionally specialized organizations at the local level, with operational autonomy allocated through deconcentration or delegation policies. Local government approaches promote territorially organized political and administrative institutions, with policy and operational autonomy allocated through devolution policies. Direct community support approaches, such as those frequently associated with community-driven development, promote resource transfer and civil society empowerment strategies that emphasize community organizations as institutions of collective action and interlocutors between people and public service providers* (ICLD, 2004)

Direct community support approaches, such as the World Bank's Capacity Enhancement Needs Assessment (CENA), reach out to communities and work through the social units found there – whether formal or informal. CENA methodology convenes stakeholder dialogues through these units in a process that engages the community to assess its own perceptions of needs and resources. Direct community support has been an effective complement to local development approaches that work through government structures or functional departments.

Strengthening direct communication between the funds and communities has led to more effective, rapid delivery of services to the intended beneficiaries. It has promoted both upstream coordination (linking community policy objectives to fiscal arrangements) and downstream coordination (linking governance to service delivery). It has also forced accountability among international organizations and government authorities – especially at the local level.

But direct community support approaches can also highlight the tension between 'participative' and 'representative' democracy at the local level. It may be the case, for example, that the effective community group is a traditional one (for example, a council of elders), which is not representative of all community members (for example, women and youth). Democratic systems and traditional systems often exist in parallel; but an essential component of good governance is transparency in the decision-making process and accountability in choices about inclusion or exclusion.

'Participative' democracy has shown that it can effectively further a pro-poor agenda by bringing decision-making closer to those ultimately affected.[26] In Porto Alegre, Brazil, the Workers' party (PT) implemented a multi-stakeholder approach to formulating municipal budgets as a way of bringing 'popular administration' to government (World Bank, 2004c). The results have not only increased services, despite budget constraints, but have tailored these to fit the particular priorities of different members of the community. Public scrutiny and questioning throughout the budgeting process also eliminated opportunities for corruption, which has previously crippled the budgeting process.

Promoting a demand 'from below' for bottom-up participation is as essential to good local-level governance as top-down initiatives to decentralize power

(Larson and Zeledón, 2004). Ultimate empowerment happens when beneficiaries are given the powers to make decisions themselves. In this process, access to information and education are essential. In the case of the UK-funded Livestock Production Programme (LPP), researcher-derived information is made available to poor farmers so that they have the ability to make decisions affecting the survival of their livestock.[27] This programme has been developed to directly contribute to the UN Millennium Development Goals by supporting the livelihoods approach for specific resource-poor livestock keepers, especially vulnerable groups, whose needs have been identified in various national and sub-national planning.

The right of stakeholders to act on the responsibilities outlined for them in global agreements provides a powerful argument for creating stronger linkages between the human rights and sustainable development frameworks.

Conclusion

The success of implementing the commitments of the global sustainable development agenda increasingly depends upon deepening the involvement of stakeholders in the process. Government's changing role and citizens' demands for greater participation are transforming traditional governance structures. New techniques and methodologies, especially those developed at the global level, are starting to infuse governance at all levels. It is a promising start.

But many questions, especially about the impact, accountability and equity of cross-sector relationships, are yet to be answered. The justification for supporting better multi-stakeholder participation is because it can create better and more long-lasting results. Strengthening the social dimension of governance requires not only creating the institutions, norms and willingness to hear new perspectives, but the ability to translate this dialogue into action for sustainable development. To summarize:

- How can the international community foster closer links between the economic development agenda, such as trade, investment and finance, and the sustainable development agenda using stakeholder participation as a means?
- How can governments and international organizations create incentives to ensure 'balanced' development of voluntary stakeholder initiatives – such as global public policy networks and partnerships?
- At the international and regional levels, how can institutions encourage political will at the national level that makes quality stakeholder processes the rule, not the exception?
- At the national level, how can governments legalize the legitimacy and influence of stakeholder processes in order to better integrate them with existing democratic processes?
- How can we strengthen methods of evaluation and monitoring of MSPs at all levels so that these further the sustainable development and pro-poor agendas?

Notes

1   With special thanks to Felix Dodds, Stakeholder Forum; Belkacem Smaili, Permanent Mission of Algeria to the United Nations; and Talat Shah, World Bank, Environmentally and Socially Sustainable Development (ESSD) Network.

2   Speech to the Council on Foreign Relations, Washington, DC, December 2004

3   The share of the world population living in democratic regimes: 38 per cent (1985), 57 per cent (2000).

4   Good governance is 'the process of decision-making and the process by which decisions are implemented (or not implemented)'. The eight major characteristics of 'good governance' are that it is participatory; consensus oriented; accountable; transparent; responsive; effective and efficient; equitable and inclusive; and follows the rule of law. UN Economic and Social Commission for Asia and Pacific (ESCAP)

5   Stakeholders are 'those who have an interest in a particular decision, either as individuals or representatives of a group. This includes people who influence a decision, or can influence it, as well as those affected by it.'

6   The nine major groups are business and industry; children and youth; women; workers and trade unions; farmers; indigenous peoples; local authorities; NGOs; and the scientific and technological community.

7   See the International Council for Local Environmental Initiatives (ICLEI), website at www.iclei.org

8   The Commission on Sustainable Development (CSD) was established by the United Nations Conference on Environment and Development (UNCED) in 1992 with a mandate to ensure effective follow-up to Agenda 21. CSD is one of the functional commissions of the Economic and Social Council (ECOSOC), the UN body with lead responsibility for coordinating the UN's efforts on sustainable development. The UN Department of Economic and Social Affairs (UNDESA) Division of Sustainable Development serves as a secretariat for the work of the CSD.

9   See International Conference on Freshwater website: www.water-2001.de/msd/stakeholders.asp.

10 The WSSS had two types of outcomes. 'Type I' are official negotiated agreements of global consensus, such as the Johannesburg Declaration and the Johannesburg Plan of Implementation (JPOI). 'Type II' are the non-negotiated outcomes to implement Agenda 21.

11 UNDESA defines them as 'voluntary multi-stakeholder initiatives contributing to the implementation of Agenda 21, Rio+5 and the Johannesburg Plan of Implementation (JPOI)'.

12 See www.johannesburgsummit.org/html/basic_info/faqs.html.

13 See UNDESA website: http://www.un.org/esa/sustdev/partnerships/partnerships.htm.

14 See UNDESA database: sector break-down of registered partnerships global (154), regional (61), sub-regional (71), national (11); available at http://webapps01.un.org/dsd/partnerships/public/browse/do

15 See Annan (2004). 95 of 266 partnerships said they were receiving funding. Of these, 18 per cent are receiving funds from international organizations, 6 per cent received grants from NGOs and an even smaller number are receiving funds from the private sector.

16 See International Forum on Partnership for Sustainable Development (2004, p5).

17 See UN Panel of Eminent Persons on United Nations/Civil Society Relations, www.un.org/reform/panel.htm

18   TheWEHAB initiative focused attention on five key issues where there has been slow progress in implementing Agenda 21: water, energy, health, food and agriculture, and biodiversity and ecosystem management.

19   The review year includes a review of obstacles to implementation; a high-level segment; a regional experience exchange; dialogue with experts; best practices; learning centres; and partnership fairs. The policy year includes an intergovernmental preparatory meeting for policy options and actions to address constraints/obstacles; the chair then prepares a draft negotiating document for consideration at the policy session, which then takes the decision.

20   Lead agencies are UNDP, UNEP and the World Bank.

21   This comprises theWFP; theWorld Bank; IFAD;WHO; ILO; UNESCO; UNICEF; UNDP; UNFPA; UNEP; UN Drugs Control Programme (UNDCP); and UNIFEM.

22   ECOSOC CSC (Economic and Social Council, Commission on Sustainable Development) (2002) *Implementing Agenda 21: Report of the Secretary-General*, E/CN.17/2002/PC2/7

23   These five regional commissions comprise the Economic Commission for Africa (ECA); the Economic and Social Commission for Asia and the Pacific (ESCAP); the Economic Commission for Europe (ECE); the Economic Commission for Latin America and the Caribbean (ECLAC); and the Economic and Social Commission for Western Asia (ESCWA).

24   E/CN.17/2002/PC.2/8

25   See   www.un.org/esa/agenda21/natlinfo/countr/czech/2003nsds_czech republic.pdf.

26   See www.democraciaparticipativa.net/documentos/NelsonCommAdvocate. htm.

27   See www.lpp.uk.The LPP is a project funded by the UK's Department for International Development and managed by NR International.

References

Annan, K. (2004) 'A more secure world:Who needs to do what?' Speech to the Council on Foreign Relations,Washington, DC

Czech Republic (2003) *Status Report*. Available at www.un.org/esa/agenda21/natlinfo/ countr/czech/2003nsds_czechrepublic.pdf

Desai, N. (2000) 'Statement to the second committee by Mr Nitin Desai, Under-Secretary-General for Economic and Social Affairs', available at www.un.org/documents/ga/docs/ 57/ac257-stusg.htm

Diamond, L. and Morlino, L. (2004) 'The quality of democracy: An overview'. *Journal of Democracy*, vol 15, no 4

Dodds, F. (2004) *Stakeholder Democracy*. Report prepared for Institutions for Sustainable Development Workshop, Barcelona

Dodds, F. and Strauss, M. (2004) *How To Lobby at Intergovernmental Meetings*. Earthscan, London

ECOSOC (United Nations Economic and Social Council) (2002) *Implementing Agenda 21: Report of the Secretary-General*. Commission on Sustainable Development tenth session, ECOSOC, E/CN.17/2002/PC2.7, E/CN.17/2002/PC.2/8

ECOSOC (2003) *Commission on Sustainable Development: Report of the 11th session (27 January 2003 and 28 April–9 May 2003)*, E/CN.17/2003/6

ECOSOC (2004) *Partnership for Sustainable Development: Report of the Secretary General.* Commission on Sustainable Development 12th session, February E/CN.17/2004/16

Ferenz, M. N. and the Consensus Building Institute at MIT (2002) *Multistakeholder Dialogues: Learning from the UNCSD Experience.* Report prepared for the Commission on Sustainable Development, Consensus Building Institute at MIT, DESA/DSD/PC3/BP4, Cambridge, MA

Goldsmith, S. and Eggers, W. D. (2004) *Governing by Network: The New Shape of the Public Sector.* Brookings Institution Press, Washington, DC

HAI Europe (Health Action International Europe) (2000) *Public–Private Partnerships: Addressing Health Needs or Corporate Agendas.* Report of the HAI Europe/BUKO Pharma-Kampagne Seminar, available at www.haiweb.org/campaign/PPI/seminar200011.html

Hemmati, M., Dodds, F., Enyati, J. and McHarry, J. (2002) *Multi-stakeholder Processes for Governance and Sustainability.* Earthscan, London

ICLD (International Conference on Local Development) (2004) 'Human Development, Social Development, and Public Sector Management Networks – World Bank'. Discussion Paper for International Conference on Local Development, Washington, DC, 16–18 June 2004, pi

International Forum on Partnership for Sustainable Development (2004) 'Chairman's Summary'. Rome, Italy, March

Iyer, S. (2002) 'Partnerships that raise more questions than answers'. *Third World Resurgence*, no 145–146

Jones, D. (2003) 'Analysing the potential of multi-stakeholder dialogue in water and sanitation sector reform'. Occasional paper series of Building Partnerships for Development in Water and Sanitation, London

Larson, A. and Zeledón, V. (2004) 'Participation and decentralized forest management: Social effects of local government initiatives' Prepared for the Tenth Biennial Conference of the International Association for the Study of Common Property (IASCP,) Oaxaca, Mexico

Livestock Production Programme, www.lpp.uk.com

Philippine Council for Sustainable Development Information Exchange and Networking Centre, www.pcsd.neda.gov.ph/nationalCSD.htm

Reinicke, W. H. and Deng, F. (2000) *Critical Choices: The United Nations, Networks and the Future of Global Governance.* International Development Research Council, Ottawa, Canada

Streck, C. (2002) 'Global public policy networks as coalitions for change', in D. C. Esty and M. H. Ivanova (eds) *Global Environmental Governance: Options and Opportunities.* Yale School of Forestry & Environmental Studies, Connecticut

UN (United Nations) (2002) *Report of the Secretary-General: Overview of Progress Towards Sustainable Development – A Review of the Implementation of Agenda 21, the Programme for the Further Implementation of Agenda 21 and the Johannesburg Plan of Implementation.* UN, New York, E/CN.17/2002/2

UN (2003) Johannesburg Declaration on Sustainable Development and Plan of Implementation of the World Summit on Sustainable Development. UN, available at www.un.org/esa/sustdev/documents/WSSD_POI_PD/English/WSSD_PlanImpl.pdf

UN (2004a) *Integrating the Priorities of the New Partnership for Africa's Development (NEPAD) into the National Development Processes: Experiences from Selected African Countries.* Office of the Special Adviser on Africa, New York

UN (2004b) *Report of the Secretary-General in Response to the Report of the Panel of Eminent Persons on United Nations–Civil Society Relations.* UN, New York

UNCTAD (United Nations Conference on Trade and Development) (2004) 'UNCTAD XI Multi-Stakeholder Partnerships: Note by the UNCTAD Secretariat'. TD/400, São Paolo

UNDESA (United Nations Department of Economic and Social Affairs), Division of Sustainable Development (2004) *Assessment Report on National Sustainable Development Strategies: The Global Picture 2003*. UNDESA, April 2004, available at www.un.org/esa/sustdev/natlinfo/nsds/nsds.htm

UNDP (United Nations Development Programme) (2002) *Human Development Report 2002: Deepening Democracy in a Fragmented World*. Oxford University Press, New York

WEHAB (2002) World Summit for Sustainable Development, WEHAB Framework papers, available at www.johannesburgsummit.org/html/documents/wehab_papers.html

World Bank (2004a) *Shaping the Future: Multi-Stakeholder Dialogues for Community Empowerment in Nigeria*. Video presentation for the International Conference on Local Development, Washington, DC, rtsp://streaming3.worldbank.org/ESSD/SDV/shaping_future.rm

World Bank (2004b) 'Summary: Local development discussion paper'. Prepared for the International Conference on Local Development, Washington, DC, 16–18 June 2004, available at www1.worldbank.org/sp/ldconference/Materials/LDDPFinal.pdf

World Bank (2004c) *Action Learning Program on Participatory Processes for Poverty Reduction Strategies: Case Study 2 – Porto Alegre, Brazil Participatory Approaches in Budgeting and Public Expenditure Management*. The Participation Group, Social Development Department, Washington, DC, available at www.worldbank.org/participation/webfiles/PEM2Brazil.pdf

Part 2

The 'WEHAB' Issues

6

Water: Water and Governance

Alan W. Hall

Introduction

The aim of this chapter is to present a coherent discussion of governance related to water management and development.[1] There are numerous definitions of governance, a word that is difficult to translate into many languages. Essentially, it relates to the broad political and administrative systems by which authority is exercised. Similarly, 'water governance' is a recent term that may not be well understood. The Global Water Partnership (GWP) defines it as follows:

> *Water governance refers to the range of political, social, economic and administrative systems that are in place to develop and manage water resources, and the delivery of water services, at different levels of society.*

Given the complexities of water use within society, developing, allocating and managing it *equitably* and *efficiently* and ensuring *environmental sustainability* requires that disparate voices are heard and respected in decisions over water. Water policy *and the process for its formulation* must have as its goal the sustainable development of water resources, and to make its implementation effective, the key actors/stakeholders must be involved in the process. Governance aspects overlap with technical and economic aspects of water; but governance points us to the political and administrative elements of solving a problem or exploiting an opportunity. Governance of water forms part of the creation of a nation's physical and institutional infrastructure and social cooperation within and between nations.

During the last few years, the concept of integrated water resource management (IWRM) has broadly been accepted as a means of ensuring a balanced and sustainable management of water resources and the provision of water services. IWRM demands a broader societal framework within which there may be a need for significant changes to existing administrative systems in order to facilitate interactions between different stakeholders. The capacity to make these changes depends, therefore, upon changes in *water governance*:

> *The IWRM approach is defined by GWP as a process which promotes the coordinated development and management of water, land and related resources in order to maximize the resultant economic and social welfare in an equitable manner without compromising the sustainability of vital ecosystems* (GWP, 2000a).

Governance and sustainable development of water resources

Governance is about the allocation and regulation of resources and is thus intensely political. It is a more inclusive concept than government *per se*, embracing the relationship between a society and its government. The concept of *water governance* relates here to government policies and actions related to water, encompassing laws, regulations and institutions; but it also relates to networks of influence, including international market forces, the private sector and civil society. It embraces both the formal and the informal institutions by which authority is exercised. All of these are affected by the political systems within which they function: national sovereignty, social values or political ideology may all have a strong impact on attempts to change governance arrangements related to the water sector. For example, land and water rights or anti-corruption measures have wider societal implications.

A term used for discussing the systems embracing all of these facets of society is *distributed governance* (Kooiman, 1993), which expresses well the dispersed nature of modern governance systems. Governance involves facing tough political realities in balancing various interests. For many years the question has been: can the state steer society? Governance in the past reflected a hierarchical system of government that steered society, directing and defining goals using political brokerage (often determined by economic power). In most developing countries, this remains the dominant model, increasing the risk of resource mismanagement and financial bad practice. The late 20th century saw a move towards stronger market-led governance systems in the richer developed countries; but this has been found problematic in countries without the ethos for self-regulation, strong and transparent government and free information.

More recently it has been recognized that the state is no longer able to solve societal problems by acting alone, particularly socio-environmental problems; nor can the private sector address the problems of the poor and the environment alone. Today, cohesive local and global networks are challenging the state's role of 'directing' society. The question currently posed is: can society coordinate and manage itself? This is what is meant by distributed *governance*, which talks about coordination of the various forms of formal and informal types of state/society/ market interaction, and the influence of civil society and policy networks. The same networks may both support the state and hold it to account in its aims to develop society. Thus, there is a dynamic (or what some call unstructured or messy) relationship between different social forces. This is a more socially centred governance system.

Why water governance matters: An international call

The World Summit on Sustainable Development (WSSD) targets and Millennium Development Goals (MDGs) regarding water cannot be achieved without better governance. These specific targets include reducing, by half, the number of people without drinking water and sanitation, and producing integrated water resources management plans by 2005; but all of the other WSSD and MDGs and targets will, to a greater or lesser extent, depend upon fulfilment of water commitments through effective governance systems.

Since the Dublin Freshwater conference and the United Nations Conference on Environment and Development (UNCED) meeting in Rio de Janeiro in 1992, goals have been set that cannot be achieved without good water governance. Calls for action on governance within the water domain have increased throughout the decade. The Hague's Second World Water Forum in March 2000 (Hague Ministerial Declaration, 2000) and the Bonn International Conference on Freshwater (Bonn Keys, 2001) highlighted the critical importance of governance for improving water resources management and delivery of domestic and productive water services. A Dialogue on Effective Water Governance is an initiative of the GWP in partnership with the United Nations Development Programme (UNDP), the World Conservation Union (IUCN) and the International Council for Local Environment Initiatives (ICLEI), which followed up these calls for better water governance and has carried out studies and country-level round tables to raise awareness and increase understanding of the reforms needed and barriers to overcome. The 2002 World Summit on Sustainable Development (WSSD) in Johannesburg gave added legitimacy and national ownership to these calls for better governance of the water sector, and the GWP dialogue was adopted as a 'Type II' implementation partnership at the WSSD.

The UNCED action plan, Agenda 21, includes commitments to support better water governance in Chapter 18 through adopting an integrated approach to water resource management (IWRM). The ten years between Rio and Johannesburg has seen a growing understanding of and commitment to IWRM, and some movement has been made towards its implementation on the ground. However, the full impacts of IWRM in relation to overall governance systems have only recently been appreciated by officials and experts alike. In the WSSD Johannesburg Plan of Implementation (JPOI), the most explicit references to governance for the water sector are in Chapter IV, which makes the specific IWRM target (Article 25) to 'develop integrated water resources management and water efficiency plans by 2005 with support to developing countries through various actions'. This commitment should help to provide greater impetus for the development of strategies for action at the national level; but in order to be really effective, such plans must set out realistic strategies for action, not just restate problems.

Chapter IV includes a list of actions that require the reform of governance systems, for example to 'employ the full range of policy instruments . . . facilitate public–private and other types of partnerships . . . establish stable transparent national regulatory frameworks . . . improve accountability of public institutions and private companies'. Elsewhere there are calls for 'effective legal frameworks . . . effective coordination among bodies and processes working on water-related issues'. The plan of implementation is general, but provides a basis for each country to develop more concrete actions for better governance in their IWRM plans.

Water governance at the international level

Water and globalization

It would be an exaggeration to suggest that water issues are directly affected by increasing globalization. Water management is usually a national or sub-national issue, but often with regional implications for those waters shared by several countries. However, some global factors can affect water indirectly. Aspects of trade and finance, including donor policy, can impact upon water resources and service provision.

For example, with the growing liberalization of trade, water services are becoming increasingly affected by international trade agreements. Often such trade agreements are negotiated under the auspices of the World Trade Organization (WTO) by trade ministry officials who know little about water and may not necessarily consult water officials. Recent concern has been expressed by some non-governmental organizations (NGOs) about the inclusion of water services in the WTO's General Agreement on Trade and Services (GATS). In a statement regarding the current experience in the Ghanaian water sector, Christian Aid made the following statement:

> Currently the government of Ghana is coming under extreme pressure to change the way it supplies water to its people. If the GATS is renegotiated, the rules of international trade may also limit the choice of governments in public-service provision. It is Christian Aid's view that this would not best serve the interests of poor people. . . Christian Aid believes decisions on water – the most vital of all development issues – must be taken freely by the national governments concerned, without outside interference and only after full consultation with those most affected, particularly poor people.

While liberalization of such services may be beneficial in raising foreign direct investment for a country, and government negotiators can place limitations on the commitments government makes in a specific service sector, developing country negotiators may not have adequate information, resources and skills to negotiate the necessary domestic regulatory restrictions to ensure clear limits for GATS obligations.

According to the neo-liberal economic theory that supports the service liberalization process, deregulation and privatization are often seen as fundamental steps for achieving efficient resource use in a market-driven economy. It is felt that competition in international trade and investments can help to create jobs, reduce national debt, raise wages and generate wealth. However, in the case of water privatization, this may actually weaken or even disrupt the call for integrated water management, favouring a single-minded economically efficient approach to water management at the cost of social and environmental factors (Kubo, 1994).

Of particular concern is balancing the promotion of trade with the need to protect domestic regulatory rights of national governments. It is generally accepted that the ability of governments to regulate water services providers is essential to ensure effective private- or public-sector provision of water services, and governments need to protect this 'right to regulate' within international agreements. Yet, specific obligations in GATS and the definition of 'public service' as specified in GATS Article 1.3 remain rather open. This may mean that where water services are either contracted out to the private sector by a public authority or procured from the private sector by a public authority – as is increasingly the case in Western Europe, and Asian and Latin American regions – they may be subject to WTO obligations, such as the requirement of 'national treatment'. This means that legitimate and democratically established legislation or service standards may be deemed 'discriminatory' under the agreement (LGIB, 2004). Other WTO agreements may also affect domestic protection of public goods, such as water – for example, the Agriculture Agreement could affect domestic policy regarding water use for livestock and crop production.

Regional trade agreements such as the North American Free Trade Agreement (NAFTA) and European Union (EU) directives can also affect water governance within a country. Similarly, debt repayments and Highly Indebted Poor Countries (HIPC) initiative agreements may skew a government's ability to allocate budgetary provisions for water services.

The WSSD calls for a more cooperative multilateral environment in providing governance for sustainable development. However, for water, the UN system does not give a good example. Over 20 UN bodies have some involvement in water affairs, with unclear lines of communication and coordination to ensure that their work is complementary. The now-defunct United Nations Administrative Coordination Committee (ACC) subcommittee on water resources is generally thought to be fairly ineffective as a coordinating body across these entities. This was alluded to in a report to the Commission on Sustainable Development (CSD) by the UN Secretary General and the committee that sought to address some of these problems (DESA, 2000).

This challenge mirrors the complexity that exists in most countries, and the call for a more integrated approach is an attempt to overcome the fragmentation that has led to a lack of coherence and resource degradation. Following the WSSD, a new inter-agency group on water – UN Water – was created to coordinate across UN bodies on water. This effectively replaces the old ACC subcommittee; but details of its role and responsibilities still remain unclear. Links between these bodies and the CSD are also uncertain. More needs to be done to achieve coherence and provide additional resources to ensure international political will. The *World Water Development Report* (UN, 2000), launched in March 2003 at the Kyoto World Water Forum, did manage to bring many UN agencies together and offered an example of how these bodies might better coordinate in the future.

Regional governance and shared waters

Given that water issues are not predominantly global in nature, it could be argued that the most important UN institutions for water are the five regional commissions (Latin America and the Caribbean; Asia and Pacific; Africa; Europe and North America; and Western Asia) that can play, for example, an important diplomatic role over shared waters. For water governance, existing bodies that are active at the national level, such as the UNDP through its national offices, could have an important coordinating role, while the specialist agencies, such as the United Nations Food and Agriculture Organization (FAO), the World Health Organization (WHO) and United Nations Environment Programme (UNEP), can provide expertise and information collection, monitoring and knowledge sharing on specific aspects of the water domain.

The legal basis for the management of waters shared between several states is mainly that of informal customary law under which 'riparian' states (states along which or through which a river flows) have rights. These riparian states are bound by 'equitable utilization', which means that they must not unreasonably injure other riparian countries; but this is inadequate in a modern world of scarce resources and increasing potential for conflict. While there are no specialized institutions responsible for international freshwater, there is a need for a system that can resolve disputes in an orderly fashion, with a more formal legal basis.

There are special governance problems related to shared or transboundary waters (at the Bonn Freshwater Conference, this was so sensitive that countries could not even agree on the term to use despite many years of debate about the issue). There is considerable experience and literature that can only be touched upon here. In the absence of acceptable international agreements, it is often force that dictates decisions and actions. There are, however, increasing examples of water being a catalyst for regional cooperation with negotiation for shared waters based on the benefits that all parties can gain from any agreement. The recent Agreement on the Incomati and Maputo Rivers in Southern Africa is an example. Recent progress on the Nile Waters Initiative is another example of a patient governance dialogue, where the catalyst for negotiations was the benefits of increased regional security and stability and consequent economic development for all parties, rather than water use as such. It is important to note that shared waters often extend to the coastal zone and UNEP's Global Programme of Action (GPA) makes this link between fresh and coastal waters (www.gpa.unep.org).

Although most negotiations over shared waters are on a bilateral basis, there are wider international laws and regional agreements. One important regional convention is the *Protection and Use of Transboundary Watercourses and International Lakes (Water Convention),* which was established in 1992 by the regional Economic Commission for Europe (UNECE). It is intended to strengthen national measures for the protection and ecologically sound management of transboundary surface water and groundwater, and obliges parties to prevent, control and reduce water pollution from point and non-point sources. However, the *UN Convention on the Law of the Non-Navigational Uses of International Watercourses,* agreed in 1997, is the only comprehensive international legal framework for guiding transboundary water conflicts. The convention consists of a set of guidelines to encourage bilateral

Box 6.1 The case of Lake Peipsi

Lake Peipsi (also known as Lake Chudskoe) is water shared by Russia and Estonia. It is a good example of using IWRM tools in managing transboundary waters and shows how political will and cooperative approaches can lead to sustainable water resources management. It demonstrates the difficulty of involving local civil society in sensitive political discourse. The first and clearest lesson is that states and governments are likely to get into serious political and social difficulties if they ignore the ideas of participation and openness. The value of distributed governance is demonstrated, although the barriers to change in many countries indicate that this will evolve slowly over many years. The Lake Peipsi case also highlights the specific issue of water governance related to the use of shared waters between nation states (GWP, 2002).

and multilateral coordination without sanctions. To date, it has been ratified by only 16 countries and is therefore not yet fully operational. The potential for conflict over water is increasing and better international efforts are needed to solve transboundary water conflicts (de Villiers, 1999).

Water governance at the national level

The Dublin Water Principles (1992) bring water resources firmly under the state's function of clarifying and maintaining a system of property rights, and, through the principle of participatory management, it asserts the relevance of meaningful decentralization at the most appropriate level of governance. There is increasing pressure to recognize and formalize water rights, and this is already happening in many countries. Formalizing rights raises complex questions about the plurality of claims and the balancing of the distribution of benefits among social groups. It also imposes responsibilities, including, in particular, pollution prevention and financial sustainability. The process of formalization is often biased in favour of the rich and powerful who may abuse the system and capture rights. Informal 'rights', defined locally with their historical rules and principles, are equally important and improper formalization without adequate consultation may lead to conflict between the formal and traditional. The capacity to defend rights against competing claimants is essential for the rights to be meaningful, whether they are formal or informal. An important matter to clarify is the extent to which the processes of devolving water rights serve the entire population.

Water law varies widely

Water governance is concerned with the functions, balances and structures internal to the water sector. It includes the framing of social agreements on property rights and the structure to administer and enforce them under the law. Effective governance of water resources and water service delivery will require the combined commitment of government and various groups in civil society, particularly at local/community levels, as well as the private sector.

There is often a marked difference between the philosophical continental European and Latin American approaches and the pragmatic US–Anglo Saxon schools of thought about water jurisdiction, as well as systems with others derived from more ancient roots, such as those of India and Islamic countries. A relatively clear original demarcation of property rights and experimentation with these rights over time has led the US to flexible approaches to water governance. This approach allows for adjustments when economic and social conditions change because it does not aspire to build institutions that cover all possible eventualities. Other examples, such as in South Africa, show real progress in introducing water governance systems, with a strong emphasis on community involvement. In South Africa, the country has been divided into 19 Water Management Areas (WMAs) (Kara, 2003). The water resources in each WMA will be controlled by a local Catchment Management Agency (CMA), which will have to make decisions on how its water is allocated and used. Public participation and cooperative governance are key tenets in the operation of CMAs (Versfeld, 2000). This approach was clearly endorsed by one of the 'Bonn Keys' developed at the international conference on freshwater in Bonn shortly before WSSD, which stated:

> *Decentralization is key. The local level is where national policy meets community needs. Local authorities – if delegated the power and the means, and if supported to build their capacities – can provide for increased responsiveness and transparency in water management, and increase the participation of women and men, farmer and fisher, young and old, town and country dweller . . . [as well as encourage] cooperation within river basins and make existing agreements more vital and valid* (Bonn Keys, 2001).

Often, modern and traditional systems exist at the same time, with traditional systems not necessarily less strong because they are manifested in cultural expectations rather than written rules. A social perception of equitable sharing is important to good governance. The notion of flexibility and equitable sharing is, however, alien to many countries whose governance systems are rigid and do not allow for '*reasonableness*'. Institutional flexibility is often not present and without enforceable sanctions, poor governance systems can tend to favour the strongest voices. This makes it very difficult and even dangerous to translate practices based on flexibility and pragmatism within many developing country governance environments unless the prevailing social system can provide adequate sanction against miscreants.

Legal mandates

Making changes to water governance systems requires an understanding of, and a distinction between, the different functional levels in water management: *operational, organizational* and *constitutional*. The operational level focuses on the use or control of water for specific purposes to fulfil specific needs, such as domestic water supply, wastewater treatment, hydropower, irrigation, environmental management and tourism, which can be in public or private hands. The organizational level deals with the coordination and mediates issues of conflict between these competing users. It also administers the rules and polices for water use and the users in a water system. This function resides within the public sector – and includes, for example, river basin authorities and regulatory bodies – the latter should be autonomous (within constitutional boundaries) if they are to act impartially. Finally, the constitutional function creates the enabling environment within which the other two functions operate. It sets the policies and legislation, taking into account governance systems outside of water institutions, as well as political imperatives.

In many countries, and with increased complexity and demands, these functions are unclear, and often governments may be unable or unwilling to exercise their full responsibilities. In this case more *ad hoc* arrangements at local government or community level are often established. These are vulnerable as they may lack any formal basis and can be adversely affected by vested interests or by central government policies and laws. A participatory and consultative approach when reforming water governance systems can help to strengthen local government and bring the positive aspects of such arrangements into the formal system, reducing vulnerability.

Allocation and regulation at the basin level

The river basin is often proposed as a basis for establishing modern water governance networks. A basin is a closed region where there are incentives for people to come to an agreement on governance systems with water as the focus. River basins can cut across formal jurisdictional boundaries; as a result, local and other government entities, which would not typically work together, could be required to do so under the auspices of a river basin commission or agency, thereby stimulating specific governing capacities and needs. National governments acting alone cannot easily allocate and regulate water at a basin level, as they are unlikely to appreciate local interests or priorities. With an integrated water resources management approach, national government should still provide the guidelines, rules and regulations to help establish the policy and legal frameworks for the basin society to operate. River basin management is not a panacea or something that is automatically established by local and regional (sub-national) governments, but it is something that needs to be based upon a broader national (and/or regional) governance framework.

Regulation within a river basin must address water quality, as well as allocate sufficient quantity to users. Extraction from or discharge into any water body must be based upon a legal permit from an authorized public authority and have time, volume and quality limits. Preventing pollution from agricultural water use (for instance, salinity and nitrates in groundwater) and from industries such as tanneries and mining is becoming increasingly critical. In the state of Sindh, Pakistan, a new water management ordinance recognizes the need to regulate irrigated agriculture. Catchment planning and management, combining land and water use, is a means of regulating at the basin level; but hitherto the tools have not been readily available to make this practical. New approaches, as found, for example, in the EU Water Framework Directive, are now starting to incorporate this within governance systems.

Financial and economic aspects of governance

Economic and other incentives should be introduced by government and by public and private service providers in order to encourage long-term sustainability of resources. Tariff structures are needed that lead to increased efficiency of use and financial sustainability, while enabling access to the poorer users. Subsidies are critical in meeting this seemingly contradictory requirement. However, these should be reviewed regularly and be carefully evaluated to ensure that they accomplish the social and economic goals upon which they are based, and do not lead to perverse use or, as is often the case, benefit the better off in society. A study in 1998 analysed subsidies in several sectors and estimated that about 90 per cent of those for water were perverse, many of them related to irrigation where water charges are low or non-existent (Myers and Kent, 1998). Often this is caused by reluctance to change old practices that may have been appropriate at the time – for example, to promote food security; but vested interests are established which can prevent any change once alternatives solutions for the problem have been developed. Of course, reforms to irrigation water charging cannot be undertaken without taking account of wider issues, such as international food trade and distortions in the world market, as these can directly influence the ability of farmers to pay for water. Furthermore, all new investments in water-using productive activities (such as industry, agriculture and domestic households) need to ensure that adequate water resources are available and that sustainable and efficient water use is guaranteed, otherwise the water will not be available or usable in the longer term. As the fourth recommendation from the 2001 Bonn Freshwater Conference points out:

> *Water should be equitably and sustainably allocated, firstly to basic human needs and then to the functioning of ecosystems and different economic uses, including food security. Allocation mechanisms should balance competing demands and take into account the social, economic and environmental values of water. They should reflect the links between surface and groundwater and those between inland and coastal water, growing urbanization, land management, the need to maintain ecosystem integrity and the threats of desertification and environmental degradation. . . Water should be treated as a valuable and finite resource* (Bonn Keys, 2001)

Corruption

Overcoming corruption is clearly an important aspect of water governance. Until recently, the lack of information and political will has made it difficult to openly discuss this problem, which is rife throughout the world and applies equally to the public and private sectors. Even more controversially, dual strategies can be used by organizations so that, while an organization appears to be thoroughly scrupulous in their home country, the same actor can be simultaneously paying out bribes to organizations overseas to gain access to resources obtained through corrupt methods (Rahaman and Varis, 2003). National law can help to address the problem of corruption; but it is a heavy and expensive instrument – a measure of last resort – as it is often difficult and costly to bring people to court. With more distributed governance, more open competition, more accountable public administrations and more transparent processes, the problem of corruption can be progressively tackled. There are many measures that can be used without recourse to legal methods, including reduced public-sector intervention in the economy, reform of public administrations, strong regulation of the private sector and fair pay for workers. All of these measures can help to reduce the temptation for corruption. Domestic and external regulators and watchdogs, including NGOs, a strong independent media and self-governance (for example, corporate social responsibility and codes of conduct) can all help to produce social sanctions that will deter all but the most unscrupulous from corruption.

Water governance at the local level

Governance and water utilities

Water laws and the regulation of water utilities are key instruments that have been discussed at length and provide many examples of weak governance. The introduction of laws and their implementation is a political process that relates to the political polarization of society. A common problem in many developing countries is that of weak regulation of utility providers. For example, when negotiations with private water utilities jeopardize benefits to the public (such as through extravagant guaranteed returns, and fixed exchange rates and interest rates), it can lead to disillusionment with private-sector involvement in service deliveries. Similarly, public utility owners are often manipulated by governments and can be job havens or cash cows, leaving them weak and under-funded with poor services for the public. Strong regulation is thus essential for both public and private utilities, with a clear definition of the respective duties of the regulator and operator.

Over 90 per cent of domestic water and wastewater services worldwide are provided by the public sector, and this is likely to remain the case. Existing services are often poor and many of those currently un-served hope that public enterprises will one day provide services. But adequate finance and efficient management may not be available to secure good-quality services through the public sector. The introduction of private utility companies has been proposed by some as a solution to increase service coverage effectively and rapidly. This approach has raised concerns with some groups, often for ideological rather than practical reasons. A focus on governance arrangements can help to overcome this fraught debate about private versus public water service delivery and the role of the community. The goal of setting in place a proper governance system can give the debate a more practical focus.

All parties accept that business should not own or control fresh water (WBCSD, 2002); however, business can take on the responsibility for managing services, service delivery and even building and owning infrastructure under government supervision and regulation. The private sector has already taken over responsibility for the management of services from weak, poorly funded public utilities in several large cities in developed and developing countries. The results have been mixed, but can show good economic outcomes and improved distribution to a wider group of citizens. However, one lesson is clear: without the necessary governance framework for regulation, water utilities, whether publicly or privately supplied, will remain inefficient. Too often the performance of the utility operator is overshadowed by the poor governance structures that are prevalent in society. In particular, the public-sector operator must work more transparently for the benefit of the consumer and not for the workers or the bureaucracy. The process for appointing private operators has to be transparent, and governments need to get the support of the user consumer.

The involvement of the private sector in Latin America has had mixed results and there are many difficulties that have to be overcome. In Cochabamba, Bolivia (Finnegan, 2002), for example, unrealistic objectives, inadequate consultation, corruption, poor contracts and the lack of transparency resulted in a fiasco that has put back the provision of services and probably condemned the local people to a continuing saga of inadequate water services possibly for decades. This was a major governance failure (and not a failure of the public administration or private sector *per se*). Similar failures are common throughout the developing world, whether the service provider is public or private. The introduction of private operators needs to take account of some general principles for good utilities governance. Such principles should allow for extensive social and parliamentary debate to reach consensus on private-sector participation and the provision of opportunities for meaningful and opportune user participation.

Governance and community participation

There is a growing perception that the governance of water resources and water services functions more effectively with an open social structure that enables broader participation by civil society, private enterprises, the media and other interest groups, all networking to support and influence government. The role of civil society and NGOs in water management and service delivery also becomes clearer as government regulation facilitates local self-governance.

It is important that in designing effective governance systems, transaction costs are not unduly increased and action is not stifled. There will always be trade-offs, and it is important to get the right balance for each situation rather than seeking the ideal system. In developed countries, governance systems are often overly bureaucratic, unwieldy and can frustrate development. In poorer countries, governance systems should probably avoid imposing too many restrictions on action beyond those necessary for essential sustainability requirements that support economic growth, environmental protection, social welfare and the provision of basic needs for the poor. The economic, environmental and social transaction costs of governance may be quite large and care should be taken to ensure that they are conducted in a balanced way and periodically monitored for their effectiveness.

More decentralization is needed in water governance, along with a stronger central role in IWRM. This must be accompanied by the necessary financial resources and human capacity development at the local level. A clear demarcation of roles and responsibilities at different levels should be agreed and understood by all parties inside and outside government. Community-level involvement is especially important to overcome local environment and development conflicts, property rights, and equity and cultural issues. Local government and municipal levels often have deep knowledge of local affairs, but can be bypassed by central authorities or powerful elites. Clear priorities are the involvement of the non-traditional players – strengthening local water associations, efficient and effective public water resource management and building the capacity of stakeholders – and ensuring attractive working conditions that keep workers in the sector and in the country.

Encouraging a water-oriented civil society is one way of encouraging voluntary water conservation and intelligent responses to classical regulatory and economic instruments. Creating such '*basin societies*' also creates local watchdogs that can both monitor and support government actions and policies or help to regulate public–private arrangements to overcome some of the institutional weaknesses at higher tiers of authority. Involving civil society in a constructive manner also makes the resolution of water conflicts more amenable to arbitration and final settlement.

Concluding thoughts

Essentially, it is possible to identify a balanced level of partnerships between key stakeholders, between centralization and decentralization and between laws and regulation to produce effective water governance. While empirical evidence suggests that there can be no dogmatic solutions, some universal attributes exist that can help to make water governance effective in practice and to fit the social, economic and cultural particularities of each country (see Box 6.2).

Too often, we search for ideal solutions that delay action or we leap enthusiastically on fashionable mantras that promise unrealistic results. Water governance demands an iterative approach that addresses critical problems in sequence according to the highest current stresses in society. Governments must take the lead but they cannot act alone. Partnerships are the key to solving complex problems, even if this requires devolving responsibilities and losing some command and control over society. This will enable countries to find solutions in a much quicker and more effective way than many developed countries have managed in the past. Achieving effective water governance cannot be undertaken hastily using blueprints imported from overseas; it needs to be developed to suit local conditions with the benefit of lessons learned from all over the world. Countries today face two specific barriers to solving their water problems: stress and simultaneity.

Box 6.2 Principles for effective water governance

- *Open and transparent:* institutions should work in an open and accessible manner with a transparent process for policy formulation. This is particularly important with regard to financial transactions.
- *Inclusive and communicative:* wide participation is needed throughout the policy chain – from conception to implementation. This will create more confidence and improve the ability of institutions to deliver policies. Transparency and accountability are built on the free flow of information.
- *Coherent and integrative:* increased diversity and complexity require more harmony and coherence in governance. Solutions often demand crossing traditional sectoral boundaries upon which government institutions are built. Coherence requires political leadership and a strong responsibility on the part of the institutions at different levels in order to ensure a consistent approach.
- *Equitable and ethical:* water governance has to be based upon the ethical principles of the society in which it functions and based on the rule of law. This manifests itself in the issues of justice, property rights for use, access and ownership of water. Legal and regulatory frameworks should be fair and enforced impartially. Equity between and among the various interest groups, stakeholders and consumers needs to carefully monitored.
- *Accountable:* roles in the legislative and executive processes need to be clear. Each institution must explain and take responsibility for what it does. The 'rules of the game' must be clearly spelled out, as should the consequences for violation of the rules, and have built-in arbitration-enforcing mechanisms. Decision-makers in government, the private sector and civil society organizations are accountable to the public, as well as to institutional stakeholders.
- *Efficient:* as well as economic efficiency, political, social and environmental efficiency need to be taken into account. It is essential that governance systems effectively balance these priorities in a way that does not impede action.
- *Responsive and sustainable:* policies must deliver what is needed on the basis of demand, and must have clear objectives and an evaluation of future impact, including, where available, an evaluation of past experience. Responsiveness also requires policies to be implemented at the most appropriate level. Most importantly, policies should be incentive based in order to ensure that there is a clear social or economic gain to be achieved by following the policy. Water governance must serve future as well as present users of water services.

Source: GWP (2003)

Stress and simultaneity

The development of water governance in the developed world was typically driven by internal forces (economy, population, declining resources, political pressures). The developing world is experiencing the same internal pressures; but the task ahead is more daunting as it faces additional stresses that the developed countries did not when establishing their own water systems. Stresses can include the high expectations that come from improved communications and greater awareness, or from an increasing scarcity and degradation of water resources, as well as through demands from external forces (such as donors, targets and NGOs) and the high expectations of domestic constituencies. It is important that governments appreciate that they cannot solve these problems by working alone but by *working with* these different groups. Such multi-stakeholder interaction, with civil society, trade unions and the market (especially the local private sector), although less orderly and structured, is the only way forward. Governance systems must permit all stakeholders to engage in solving the growing water problems.

The current rapid pace of economic, social and environmental change threatens to overwhelm the capacity of developing countries to develop laws and institutions at a more measured pace. Many water-short developing countries are facing, *simultaneously*, many pressing development issues. The water crisis requires nations to act now to put their governance systems in order. Apart from the severity of the crisis that many countries face, the most efficient moment to build sustainability into a water system is during the early stages of its planning and design. This *simultaneity* of problems does not allow governments to remain entrenched in the old hierarchical governance systems.

To solve these problems governance systems must facilitate partnerships, use IWRM tools and set out a sequence of priority actions. As required under the Johannesburg Plan of Implementation (JPOI) of the WSSD, each country must develop IWRM plans and strategies that set out the sequence of changes needed to meet the specific pressures they face. The international circle of experienced water managers can provide practical help to those facing intensely stressful situations by putting into practice the principles of IWRM.

Using integrated water resource management tools

The IWRM approach overcomes the traditional fragmented and sectoral approach to water and makes a clear distinction between resource management and the water service delivery functions. IWRM is a political process because it deals with reallocating and regulating water, the allocation of financial resources, and the implementation of environmental, social and economic goals. There is a general agreement in the water community that IWRM provides the only viable way forward for sustainable water use and management – although there are no universal solutions or blueprints and there is much debate on how to develop and implement IWRM in practice. Moreover, IWRM is not applied in a vacuum and the broader picture, as described by governance, provides the context in which the IWRM approach can be applied. Much more work remains to be done to establish effective water governance regimes that will enable IWRM to be employed.

In order to establish effective water governance systems and put IWRM into practice there is a variety of tools available to policy-makers and practitioners as described in a range of literature. The GWP *Toolbox for Integrated Water Resources Management* (GWP, 2003) brings together an array of over 50 tools and references that can be used by practitioners to strengthen governance and is supported by experiences from around the world. Different countries will need to identify which management tools or instruments are most important and appropriate given their specific circumstances.

Sequencing

Institutions, laws and management systems develop slowly and adapt to rapidly changing environmental conditions. It is important that countries tackle critical issues first and adopt a more pragmatic approach. Because of the simultaneity of pressing development issues, nations must resist the temptation to follow the example of developed countries. They cannot afford to postpone sustainability goals or follow such gradual sequencing of concerns seen in earlier historical cases such as in the US or Europe. Under present conditions, sustainability and socio-economic development cannot be viewed as separable. The response must be to prepare a sequence of actions to tackle the truly critical demands in a flexible manner that allows for learning through doing and not delaying action in order to wait for ideal solutions.

Partnerships

While distributed governance and the need to involve stakeholders is promoted, the key role of government and the public sector is recognized as critical for the proper stewardship of water as a common pool resource. The role of government in sponsoring civil society can be pivotal in good outcomes. Partnerships at the regional level based on shared benefits can be helpful in building good relations and overcoming shared water problems.

Reform

The WSSD Plan of Implementation for water cannot be achieved without reforming governance systems in many countries. The investment needed to meet the MDGs and WSSD targets will not be forthcoming without good governance. The reform of policies and institutions and increased investment in infrastructure and technology are inseparable. Innovative means to find the needed investments are being investigated – for example, through the World Panel on Financing Water Infrastructure; but without the appropriate governance systems and the stability that this brings to the country investment will remain depressed and capacity will drain away from the poorer countries.

Questions for change

- Do countries currently have sufficient capacity and knowledge of their current water resources situation to adopt IWRM plans and strategies for achieving better water governance?
- Which simple indicators should the United Nations select, through the MDGs' Task Force, to be used by the CSD and others to monitor progress on better water governance?

- How do the current policies, rules and regulations of the multilateral development banks and donors need to change to increase support for water governance and help provide greater support at the sub-national level?
- How can governments better integrate water as a priority and as an integral part of their poverty reduction and development strategies towards meeting all of the MDGs?
- How can governments improve their governance systems so that there is less fragmentation and fewer contradictory policies and laws related to water at all levels?

Note

1   The chapter is based extensively on Rogers and Hall (2002).

References

Bonn Keys (2001) International Conference on Freshwater, Bonn, 3–7 December 2001. Synopsis document, available at www.water-2001.de/outcome/bonn_keys.asp

Cesano, D. et al (2000) *Water Policy: Impact of Economic Globalization on Water Resources – A Source of Technical, Social and Environmental Challenges for the Next Decade*. Royal Institute of Technology, KTH, 100 44, Stockholm, Sweden, January, Canada Mortgage and Housing Corporation (CMHC), Government of Canada, available at www.cmhc-schl.gc.ca/en/imquaf/himu/wacon/wacon_070.cfm

Christian Aid (2001) 'Master or servant? How global trade can work to the benefit of poor people'. Indepth briefing paper, available at www.christian-aid.org.uk/indepth/0111trme/master2.htm#Water

Coyle, D. (2002) 'Developing countries need stability more than handouts'. *The Independent Newspaper*, 27 August 2002

DESA (United Nations Department for Social and Economic Affairs) (2000) 'Review of the ACC Subcommittee on Water Resources'. Note by the Secretary General. Commission on Sustainable Development, eighth session, 24 April–5 May 2000, E/CN.17/2000/18, available at http://ods-dds-ny.un.org/doc/UNDOC/GEN/N00/390/44/PDF/N0039044.pdf?OpenElement

European Commission (2002) *Water Framework Directive: Integrated River Basin Management for Europe*, available at www.europa.eu.int/comm/environment/water/water-framework/index_en.html

Federal Ministry for the Environment and Federal Ministry for Economic Cooperation and Development (2001) *Ministerial Declaration, The Bonn Keys and Recommendations for Action*. International Conference on Freshwater, Bonn, Germany, December 2001

Finnegan, W. (2002) 'Letter from Bolivia: Leasing the rain'. *New Yorker*, April 2002

GWP (Global Water Partnership) (2000a) 'Integrated water resources management'. GWP TEC Background Paper no 4, 2000

GWP (2000b) *Towards Water Security: A Framework for Action*. GWP, March 2000, available at www.hrwallingford.co.uk/projects/gwp.fau/documents.html

GWP (2002) *Estonia and Russia: Managing Transboundary Waters in the Lake Peipsi/Chudskoe Basin, Case No16*, available at www.gwp.ihe.nl/wwwroot/ZappEngine/objects/ACF1A6E.pdf

GWP (2003) *Toolbox for Integrated Water Resources Management.* GWP, March 2003, available at http://gwpforum.netmasters05.netmasters.nl/en/index.html

Hague Ministerial Declaration (2000) *Ministerial Declaration of The Hague on Water Security in the 21st Century.* Agreed to on 22 March 2000, available at www.thewaterpage.com/hague_declaration.htm

International Law Commission (1997) *Law of the Non-navigational Uses of International Watercourses.* International Law Commission, Helsinki

Kara, I. (2003) *Governance in Water Resources Management: Progress in South Africa.* Department of Water Affairs and Forestry, Third World Water Forum: INBO session, 20 March 2003, available at www.riob.org/wwf/EKarar_SA.pdf

Kaufmann, D. et al (1999) 'Governance matters'. Policy Paper 2196, World Bank, Washington, DC, October 1999

Kooiman, J. (ed) (1993) *Modern Governance: New Government–Society Interactions.* Sage Publications

Kubo, T. (1994) *Reorganisation of Water Management in England and Wales 1945–1991.* Japan Sewage Works Association

LGIB (Local Government International Bureau) (2004) *General Agreement on Trade in Services.* Councillor Briefing, June 2004. LGIB, London

Myers, N. and Kent, J. (1998). *Perverse Subsidies.* International Institute for Sustainable Development, Winnipeg, Manitoba, Canada

Pierre, J. (ed) (2000) *Debating Governance, Authority, Steering and Democracy.* Oxford University Press, Oxford

Rahaman, M. and Varis, O. (2003) *The Ethics of Water: Some Realities and Future Challenges.* Water Engineering, Department of Civil and Environmental Engineering, Helsinki University of Technology, available at www.water.hut.fi/pdl/Publication_3.pdf

Rogers, P. and Hall, A. W. (2002) 'Effective water governance'. GWP Background Paper no 7, Global Water Partnership, Wallingford, UK

UN (United Nations) (1997) *The UN Convention on the Law of the Non-Navigational Uses of International Watercourses,* available at www.un.org/law/ilc/texts/nnavfra.htm

UN (2000) *Water for People: Water for Life.* World Water Development Report, available at unesdoc.unesco.org/images/0012/001295/129556e.pdf

UNECE (United Nations Economic Commission for Europe) (1992) *The Protection and Use of Transboundary Watercourses and International Lakes (Water Convention).* UNECE, Geneva

Versfeld, D. (2000) *Sharing South Africa's Water: Uncovering Challenges for Development through Strategic Environmental Assessment.* Department of Water Affairs and Forestry: Team for Strategic Environmental Assessment. Paper prepared for the International Symposium on Contested Resources: Challenges to Governance of Natural Resources in Southern Africa, Cape Town, 18–20 October 2000, available at www.dwaf.gov.za/sfra/Articles/sharing_sa-water.pdf

de Villiers, M. (1999) *Water Wars: Is the World's Water Running Out?* Weidenfeld and Nicholson, London

WBCSD (World Business Council for Sustainable Development) (2002) *Water for the Poor.* WBCSD, August 2002

Winpenny, J. (ed) (2003) *Financing Water for All, Report of the World Panel on Financing Water Infrastructure.* GWP/WWC/3WWF, March 2003, available at www.gwpforum.org

WSSD (United Nations World Summit on Sustainable Development) (2002) *Johannesburg Plan of Implementation,* September 2002

WWC (World Water Commission) (2000) *World Water Vision: A Water Secure World.* WWC, March 2000

7

Energy: Energy Governance, Poverty and Sustainable Development

Richard Sherman

Introduction

Energy poverty in the midst of plenty is one of the central sustainable development challenges in today's globalized society. Access to energy services is a prerequisite to achieving the United Nation's poverty alleviation goal to 'reduce by half the number of people living under US$1 a day, by 2015'. It is therefore no surprise that energy and its relationship to poverty eradication and sustainable development attained a high profile throughout the World Summit on Sustainable Development (WSSD). This chapter provides an overview of the national and multilateral governance challenges in relation to prioritizing the energy needs of the poor, increasing financing for energy access and the share of renewable energy technologies, and the governance of international financial institutions. The chapter highlights considerations for governments and other stakeholders in support of innovative energy poverty-eradication strategies. The recommendations speak to the actions that need to be considered by national governments, in particular ministries responsible for energy, social development, trade and finance, environment and sustainable development, and the actions that need to be considered by international financial institutions such as multilateral development banks (MDBs) and export credit agencies (ECAs).

Multilateral challenges

In accordance with the various international energy decisions prioritizing the energy needs of the poor, policies and measures that address energy access must now be given the highest priority in global energy sector planning. A high priority is to seek out good practice policies and instruments across the world and adapt them to particular country characteristics. There is also considerable scope for governments, international financial institutions (IFIs) and the private sector to support energy access through the development of energy efficient and renewable energy technologies. New delivery and financing structures need to be tested, developed and adapted, and implemented. Many of the new energy technologies needed for an energy revolution already exist. But the pace of change will be heavily reliant on the ability of society to overcome the political barriers that remain entrenched in our current energy habits.

The level of worldwide investment in the energy supply sector, US$450 billion per year, is projected to increase to perhaps US$750 billion per year by 2020, about half of which would be for the power sector (WEC, 1995). The key challenge is to ensure that significant portions of these finances are targeted towards energy access, with a focus on clean and renewable energy resources. The refocusing of energy-sector financing priorities could be supported by actions at the national and regional level to create innovative financial mechanisms and to establish national energy poverty-eradication targets and strategies.

Early policy action is needed to establish a credible commitment to energy poverty eradication and to reverse years of policy choices that have favoured indus-trial and urban energy needs. Without credible policy signals, the required changes in investment toward energy access and renewable alternatives will not occur. Opportunities to redirect technological advances towards more rapid development of renewable technologies will also be delayed. Without early action, the potential additional benefits from sustainable development, including climate protection, health, reduced air pollution and savings from energy efficiency, will be lost.

Addressing the role of multilateral development banks and export credit agencies

The energy sector is traditionally one of the largest lending portfolios for multilateral and bilateral development and export credit agencies, with unsustainable technologies such as fossil fuels, nuclear power plants and large dams having comprised the bulk of energy lending. Since 1992, multilateral development banks, such as the World Bank, and export credit agencies have invested billions of dollars into unsustainable energy investments, with little priority for energy access and clean and renewable energy technologies. It is estimated that the World Bank Group has spent US$13.6 billion on fossil fuel projects, which will, over their lifetimes, release 37.5 billion tonnes of carbon dioxide (CO_2) into the Earth's atmosphere.[1] With regard to ECAs, the World Resources Institute (WRI) has noted that from 1994 through the first quarter of 1999, ECAs from Europe, Japan, Canada and the US supported US$103 billion in exports or investments for fossil-fuelled power generation, oil and gas development, transportation infrastructure, aircraft sales and energy-intensive manufacturing (such as petrochemicals, pulp and paper, and iron and steel) in developing countries. They noted, in contrast, that renewable energy projects co-financed by ECAs totalled only about US$2 billion (Maurer and Bhandari, 2000).

Among the concerns of public interest groups is the fact that the majority of ECA financing undermines the formal commitments that industrialized governments have made to facilitate the transfer of environmentally sustainable technologies that can help developing countries grow in a less carbon-intensive fashion, such as those outlined in the United Nations Framework Convention on Climate Change (UNFCCC) and decisions of the Commission on Sustainable Development (CSD). Overall, flows of trade and project finance going to developing countries are concentrated in sectors with important implications for future greenhouse gas (GHG) emissions. Another concern is the lack of accountability and transparency in the operations of ECAs. ECAs are required to disclose little or no information about their operations or decisions, despite the fact that they are publicly funded. Of 12 Organisation for Economic Co-operation and Development (OECD) ECAs, only three – the Japanese Bank for International Cooperation (JBIC), the US Overseas Private Investment Corporation (OPIC) and the US Export Import Bank (US ExIm Bank) – have information reporting policies of any kind. This lack of transparency can also contribute to the very political instability and poor business environment within developing countries against which export insurance is designed to guard. The result is a vicious circle of public mistrust and public suspicions about the designs of foreign corporations (Monsarrat, 2002).

The last few years have seen the growing recognition by a number of government and international institutions that rapid energy development in developing countries will need to be accompanied by significant reform of multilateral development banks and export credit agencies. Article 27 of the G8 Genoa Communiqué (2001) contains statements relevant to the role of energy financing. It calls on MDBs and national development assistance agencies to adopt an innovative approach and to develop market-based financing mechanisms for renewable energy. Throughout the WSSD process, non-governmental organizations (NGOs) focused on energy subsidies; at the Bali WSSD PrepCom a coalition of 14 international NGOs called for a target of 20 per cent of OECD country energy-sector lending and export credit guarantees to be redirected towards renewable energy development and energy efficiency programmes and the phasing-out of support for non-sustainable energy activities by 2007. The NGOs also called on IFIs to prioritize: development of developing country research; development and manufacturing of renewable energy; and access to energy and creating a favourable regulatory and fiscal framework for renewable energy and energy efficiency. The NGO coalition emphasized that the international financial institutions should identify and foster local intermediaries with a sustainable development mandate that can provide financial and technical assistance, including concessional finance and grants, training, capacity-building and other resources for the development of small- and medium-sized enterprises (SMEs).[2] During the WSSD, the parliamentary NGO Global Legislators Organization for a Balanced Environment (GLOBE) launched its voluntary initiative Renewable Energy Now through Export Finance Worldwide (RENEW), which aims to target at least five of the Group of 8 (G8) countries to devote 10 per cent of their energy-export finance lending portfolios to renewable energy by the year 2010.[3]

The issue of IFI reform has also been raised within the context of the climate change negotiations. The Climate Action Network (CAN) has argued that a necessary aspect of gaining the participation of affected stakeholders in decision-making processes is the disclosure of information about projects and processes in order to build transparency and accountability. CAN proposed that a process addressing IFI and ECA energy related investments should be developed under the auspices of the Conference of the Parties (COP) to the UNFCCC. The network lobbied COP-5 in 2000 to instruct the Intergovernmental Panel on Climate Change (IPCC) to provide, by COP-6, a transparent methodology by which IFIs and ECAs calculate the full life cycle climate-change impacts of their development lending and loan guarantees. This exercise is vital for two reasons: first, calculations of GHG emissions are currently being conducted only in an *ad hoc* manner; and, second, it is essential that a system be installed to ensure that the public money lent by IFIs does not undermine the goals of the Kyoto Protocol. CAN has suggested that the ECAs report annually to COP on such activities and that they should track and report annually on all direct and indirect greenhouse gas emissions related to power plants, upstream oil, mining and gas, and transport projects that receive their support.

One of the most important contributions to meeting the Millennium Development Goals (MDGs) and the WSSD goals would be the redirection of energy funds in international financial institutions towards investments that support energy access and the use of clean and renewable energy resources. The G8 governments, who are the primary decision-makers of these institutions, should mandate and provide guidance to the multilateral financial and bilateral financing institutions to place a larger share of investments into energy access projects. These measures would be consistent with the recommendations of the G8 Renewable Energy Task Force, which recommended that the G8 countries should support access to renewables by the rural poor, such as through strengthening micro-finance organizations and competitive rural concessions. Through this, SMEs, NGOs and community-assisted energy programmes in the developing countries should look to access dedicated funds and adopt renewable energy applications with micro-financing opportunities. Given the important role that ECAs play in directing (and subsidizing) private foreign direct investment (FDI) in the energy sector, governments should set targets for a share of ECA energy-sector funds (or an absolute amount) that will support access investments (as opposed to only traditional supply investments).

They should also ensure that energy-sector Official Development Assistance (ODA) for the poorest countries will include a focus on access programmes. The G8 Renewable Energy Task Force recommended that modern energy access and environmental considerations should be integrated within the IFI's energy sector dialogue and investment programmes. Thus, current instruments and agency programmes should be adapted to provide increased support for renewable energy projects, which, although economically attractive, may be small and have long pay-back periods. Guarantee funds, refinancing schemes for local banks and *ad hoc* loan facilities to local small private operators should be considered in this respect. The task force also recommended that the G8 should extend so-called 'sector arrangements' for other energy lending to renewables and develop and implement common environmental guidelines among the G8 ECAs. This could include identifying criteria to assess environmental impacts of ECA-financed projects and establishing minimum standards of energy efficiency or carbon intensity for these projects; as well as developing a common reporting methodology for ECAs to permit assessment of their local and global environmental impacts.

Options for coordination in the United Nations system

There is no international agency with a broad mandate to focus on energy and sustainable development, although noteworthy contributions are being made by several institutions, including the United Nations Development Programme (UNDP), the United Nations Environment Programme (UNEP) and the United Nations Food and Agriculture Organization (FAO), amongst others. Despite the lack of clear coordination structure and even an organizational home, issues concerning the need for a global institutional structure for energy within the UN remained on the periphery of the discussions on energy and governance for sustainable development during the WSSD. While many of these proposals lack general political support from governments, their mention in a future discussion on multilateral governance frameworks remains relevant.

The Action Plan for the Global Proliferation of Renewable Energy, developed and proposed by the World Council for Renewable Energy, contains the farthest breadth of proposal for international energy governance. Among the 12-point plan are proposals for a renewable energy proliferation treaty, an international renewable energy agency and integrated strategies of UN organizations. The Renewable Energy Proliferation Treaty would be developed as a supplementary protocol to the Nuclear Non-proliferation Treaty (NPT), which should be passed at the review conference by the signatory states in 2005. The supplementary protocol in form of a Renewable Energy Proliferation Treaty should be the basis of an international treaty for the introduction of renewable energies and should internationally legitimize an International Renewable Energy Agency (IRENA). The World Council for Renewable Energy notes that among international organizations, one is missing that concentrates its entire strength on promoting renewable energies and is thus an international point of reference: an International Renewable Energy Agency. The function of this agency is, in particular, to assist in building 'human capacity' in the field of renewable energies, including cooperation by establishing 'centres for the application of renewable energies' on a regional level for the transfer of technology (World Council for Renewable Energy, 2002).

Other proposals for new institutions include a proposal from the NGO Energy and Climate Caucus of the CSD, which called for the establishment of an International Sustainable Energy Fund (ISEF). The general function of the ISEF would be to support projects to promote energy conservation and sustainable forms of renewable energy, with 80 per cent of the fund's income, in accordance with commitments to provide renewable energy to the world's poor, used to support sustainable energy programmes in poor and low-income areas of developing countries and economies in transition, such as micro-credit and credit exchange programmes that integrate sustainable energy projects with poverty eradication. They have also called on governments, international agencies and intergovernmental entities to commit to financing, such a fund with at least 20 per cent of the monies saved from phasing out governmental subsidies that support unsustainable forms of energy.[4] During CSD-9, the Energy and Climate Caucus has proposed the establishment of International Sustainable Energy Organization (ISEO), which would have three primary tasks: to assist countries in identifying and ending government subsidies for unsustainable forms of energy; to fund conservation and sustainable energy programmes in developing countries, and especially to focus on providing sustainable energy access for people in rural and low-income areas, as well as assisting major fossil-fuel producing countries to diversify into sustainable forms of energy; and to disseminate information on sustainable energy policies and practices, facilitating international technology transfer and cooperation and all means of sustainable energy capacity-building.

There are some proposals that warrant further attention of the CSD. One such proposal deals with the issue of monitoring and reporting, and recommends that the CSD invite governments to report on their energy access and clean energy development in the context of the national strategies on sustainable development (NSSD) and MDGs reporting processes. Tracking progress towards these goals is essential and should include reporting all public funding (for example, R&D and export credit agencies) to support different energy technologies, as well as timetables for a shift towards renewable energy and energy efficiency. The CSD could also invite annual reports from the OECD on relative financial flows and donor assistance patterns in order to support renewable energy. There is also a need to discuss the role of public policy networks in assisting energy decision-makers. Since 2000, the energy sector has had the benefit of several high-profile global public policy networks, which have included the World Commission on Dams, the G8 task force, the Minerals and Mining Sustainable Development process and, more recently, the World Bank's Extractive Industries Process. Another recommendation for international energy architecture was a call for a structured, ongoing dialogue on energy access and development through a Global Energy Forum. This would be a non-UN, multi-stakeholder group, similar to the current Global Forum on Sustainable Energy, but with broader international support and participation and explicit focus on financing access. The forum agenda would cover both widening energy access and cleaner energy issues, including funding/financing mechanisms. This body could be expanded to cover all aspects of energy access, cleaner energy and funding/financing mechanisms.

Other proposals deal with inter-agency cooperation and cooperation between UN bodies and the Bretton Woods organizations. One innovative proposal has suggested the development of a joint strategic plan of action for implementation, which would have as its objective streamlining the activities of the IFIs and the UN, to provide financial and technical support for implementing international energy decisions and instruments in accordance with national plans, priorities and programmes. The plan would aim to enhance the UN's coordinating role in support of country policy and programming dialogue in close cooperation with the UNDP and UNEP. In accordance with its mandate as the leading implementation agency of the MDGs, the UNDP should, in close cooperation with other relevant UN agencies and the financial institutions, ensure the implementation of the strategic plan. The UN Development Group should play an important role in preparing and implementing the plan and contribute to clarifying the roles and functions of the responsibilities of different institutions. While partnership and cooperation should be emphasized, a greater specialization with lead responsibilities assigned to the UNDP might serve to streamline the system and increase impact. The strategic plan of action could include measures to finance and support capacity-building and technology transfer; technology assessment, and monitoring and information; energy policy development and planning; mainstreaming of energy access into overall development/poverty/sectoral strategies and plans/national strategies for sustainable development; financing the implementation of energy access projects and programmes at regional, sub-regional, national and local levels, with a particular focus on poverty reduction and development; and the development of partnership with business, NGOs and other relevant stakeholders.

Addressing corruption in the energy sector

There is also a growing need to address the relationship between multinational corporations and corruption in the energy sector. In a recent open editorial in the *Financial Times*, global financier George Soros argued that a close connection between the exploitation of natural resources and the prevalence of corrupt and oppressive regimes exists. He noted that while oil and mining companies play an important role in many developing countries, they are often the main source of budget revenues and foreign currency earnings (Soros, 2002). Soros is pushing a proposal known as 'publish what you pay'. The idea is to require natural resource companies to make public disclosure of taxes, fees, royalties and other payments to governments as a condition of being listed on leading stock exchanges.[5] The World Energy Council (WEC) has stated that corruption adds to the cost of energy by creating tremendous economic inefficiency and the loss of opportunities to achieve the three goals of energy accessibility, energy availability and energy acceptability. Corruption adds to the cost of energy, creates an inefficient economy and compounds the difficulty of meeting WEC's goal of bringing commercial energy to the poor. The WEC has called for its members to 'make ethics a strong component of energy system governance', recommending that the ingredients of the global ethical approach include voluntary governmental and corporate energy and/or environment audits; transparent contractual relationships; common safety and environmental rules, as well as best business practices for company plants in all countries where they operate; and respect for energy workers and customer choice.[6]

National governance challenge

People living in the conditions of energy poverty have benefited very little from conventional energy policies Most investments in the energy sectors of developing countries have targeted the urban energy sector, and the pace of the transition from the use of traditional to modern energy sources in rural areas has generally lagged behind. Therefore, significant rural–urban inequalities in energy supply and consumption are common, with the per-capita consumption of energy by the rural population invariably lower than that of the urban population. In the majority of cases, hopes that improvement would 'trickle down' from the more advanced sectors of the economy have not been realized (World Energy Assessment, 2000). Drawing on the objectives identified by the MDGs and the WSSD, the first priority of national energy policy should be to satisfy the basic needs of a population without modern energy services.

National energy access strategies

Targeting the goal of universal access to electricity over the next two decades will require the launching of ambitious national electrification programme as integral elements of national sustainable development frameworks. At the national level, all governments should agree to launch national programmes and initiatives on renewable energy and efficient clean energy technologies in order to provide energy services to people, mostly in rural and remote areas, who currently have no access to modern energy services, and improve the services of the people who are currently inadequately powered. In countries that have not yet completed their national sustainable development strategies, consideration should be given to include energy access strategies and targets as part of these processes, or, where appropriate, included in poverty reduction strategy papers (PRSPs). Alternatively, national ministries could develop stand-alone strategies.

The access strategies should also include targeted actions by governments to develop capacity (human and institutional) in the energy sector at all levels. Capacity-building programmes should focus on areas that will catalyse greater investment by both public and private sectors. Among the areas that need to be prioritized for capacity-building initiatives include policy and strategy development; intra-governmental coordination; regulatory capacity market restructuring; project development capacity; and innovative local financing mechanisms and institutions. Activities should also support local energy centres that promote access to energy, disseminate information and serve as a focus for capacity-building and job creation, and the networking of centres of excellence on solutions to cleaner energy and access problems. The strengthening of research, development, demonstration and institutional capacities in the field of renewable energy utilization, as well as capacity development for the transfer of environmentally sound and advanced technologies, are also required. Linked to these national programmes, governments need to build institutional capacity at all levels in order to undertake and develop resource assessments; market assessments; pre-feasibility and feasibility studies; environmental impact assessments and technology guidelines; public awareness and education programmes; training of local people in technical and maintenance skills; training for financial institutions in renewable energy projects' appraisal and micro-financing packages; and support of private-sector engagement in the renewable energy industry.

There is also a need to create policies, programmes and an institutional framework that can facilitate community-based financing to support community energy services. This process should include the identification of new and innovative financial mechanisms that reward rural communities for their role as stewards of environmental services and functions. Some of the priorities for national-level activities include the creation of support mechanisms to help fund demonstration projects by the provision of grants and soft loans, provision of grants and soft loans for large-scale projects, and the provision of backing and loan guarantees for users in rural areas. Bilateral development assistance and other concessionary funds should help to strengthen policy-making and regulatory capacity, reduce investment risks, demonstrate potentially viable investments and build the capacity to support project investments. Micro-credit programmes that integrate renewable energy technologies and projects with poverty alleviation should be emphasized. There are already some promising financing initiatives in existence, with others in the process of being developed in a number of countries. Successful examples of revolving loan funds or micro credit for renewable energy already exist in many developing countries. Experience has shown that innovative financing mechanisms and financial intermediaries can connect end users to sources of capital and bundle small projects for commercial financing. Intermediaries can take many forms, including local development NGOs and energy service companies. According to the International Energy Agency (IEA), innovative financing arrangements must be more widely employed to accelerate the deployment of clean technologies and to increase access to energy services. Grants, concessional loans, financial intermediaries such as energy service companies, accessible credit for small clean energy producers and micro credit for users are some of the financing devices that can be deployed (IEA, 2002).

Strong institutions are the backbone of an efficient and effective renewable energy sector. However, many countries face enormous challenges in developing the appropriate policy, legal, fiscal and administrative frameworks to mobilize and unlock the potential of the renewable energy sector to contribute to sustainable development. One proposal for supporting national renewable energy development is for the creation of a national renewable energy organization to assist and coordinate national programmes for increased use of renewables, to support the assessment of energy options, and to assist centres of excellences in specialized areas of renewable energy research. The proposed mandate of a national renewable energy organization could include:

- supporting independent renewable energy analysis and capacity-building/ training centres that provide support for local governments and other institutions;
- providing technical and business management training for renewable energy system producers, distributors and service technicians;

- establishing effective demonstrations of good-practice technologies and delivery systems;
- initiating or supporting promotional campaigns on the benefits of renewable energy aimed at all potential markets (from the formal business and financial sectors to households and other small-scale users);
- developing and disseminating good quality information about renewable energy options for health, education, agriculture, water and other development sectors;
- providing good-quality technical assistance on the design, production and commercialization of important small-scale renewable energy technologies;
- conducting reviews of actual and good practices on energy prices, taxes and incentive schemes and their impacts on renewable energy adoption;
- supporting a national network of renewable energy expertise; and
- supporting the participation by major groups in energy decision-making.

Renewable energy and energy access

For supporters of renewable energy, the WEHAB (water, energy, health, food and agriculture, biodiversity) agenda presents an important opportunity to accelerate policy reforms and spur the development of new markets for the rapid deployment of modern, clean and affordable energy sources. The decade since the United Nations Conference on Environment and Development (UNCED) in 1992 has witnessed great enthusiasm in both public and private sectors for expanding the use of renewable energy technologies. In particular, the global climate policy process has already contributed to the build-up of a sizeable market for renewable energy in Europe and Japan, nurturing industries now poised to capture export opportunities in the 'emerging markets' of the developing world. There have also been some significant steps in India, China and Latin America and, to a certain degree, in Africa.

Despite these positive signals, several barriers to implementing renewable energy technologies remain. The most common barriers to the increased use of renewable energy technologies are economic, political and informational. Because most of the costs for renewable energy technologies are upfront capital costs, there is a general perception that they are expensive. Many apparent economic barriers are actually due to government policy that is still very strongly influenced by the powerful oil and gas lobbies. This is evident in the small amount of research and development funding spent on renewables compared to fossil fuels and nuclear energy. Renewables are also penalized by the generous tax subsidies enjoyed by the oil and gas industry. Many renewable technologies become considerably more competitive relative to conventional fossil fuels when decisions are made on the basis of full-price costing, which takes into account all environmental externalities, such as life-cycle greenhouse gas emissions, land use, toxic waste disposal and water pollution. Barriers to renewable energy cannot be seen in isolation from underdevelopment in Southern countries and the need for increased service provision and access to income-generating sustainable livelihoods. In most developing countries, inadequate attention is given to barrier removal activities, in general, and to rural energy needs, in particular.

The prioritization of renewable energy technologies under the WEHAB initiative follows from the outcomes of both the CSD-9 and the G8 Renewable Energy Task Force. The CSD-9 decision on renewable energy calls on governments to develop and implement appropriate national, regional and international policies and measures to create an enabling environment for the development, utilization and distribution of renewable energy sources. It emphasizes the need to develop domestic programmes to increase the contribution of renewable energies to total energy consumption and encourages the use of indigenous sources of renewable energy, where appropriate. The G8 Renewable Energy Task Force (2001), set up after the G8 Okinawa Summit in 2000, concluded that, over the coming decade, concerted action by G8, other countries, the private sector, IFIs and others could result in a significant improvement in the efficiency of traditional biomass use for cooking purposes by up to 200 million people in developing countries; provision of access to electricity from renewable sources to up to 300 million people in rural areas of developing countries; and service up to 500 million people connected to electricity grids worldwide, 300 million of whom could be in developing countries.

At the core of governments' challenge to implement a sustainable energy future is the obligation to create an enabling environment in order to stimulate the design, production, distribution and marketing of sustainable energy technologies and services. Two prerequisites for successful technology transfer and the building of leadership capacity for renewable energy technologies are the establishment of an appropriate legal and regulatory framework and the rational pricing of energy. The framework must also address such elements as social, labour and environmental concerns in order to shape the technology transferred to conform to national and international sustainable development objectives. Renewable energy systems cannot compete in open markets as long as the playing field is tilted to favour conventional energy resources. Government energy policies must ensure that the playing field is levelled to support the wide dissemination of renewable energy technologies and services. An energy market that considers the total cost to society of its energy choices would greatly encourage the deployment of renewable energy technologies. Governments also need to create the enabling conditions to support national systems of innovation and technology transfer. Such conditions could include targeted capacity-building, information access, and training for public and private stakeholders and support for project preparation; strengthening scientific and technical educational institutions in the context of technology needs; technology assessment, promotion of prototypes, demonstration projects and extension services through linkages between manufacturers, producers and end users; and local and regional partnerships between different stakeholders for the transfer, evaluation and adjustment to local conditions of sustainable energy technologies.

Probably the most substantial measures that could be adopted to increase the share of renewable energy technologies are the establishment of renewable energy set-aside programmes at the national level. These programmes require that all energy distributors or generators (depending upon how the standard is designed) use renewable energy to meet a specified percentage of electricity sales or total generation. The standard ensures that a minimum amount of renewable energy is included in the country's energy portfolio. Standards can be dynamic, designed to increase the renewable energy market share over time, in order to expand the renewables market. By establishing long-term market demand for renewable energy, this type of policy encourages investors to develop renewable resources. This measure is similar to the Renewable Portfolio Standard (RPS) innovation under active consideration in some developing countries and adopted by six states in the US and by several European countries. The RPS is a new concept, first promoted during the mid 1990s. If properly implemented, the RPS can be a cost-effective policy for developing a significant market for renewable energy applications.

The potential benefits and costs for clean energy and renewable energy development needs to be well explained to a wider audience of government officials, parliamentarians, energy industry officials, potential investors and consumers. Education and training are also important to improve the skills and capacities of the renewable energy industry. The challenge lies in creating a popular basis for change – and this involves a large number of aspects. Amongst these are the general popular acceptance and active involvement based upon environmental awareness, strengthening of social relations, self-sufficiency, local production and development, and creation of new industries and employment. An innovative approach to these and other renewable energy tasks is the establishment of national renewable energy organizations. Another important activity at the national level is the encouragement of the private sector to support renewable energy. Promoting energy access and clean and renewable energy at the national level is not just about governments, environmental NGOs and the renewable energy sector; it must also include incentives and policies targeted at the private sector. The private sector needs to promote the case of eradicating energy poverty much more aggressively if it expects governments to take the necessary supporting steps, such as creating incentives.

The next steps for energy governance

Despite being identified as one of the most politicized and contentious negotiating issues on the international sustainable development agenda, international decisions on energy have steadily increased, with key decisions, including targets and time frames, now contained in the decisions of the Commission on Sustainable Development and the World Summit on Sustainable Development. However, a large implementation gap exists between these international decision-making forums and the implementation of energy and sustainable development policies at the national level. Both the Millennium Declaration and the WSSD Declaration recognized the alarming discrepancy between international commitment and action in the field of sustainable development. Goals and targets agreed by the international community, such as increased support for developing countries, have not been implemented as decided. The disturbing gap between these commitments and their implementation needs to be addressed at the national level.

As lengthy and as convoluted as producing the text of an energy decision can be, ensuring that the provisions of these agreements are fully implemented is an even more lengthy and, at times, more difficult task. The first and most important action, which governments and international organizations can take towards the implementation of these agreements, is, of course, to implement them domestically. A more strategic, coherent and coordinated framework for supporting national implementation should be developed with time-bound action-orientated goals for the eradication of energy poverty. The success of these measures will, in part, depend upon the ability of governments to engage key stakeholders, including the media, local governments and academia, as well as the key sectoral ministries and national parliaments, in the development and implementation of national energy access and clean energy strategies.

There is also a need to ensure that these energy access plans include actions for regional and sub-regional cooperation, including regional policies and programmes to create an enabling environment for such cooperation. Regional- and country-level support structures would include commitments from regional development banks to support the programme of action and direct financing appropriately; energy and development specialists in national UNDP and World Bank offices; collaboration with regional economic and political integration organizations and programmes; and close interaction with and guidance from NGOs, civil society organizations and private-sector associations/partners.

At the multilateral level, there is a need for negotiations to address the relationship between international energy financing and eradicating energy poverty in developing countries. There is little doubt that one of the most constructive contributions to meeting the Millennium Development Goals and the WSSD goals would be the redirection of energy funds in international financial institutions towards investments that supports energy access. There is also a need to develop a coherent and coordinated approach within the UN system related to energy-implementation issues. The follow-up discussions on the WSSD, the MDGs and the Monterrey Consensus provide an appropriate venue to continue negotiations on energy issues and action to be taken at the international level. Further opportunities exist at the annual meetings of the Bretton Woods Institutions (BWI). These international fora should therefore focus their attention to address the following challenges:

- How can they ensure that energy access and clean and renewable energy technologies are prioritized within the decision-making process of multilateral development banks and export credit agencies?
- What measures are required to secure the transparency and accountability of decision-making in the allocation of resources of multilateral development banks and export credit agencies?
- What is the relevance, future and possible structure of international energy decision-making within the United Nations General Assembly, and particularly the need for a high-level energy forum for policy dialogue and coordination among energy and other relevant ministries?
- What are the necessary measures to ensure the coherency and coordination of activities implemented by UN bodies, including the Global Environment Facility (GEF), and those of multilateral development banks and export credit agencies?

• Is there a need for a high-level dialogue between developing country governments, energy stakeholders and international financial institutions on investment and export priorities that are supportive of energy access goals?

Conclusion

This chapter has presented an overview of the key energy governance challenges and proposals facing national and global decision-makers. It has proposed options to highlight the measures that national governments could undertake as part of a comprehensive and concerted effort to accelerate progress and more effectively address the causes of energy poverty at country level, including national energy access targets and renewable energy set-aside programmes. It has argued that developing and maintaining national and international energy access strategies must now be at the core of all intergovernmental efforts to address sustainable development and poverty eradication. It further notes that poverty eradication and improved living standards cannot be achieved sustainably without major changes in the current international energy finance system. It has called for a new international strategy for energy finance that targets resources towards energy access and the increased utilization of clean and renewable energy technologies, and has suggested processes to ensure the coordination and coherence between the energy programme of the United Nations and those of international financial institutions.

Notes

1 *The World Bank and the G7: Still Changing the Earth's Climate for Business, 1997–98.* Sustainable Energy and Economy Network (Institute for Policy Studies, US) and the International Trade Information Service (ITIS), available at www.seen.org/wbstill/index.html.

2 'Clean and affordable energy in the WSSD', Statement released by 14 NGOs, July 2002, available at www.climnet.org/WSSD/energyletjun02.pdf.

3 Partners involved in RENEW include the Global Environment Facility (GEF); the United Nations Environment Programme (UNEP); the Tata Energy Resources Institute; the World Resources Institute (WRI); the World Watch Institute; the World Conservation Union (IUCN); World Wide Fund for Nature (WWF) and the National Wildlife Fund; the American Wind Energy Association; the Business Council for Sustainable Energy; and the Solar Energy Industry Association.

4 NGO Energy and Climate Caucus of the CSD, 2002.

5 'Transparent Corruption Oil and natural resource companies should make clear how much money is being taken by officials, says George Soros', *Financial Times* open editorial, 13 June 2002.

6 World Energy Council, www.worldenergy.org/wec-geis/publications/reports/etwan/policy_actions/chap_5_action10.asp.

References

IEA (International Energy Agency) (2002) *Making Markets Work*. Brochure for the WSSD, available at http://.spider.iea.org/envissu/johannesburg/brochure2.pdf

Maurer, C. and Bhandari, R. (2000) *Climate of Export Credit Agencies*. World Resources Institute, Climate Protection Initiative, May 2000, Washington, DC, available at http://pdf.wri.org/eca.pdf

Monsarrat, A. (2002) *From Rio to Johannesburg: Export Credit Agencies – The Environmental Impact*. GLOBE International and the World Watch Institute, available at www.globe international.org/newsevents/wssdecabrief.htm

Soros, G. (2002) 'Transparent corruption'. Comment, *Financial Times*, 13 June 2002

WEC (World Energy Council) (1995) *Financing Energy Development: The Challenges and Requirements of Developing Countries*. World Energy Council, London

World Council for Renewable Energy (2002) *Action Plan for the Global Proliferation of Renewable Energy*, available at www.world-council-for-renewable-energy.org/downloads/actionplan.pdf

World Energy Assessment (2000) 'How to encourage more sustainable delivery of energy services'. UNDP/UNDESA/World Energy Council/Sustainable Energy and Development Division (SEED), 2000, available at www.undp.org/seed/eap/activities/wea

8

Health: Health and Sustainable Development – Addressing the Challenges Post-Johannesburg

Yasmin von Schirnding

Introduction

Today countries face a myriad of health-related problems relating, on the one hand, to poverty and a lack of access to basic services and resources, and, on the other, to large-scale, rapid industrialization, urbanization, demographic change and technological development. The problems facing the health sector are increasingly complex, multidisciplinary in nature, often ill defined and have uncertain solutions. The emergence of the concept of sustainable development as a guiding principle for policy formulation in health and other sectors, the adoption at the United Nations Conference on Environment and Development (UNCED) in 1992 of Agenda 21, the subsequent adoption of the Programme for the Further Implementation of Agenda 21, and the Johannesburg Plan of Implementation (JPOI) negotiated at the World Summit on Sustainable Development (WSSD) (UN, 2002a) have been important stimuli at international, national and local levels for putting health high on the international development agenda.

For the first time, meetings of the Group of 8 (G8), the United Nations Security Council, the World Economic Forum and the Organisation for Economic Co-operation and Development (OECD) have explicitly addressed health issues requiring attention as development issues. Health has, in effect, become recognized as a resource for, and as an indicator of, sustainable development. Back in 1992, the Rio Declaration stated that 'Human beings are at the centre of concerns for sustainable development. They are entitled to a healthy and productive life in harmony with nature'. This stressed the important inter-linkages between the social, economic and environmental pillars of sustainable development, all of which are underpinned by good health. Furthermore, Chapter 6 of Agenda 21 emphasized the fundamental commitment within sustainable development to 'protecting and promoting human health' (UN, 1993). At the WSSD, health was singled out by the UN Secretary General as one of the five priority issues to be addressed, along with water, energy, agriculture and biodiversity (Annan, 2002). A key message in the wide-ranging health agenda was that sustainable development cannot be achieved where there is a high prevalence of debilitating illnesses, and the health of the population cannot be maintained without a healthy environment. A major challenge lies ahead for both the health sector, as well as sectors outside of health, in implementing the agreements reached in Johannesburg.

Environment and poverty links

In Johannesburg, particular emphasis was placed on health issues in relation to environment and poverty concerns. The environment can be a source of ill health for many of the world's people, particularly the poor. At least a quarter of the global burden of disease can be attributed to environmental factors. Many infectious diseases are associated with poor environmental quality and lack of access to basic services, such as water and sanitation. Many non-infectious diseases are also environment-related cancers and respiratory illnesses. Indoor air pollution from cooking and heating with biomass and other dirty fuels such as coal contribute to nearly 2 million excess deaths a year, most of them in children under the age of five.

In addition, the emerging burden of environmental disease is associated with risk factors such as chemicals in food, the air and water; deteriorating air and water quality; physical factors such as noise or radiation; and unhealthy working conditions, both in the formal and the informal sector. The link between health and the environment is most evident amongst the poor, who frequently live in unsafe and crowded settlements, in underserved rural areas or in slums on the edges of cities (von Schirnding, 2000). They are more likely to be exposed to pollution (both indoors and outdoors) and other health risks at home, at work and in their communities. They are more likely to consume insufficient or poor-quality food, to smoke cigarettes and to be exposed to other health risks. Although concerted action over the past 50 years has led to significant improvements in human health, average life expectancy has increased and infant and child mortality rates have declined, not all regions of the world have shared equally in these improvements (von Schirnding, 2001). Poor health continues to be a major constraint on development efforts. Improving access to safe water, sanitation, clean air, improved waste management and sound management of chemicals were among the key issues that received special attention in Johannesburg. Of particular note was the call for increasing access to sanitation to improve human health and reduce infant and child mortality, prioritizing water and sanitation in national sustainable development strategies and poverty reduction strategies where they exist. A new target was agreed – namely, to halve by the year 2015 the proportion of people who do not have access to basic sanitation. This new target complements the Millennium Development Goal (MDG) on access to safe drinking water.

Another important agreement was to aim, by 2020, to use and produce chemicals in ways that lead to the minimization of significant adverse effects on human health and the environment, taking into account the precautionary approach. Also called for was the promotion of reduction of risks posed by heavy metals that are harmful to human health and the environment. An agreement to diversify energy supply and substantially increase the global share of renewable energy sources with the objective of increasing its contribution to total energy supply was significant (especially for its health implications), even though the WSSD failed to reach agreement on a specific time-bound target. There was also an agreement to improve access to *inter alia* reliable and affordable energy services for sustainable development and resources sufficient to achieve the MDGs.

Other aspects of note were the call to enhance health education (with the objective of achieving improved health literacy on a global basis by 2010), and an emphasis on capacity-building to better assess health and environment linkages. The need to strengthen occupational health programmes was highlighted, as was the necessity of reducing air pollution exposures and related health impacts (including through the use of cleaner fuels, modern pollution-control techniques and reducing dependence on traditional fuel sources for cooking and heating), as well as controlling lead exposure through phasing out lead in petrol, paints and other sources of human exposure.

The role of health in development

The Johannesburg agenda also reflected a major shift in recent thinking regarding the role of health in poverty reduction and development. Health is far more central to poverty reduction than previously thought, and that realization is now beginning to shape national and global policies. It has been known for years that people who are poor are more likely to get sick. But now knowledge is accumulating about how ill health creates and perpetuates poverty, triggering a vicious cycle that hampers economic and social development and contributes to unsustainable resource depletion and environmental degradation. Evidence suggests that health gains trigger economic growth: if the benefits of that growth are equitably distributed, this can lead to poverty reduction.

The Commission on Macroeconomics and Health (CMH) (WHO, 2001), appointed by the World Health Organization (WHO), has assembled powerful evidence suggesting that the role played by health in determining the economic prospects of the world's poor communities has been significantly underestimated. The main causes of avoidable death in low-income countries include HIV/AIDS, malaria, tuberculosis (TB), childhood infectious diseases, maternal and peri-natal conditions, micronutrient deficiencies and tobacco-related illnesses. Recent evidence shows how disease undermines economic progress. Major diseases, such as HIV/AIDS, malaria and TB, directly affect the poorest countries' ability to develop. They function as a drag on economic growth and they perpetuate poverty. Childhood illnesses and maternal morbidity and mortality keep the most vulnerable groups trapped in vicious cycles of deprivation and despair. In Johannesburg a call was made to strengthen the capacity of healthcare systems to deliver basic health services to all, aimed at improving access to essential drugs, immunization services, vaccines and medical technology, improving maternal and obstetric care, and reproductive and sexual health. These commitments were made with an emphasis on meeting the MDGs related to health, including reducing maternal and child mortality. Specific measures to combat and treat HIV/AIDS, malaria, TB and other diseases were called for, with special emphasis placed on the need to mobilize financial resources and to support the Global Fund to Fight AIDS, TB and Malaria.

Good health can no longer be seen as an expense that only rich countries can afford, but instead as a necessary investment by all countries, including the poorest countries of the world. The massive effort envisaged to fight against the major disease burdens of the poor will require substantially increased funding, including a greater share of domestic budgets devoted to health. This will need to go into disease specific programmes, as well as into the health system itself. More effective coordination of donor funding and assistance is also needed to ensure that essential links are maintained in the chain of reduction of disease trends and building of health systems. In addition to higher allocations from national budgets, increases in bilateral and multilateral assistance are needed. It has been estimated that, at a minimum, US$30 to $40 per person is needed to cover essential personal interventions, including for HIV/AIDS (WHO, 2001). This contrasts with actual spending in the order of US$13 per person in the poorest countries. An increase in domestic budgetary resources of 1 per cent of gross national product (GNP) by 2007 and 2 per cent by 2015 has been called for. In addition, donor grants of US$27 billion per year will be needed by 2007, rising to US$38 billion in 2015 (WHO, 2001). The CMH also recommended that investment should focus on research and development towards new drugs, vaccines and diagnostics for tackling diseases of the poor. Decreasing prices of drugs through full use of the safeguards contained in the Agreement on Trade-related Aspects of Intellectual Property Rights (TRIPS) were also called for.

The aggregate additional cost of scaling up interventions in low-income countries is in the order of US$66 billion per year, about half of which comes from donors. This is expected to result in a saving of 8 million lives per year and provide economic benefits that yield a sixfold return on investment. This applies whether the risks are from communicable diseases, maternal and child health conditions, poor nutrition, reproductive ill-health, non-communicable diseases or unhealthy environments. Significant funding pledges were announced by many countries in various areas of sustainable development (for example, in water and energy), and at the WSSD itself some 16 partnership programme and projects were announced in health. This included a special initiative launched by the director general of WHO (Brundtland, 2002) on healthy environments for children, which aims to galvanize global action on some of the major environmental risks to children in the settings where they live, learn and play.

The burden of communicable diseases

Special emphasis was placed in Johannesburg on communicable (infectious) diseases, as these occur mainly in developing countries where poverty and poor environments greatly increase the risk of disease. The poorest billion people in the world are particularly vulnerable to such diseases. Of those communicable diseases that contribute to and deepen the poverty of the world's poorest people, HIV/AIDS has the greatest potential and actual impact on individuals, families, sectors and nations. About 40 million adults and children are now living with HIV/AIDS (UNAIDS, 2001), 95 per cent of whom are in developing countries. HIV/AIDS has had its most severe impact on the most vulnerable groups, including the poor, women and children. In sub-Saharan Africa, for example, over 25 million people are infected with HIV/AIDS (WHO, 2002). In stark contrast to trends in other regions, children in Southern Africa can expect to live shorter lives than their grandparents. More than 12 million Africans have died of AIDS to date and many millions orphaned as a result. HIV prevalence rates of 10 to 15 per cent can translate into a reduction in growth rate of gross domestic product (GDP) per capita of up to 1 per cent per year.

Through its widespread impact on demography, households, communities, sectors and the economy, AIDS is now seen as more than a health crisis. It is recognized as a threat to development and security throughout the world, and the Secretary General of the UN has highlighted the fact that the devastation brought by HIV/AIDS is now so acute, it has itself become one of the main obstacles to development.

Malaria is another key health threat associated with poverty that was highlighted in Johannesburg. Several hundred million people continue to be infected annually with malaria, resulting in almost 300 million clinical cases worldwide each year (WHO, 2002). Malaria is increasing in many countries, partly because of deterioration in public health infrastructure, but also because of climatic and environmental changes, conflict-related human migration, widespread poverty, and the emergence of drug-resistant parasites. Africa's GDP would probably be in the region of US$100 billion higher if malaria had been tackled 30 years ago, when effective control measures first became available (Brundtland, 2000). Even today, half a billion cases of malaria each year lead to the loss of several billion days of productive work. The estimated costs of malaria, in terms of strains on the health systems and economic activity lost, are enormous. In affected countries, as many as three in ten hospital beds are occupied by victims of malaria.

Non-communicable diseases

While many countries continue to see their development efforts hampered by the burden of communicable diseases, at the same time they are faced with the rising incidence of non-communicable diseases (NCDs). In this regard, Johannesburg called for programmes to combat non-communicable diseases, mental health problems, injuries and violence, and associated risk factors such as tobacco, alcohol, unhealthy diets and lack of physical activity. In 1999, NCDs were estimated to have contributed to almost 60 per cent of deaths in the world (Yach and Bettcher, 2000) and 43 per cent of the global disease burden. Based on current trends, these diseases are expected to account for 73 per cent of deaths and 60 per cent of the disease burden in the year 2020.

The rapid rise of NCDs is threatening economic and social development, as well as the lives and health of millions of people. They represent a major health challenge to global development in the coming century. Low- and middle-income countries suffer the greatest impact, and the rapid increase in these diseases disproportionately affects poor and disadvantaged populations, contributing to widening health gaps between and within countries. Four of the most prominent NCDs – cardiovascular disease, cancer, chronic obstructive pulmonary disease and diabetes – are linked by common preventable risk factors related to lifestyle: tobacco use, an unhealthy diet and physical inactivity. The alarming growth rate of tobacco consumption, for example, threatens sustainable development everywhere. In 1999, there were over 1.25 billion smokers in the world (representing one third of the world's population aged 15 and over), and tobacco consumption was responsible for 4 million deaths. Recent trends in tobacco consumption indicate rising prevalence rates, especially among children, young people and women.

The call for integrated strategies

Other aspects emphasized in the JPOI included the need to integrate health concerns within strategies, policies and programmes for poverty eradication and sustainable development, implementation of the WHO Health for All strategy, and creating more effective national and regional policy responses to environmental threats to human health, as well as encouraging health-promoting production and consumption policies.

The Millennium Declaration, adopted unanimously by world leaders in September 2000 (UN Millennium Assembly, 2000), sets a number of interrelated goals and targets that are based on principles of sustainable development and are aimed at making further progress in eradicating poverty and advancing healthy and sustainable human development. Three of the eight goals directly relate to health: reducing child mortality, improving maternal health, and combating HIV/AIDS, malaria, TB and other diseases. However, several other MDGs are of central importance to realizing health goals. For example, the goal of eradicating extreme poverty and hunger has an obvious and direct impact on people's health. Universal primary education, the second MDG, is also key to improving health, as is the MDG related to environmental sustainability. At the WSSD, many of these goals were confirmed. New targets were also set. A recommitment was made to the Health for All strategy. This was declared as the main health goal of governments in 1977 – namely: 'Attainment by all the people of the world by the year 2000 of a level of health that will permit them to lead a socially and economically productive life'. However, various trends, including globalization of trade, travel and technology; urbanization and the growth of megacities; widening gaps between the rich and poor; the continuing burden of infectious diseases; the rise in non-communicable diseases; and growth in environmental threats made a reassessment of this Health for All (HFA) strategy necessary in 1995.

The renewed Health for All in the 21st Century strategy adopted at the World Health Assembly in 1998 (WHO, 1998) set out global priorities and targets for the first two decades of the 21st century, which aim to create the conditions for people worldwide to reach and maintain the highest attainable level of health throughout their lives. The strategy is based on the principles of social justice, equity and human development, and emphasizes the prevention of ill health, the minimization of health risks and the promotion of population health. Conceived in these terms, the improvement of health requires more than the services delivered by the health sector alone; the contribution of other sectors is explicitly recognized as being vital for improving the health and well-being of the population.

The need for inter-sectoral action

Many of the key determinants and solutions to health and disease lie outside the direct realm of the health sector, in sectors concerned with environment, water and sanitation, agriculture, education, employment, urban and rural livelihoods, trade, tourism, industrial development, energy, and housing. Addressing the underlying determinants of health through inter-sectoral efforts is thus key to ensuring sustained health improvements and ecologically sustainable development (von Schirnding, 1997a). In this regard, Johannesburg called for increased action from the international community, non-governmental organizations (NGOs), the private sector and local communities to implement sustainable development objectives through partnerships and alliances at all levels, global to local.

Preventing disease through inter-sectoral action

Inter-sectoral approaches and partnerships have been successfully developed to tackle particular diseases, both communicable (infectious) and non-communicable. Effective tools are available and many low-income countries have shown that by using these tools wisely, the disease burden can be reduced dramatically (von Schirnding and Mulholland, 2002). Increasingly, policies and programmes to combat communicable diseases are focusing on integrated strategies. Such strategies simultaneously address the underlying causes of disease, often found in the broad socio-economic, cultural and physical environment, as well as addressing issues relating to the treatment of the disease condition itself.

In the field of malaria, the failure of past efforts is due, to a large extent, to inadequate collaboration of malaria control programmes with non-health sectors and insufficient attention paid to the political, economic and social aspects of people's experiences of malaria. Successful malaria-control efforts now involve contributions from community members and people working in education, environment, water supply, sanitation and community development. Better environmental management can contribute to malaria control through improved water management strategies, as well as interventions to address habitat modifications such as land conversion and forest clearance for roads and agriculture. For success to be sustained, such efforts should be an integral part of national health development and community action efforts, supported by inter-sectoral collaboration at all levels and by monitoring, training and evaluation.

With respect to environmental diseases and NCDs, global instruments are increasingly needed – for example, in the field of tobacco and chemical safety. Solutions to global environmental problems require increased international cooperation, particularly through implementation of international laws and conventions.

Tobacco and chemical control

The globalization of tobacco consumption restricts the capacity of countries to unilaterally control tobacco within their borders. Transnational tobacco control issues (including trade, smuggling, advertising and sponsorship, prices and taxes, control of toxic substances, and tobacco package design and labelling) require multi-sectoral cooperation and effective action at the global level. The development of an international legal instrument, the Framework Convention on Tobacco Control (FCTC), represents the first time that countries have enacted their constitutional right to develop binding international legal instruments to protect and promote global public health. Formal negotiations of the convention began in October 2000, and it was adopted in 2003. The FCTC process is a catalyst for multi-sectoral cooperation, as well as supporting national action to develop comprehensive tobacco-control policies. Within national governments, the creation of the FCTC has provided the opportunity for the tobacco-control debate to expand to ministries other than health, including foreign affairs, trade and agriculture.

Concern is mounting about the safety of chemicals. A number of useful partnerships have been built, including the Intergovernmental Forum on Chemical Safety (IFCS), formed in 1994 as a non-institutional arrangement in which national governments, intergovernmental organizations and NGOs can meet to consider issues associated with the assessment and management of chemical risks. An example of how this mechanism has borne fruit was its efforts to develop recommendations on Persistent Organic Pollutants (POPs) to the United Nations Environment Programme's (UNEP's) Governing Council, which subsequently led to the negotiation and adoption of the Stockholm Convention. Another partnership example is the Inter-organization Programme for the Sound Management of Chemicals (IOMC), which was formed in 1995 as a mechanism to coordinate the work of intergovernmental organizations active in chemical safety: UNEP; WHO; the International Labour Organization (ILO); the United Nations Food and Agriculture Organization (FAO); the United Nations Industrial Development Organization (UNIDO); the United Nations Institute for Training and Research (UNITAR); and the OECD. The successes of this partnership have been numerous, including a globally harmonized system for classification and labelling of chemicals, increasing the numbers of risk assessments developed, and work to address the dangers of chemical accidents. In many such partnerships the private sector has had an important role to play in encouraging safer production and use of chemicals. Responsible Care is one of the oldest and best established initiatives in the industry, and could be seen as a complementary governance framework based on peer pressure and public transparency, establishing clear guidelines for participating companies even in countries with weak regulatory standards.

While there are practical and achievable ways of improving health, alleviating poverty and furthering sustainable development, many obstacles are still hampering effective efforts in the prevention and control of diseases. These include:

- lack of funding;
- lack of attention to the health impacts of activities in other sectors;
- economic incentives for non-sustainable practices;
- weak health systems;
- low priority given to health;
- lack of political commitment;
- lack of inter-sectoral action;
- lack of institutional cooperation – vertical and horizontal.

Strengthening health system performance

Health systems must be able to respond to the health needs of people throughout their lives and at the same time make efficient use of limited resources. Building on primary healthcare, sustainable health systems need to guarantee equity of access to essential health functions. These functions include:

- quality care (diagnostics and treatment) across an individual's lifespan;
- preventing and controlling disease, and protecting health;
- providing education and health information to enable citizens to act responsibly in the interest of their own health.

In order to build a sustainable health system that delivers against these minimal requirements, it is necessary to (Buch, 2001):

- promote legislation and regulations in support of health systems, including a framework for private-sector activities that are in line with system priorities;
- develop health information systems and ensure active surveillance;
- foster the use of, and innovation in, health-related science and technology;
- build and maintain human resources for health;
- secure adequate and sustainable financing on a macro- and micro-economic level;
- share knowledge and expertise, nationally and internationally.

In 2000 (WHO, 2000), the WHO carried out the first-ever global analysis of the world's health systems – that is, all organizations, institutions and resources devoted to producing health actions (any effort, whether in personal healthcare, public health services or through inter-sectoral initiatives, whose primary purpose is to improve health). Five performance indicators were used to measure performance of health systems in 191 member states in trying to achieve three overall goals: good health, responsiveness to expectations of the population and fairness of financial contribution. It was found that progress towards these goals depends crucially upon how well systems carry out four vital functions: service provision, resource generation, financing and stewardship. Special emphasis was placed on stewardship, which has a profound influence on the other three aspects. The ultimate responsibility for the overall performance of a country's health system lies with government, which in turn should involve all sectors of society in its stewardship function. This is a major challenge for ministries of health.

Moving beyond the health sector

Much progress has been made in forging closer links between national healthcare and other sectors, particularly through:

- local and national inter-sectoral health and development planning;
- increased use of planning tools, such as health impact assessment procedures;
- integrated monitoring and surveillance systems;
- improved health information systems and indicators.

The policies of all sectors that affect health directly or indirectly need to be analysed and aligned in order to maximize opportunities for health promotion and protection. This will require health professionals to be more responsive to the primary motivations of professionals from these other sectors, and to be willing to negotiate for policies that are mutually beneficial.

Joint action

Education

Stronger joint action by health systems and the education sector could contribute substantially and rapidly to the overall improvement of the health status of populations, and to a long-term reduction in health and economic inequalities between groups.

Finance

Economic and fiscal policies can significantly influence the potential for health gains and their distribution in society. Tax incentives can be set so that they contribute to a healthier lifestyle (for example, healthy nutrition) and discourage the use of harmful products/substances such as tobacco and alcohol. Such policies, when combined with appropriate legislation and health education programmes, can retard and even reverse negative trends, particularly in the area of non-communicable diseases and trauma.

Agriculture

Agricultural policies can incorporate specific disease prevention measures in irrigation schemes; actively promote integrated pest management in order to minimize the use of toxic chemicals; establish land-use patterns that facilitate rather than discourage human settlements in rural areas; encourage substitution for crops that harm health; and ensure the production of safe and sufficient foods. An energy policy that favours health should support the use of cleaner energy sources. It should ensure that less hazardous and toxic waste is produced, that cleaner and more energy-efficient transport is available and that buildings are designed to be energy efficient. The cumulative impact of such policies can be substantial. Their enactment can ensure that health is not sacrificed for narrow short-term sectoral or economic gains.

Industrial policy

The business sector should be encouraged to not only endorse and implement sustainable occupational health strategies, but to provide additional services such as education, disease prevention and other types of care to employees in a cost-effective manner. Existing programmes can serve as good practice examples and should be promoted through the Global Compact and within business associations.

Inter-sectoral planning at a national level

Johannesburg and Rio emphasized that new planning approaches are needed in order to achieve sustainable development. A number of elements, in particular, are necessary for the integration of local and national health concerns within environment and development planning. These are:

* identification and assessment of health hazards associated with environment and development;
* development of environmental health policy incorporating principles and strategies for all sectors responsible for development;
* communication and advocacy of this policy to all levels of society; and
* a participatory approach to implementing health and environment programmes.

Many countries have instituted new policy and planning frameworks over the past decade, and have developed tools to make health and environment concerns an integral part of the planning process. On a worldwide basis, measures to incorporate health and environment issues within national plans and programmes have varied from country to country, depending upon priorities, planning mechanisms and the way in which planning responsibilities are divided (von Schirnding, 1997a). This has led to a wide variety of approaches being adopted, including:

- preparation of health and environment plans for inclusion in the national plans for sustainable development;
- integration of environmental protection and health plans into national economic and social development plans;
- review and modification of sectoral plans to include health and environment concerns;
- incorporation of health considerations within national environmental action plans;
- inter-sectoral input into national health policy and plans.

Of particular interest is the development of national environment and health action plans (NEHAPs), which aim to incorporate health and environment issues within national action plans.

National environmental health action plans

National Environmental Health Action Plans emerged after the adoption of Agenda 21 during the mid 1990s, and were first developed by a number of pilot countries in Europe. The NEHAP planning process has also been adopted in other regions of the world. In developing countries, NEHAPs were often preceded by World Bank-promoted national environmental action plans (NEAPs). NEHAPs have encouraged a process of inter-sectoral consultation and collaboration. This, in turn, has led to a greater understanding of the importance of environment and development issues within health ministries, and a greater understanding of the importance of health issues within environment and other ministries. Reviews of the NEHAP planning process have identified a number of strengths, among which are:

- increased awareness and understanding of health, environment and development problems;
- increased focus on prevention;
- adoption of broader approaches;
- improved collaboration between sectors; and
- formation of viable partnerships.

Adoption and implementation across the world has, nevertheless, been uneven, and weaknesses still remain. These include:

- gaps in data availability and quality;
- difficulty in detecting health and environment trends;
- poor linkages between health and environment data;
- emphasis on symptoms, rather than causes of problems;
- little focus on analysis of management structures;
- lack of capacity for implementation; and

- lack of clarity regarding priority-setting processes (von Schirnding and Mulholland, 2002).

In addition to these commitments, health, sustainable development and poverty reduction have being addressed at country level in comprehensive development strategy and planning tools, such as the United Nations Common Country Assessments (CCAs) and the United Nations Development Assistance Frameworks (UNDAFs).

Inter-sectoral planning at a local level

Key to the Agenda 21/WSSD process has been the development of initiatives on the local/municipal level through dialogue between local government and its citizens, organizations and private enterprises, and the subsequent formulation of strategies based upon information gathered through the consultation process. Local Agenda 21 and related activities include, among others, the WHO Healthy Cities Movement, and the United Nations Human Settlements Programme's (UN-Habitat's) and UNEP's Sustainable Cities Movement. Local planning initiatives that address health and environment concerns in sustainable development have been collectively referred to as Local Environment and Health Action Plans (LEHAPs). These include local Agenda 21 initiatives, which address health issues and/or involve the health sector in local development planning, as well as 'Healthy Cities' types of approaches (von Schirnding, 1997b).

The Healthy Cities Movement started as a small-scale project of the WHO European office in 1987. It has now become a major movement, involving thousands of cities throughout the world. Key successes of the Healthy Cities type approaches include:

- efforts to place health higher on the agenda of local decision-makers in cities and other settings;
- building a strong local lobby for public health concerns;
- dealing with health, environment and development problems through local participation;
- ensuring that all development sectors and agencies, including those dealing with housing, local government, industry, transport and planning, address health issues in their work.

The Healthy Cities concept and approach has been translated in different ways according to the different emphasis of different localities: Healthy Cities in Europe and Africa, Healthy Islands in the Western Pacific Region, Healthy Municipalities and Communities in North America, Healthy Villages in the Eastern Mediterranean, as well as healthy 'settings', which encompass schools, marketplaces and many other sites and settings where people live, work and recreate.

A significant innovation in addressing development problems during recent years has been the emergence of Local Agenda 21 initiatives (LA21). Local Agenda

21s were seen as the means by which local action plans could be developed within each city and town to implement the many recommendations that were within the Agenda 21 programme of action. The LA21s implemented since 1992 have particular importance for three reasons (McGranahan, 2001):

1 They represent concrete experiences that have sought to address the many problems associated with development.
2 Most are locally developed and driven, not developed or imposed from outside, and they generally rely more on locally generated resources than external resources.
3 They support (and reinforce) 'good local governance' for environment and development.

Although more common in Europe and North America, there are growing numbers of cities with Local Agenda 21s (in Africa, Asia and Latin America). Nevertheless, in higher-income areas, more needs to be done to ensure that locally driven agendas take the regional and global impacts of local activities into account. In low-income areas, securing governmental and international support for local agendas that meet the needs of the more vulnerable groups remains an important challenge. Across the board, LA21s still face the challenge of entering the mainstream of development politics and policies, without losing their inclusive and consultative character.

One of the major weaknesses of LA21s is that health is typically not a central concern of most of these initiatives. There are a number of untapped synergies between the LA21 processes and health improvement, which could be built on the following:

• The multi-sectoral and inclusive approach of LA21s provides a potentially important means of achieving health improvement in Africa, Asia and Latin America.
• Strengthening the health dimension of LA21s could help to ensure that the more vulnerable groups have a better opportunity to articulate their interests.

The difficulties encountered to date suggest that LA21s require stronger regional and national frameworks to support the action needed to address regional and global goals (McGranahan, 2001). Furthermore, health has emerged as an important motivating factor in local initiatives in many high-income areas. Of more concern in less affluent settings, despite being local, LA21s often fail to address issues that threaten the health of the most vulnerable groups. One might therefore expect public health issues to emerge at the top of LA21s in the future – or at least for most of the measures that emerge to be directly relevant to public health. So far, this has rarely been the case. This suggests that LA21s require more active involvement from the health sector in order to ensure that widely acknowledged local health priorities are addressed, especially in relation to poverty (McGranahan, 2001).

The need for new planning tools

Effective health, environment and sustainable development policies and programmes depend upon convenient access to information about a large variety of hazards, ranging from biological hazards in food and water, to chemical hazards such as pesticides, to various physical and social factors. This is necessary if health authorities are to effectively discharge their responsibility to protect public health. But it also serves to clarify the extent to which health hazards are attributable to environmental conditions and/or to the activities of sectors other than health.

Environmental monitoring systems need to be designed to ensure that the exposure information collected is relevant to health concerns, and not merely used to monitor effectiveness of environmental control measures. Currently, few monitoring systems are set up with the aim of comprehensively assessing the various exposure routes (such as air and water) of potential contaminants. Moreover, integrated pollution control mechanisms are usually lacking. In general, knowledge of environment and health risks is segmented and incomplete. Mechanisms to ensure coordination at national, regional and local levels regarding health effects assessment and the development of adequate reporting systems are commonly lacking. Equally, mechanisms are frequently not in place to ensure that such information, once obtained, is transmitted to the various relevant sectors for action. Integrated databases on development hazards, environmental exposures and health are urgently required. Well-developed health and environment information systems, based on relevant data sets, are essential if scientific monitoring information is to be provided in support of policy- and decision-making, planning and evaluation (von Schirnding, 2002).

Improving environmental health management: Towards sustainable health management

In order to improve sustainability in health management in a complex and interlinked environment, a rethink of current organizational approaches is needed. Principles for such a reorganization might include the following:

- decentralization;
- inter-sectoral/interdisciplinary teams and task forces;
- clear and measurable objectives, developed using a multi-stakeholder approach;
- transparency of objectives, process and outcome.

There is a need to develop capacity in order to implement inter-sectoral policies and plans at all levels. This includes managerial, legal, administrative, institutional, human resource, financial and other aspects of capacity development. A new orientation and approach to service delivery is required. Present systems of organization in many government authorities worldwide are still based on concepts of bureaucracy, hierarchy, professional authority, disciplinary specialization and sectoral analysis. In order to facilitate implementation of inter-sectoral plans, there may be a need for institutional restructuring and readjustment. This may involve internal reforms within government departments in order to support a partnership-based approach. Issues that need to be addressed include mechanisms for inter-jurisdictional cooperation in implementing policies and plans, decentralization of structures to facilitate community involvement of sectors, and better coordination within and between governance structures.

The root causes of problems often need to be addressed outside of existing jurisdictional boundaries, with different organizations and agencies having different jurisdictional boundaries. For example, air quality problems usually need to be addressed at local, regional and national levels, depending upon the nature of the problem and the solution required. Other issues may demand more local approaches and solutions, such as dealing with drainage problems in a particular neighbourhood. In situations where there are complex jurisdictional arrangements, with responsibility for health and related services divided between national, regional and local authorities, implementation of inter-sectoral approaches have been complicated. Various types of jurisdictional reform can take place – for example, extension of geographical boundaries, amalgamation of multiple jurisdictions, transfer of powers and functions and so on. Inter-jurisdictional coordinating mechanisms can also be formed. While there is no universal understanding of what precisely constitutes an environmental health service, it is essentially concerned with developing and implementing environment and health policies, largely through monitoring and control activities, but increasingly through environmental health promotion activities. Environmental health services worldwide have been established and developed within a complex framework of policies, institutions and legislation. The concept of environmental health, the problems to be addressed, the way in which services are delivered and the way in which governments are organized differ considerably throughout the world.

In most countries, a range of different agencies have responsibility for various aspects of environment and health concerns, at different levels of government. While there is no optimum arrangement for environmental health services, there is a need to develop organizational structures that facilitate the movement of professionals across different sectors and organizations, in the ambit of environmental health services, and that facilitate coordination. Local government usually takes the lead in service delivery, sometimes through Local Agenda 21 programmes. The nature and complexity of environmental health problems and the strategies needed to address these will differ and will, to some extent, determine the institutional requirements. In some contexts key responsibility will rest with the health department, with the environmental health officer playing a traditional role regarding environmental sanitation, while in others (for example, in large metropolises) more specialized environmental health professionals may be needed to tackle complex and diverse problems, with roles and responsibilities of different sectors and administrative structures more precisely defined. Many of the larger cities around the world have now formed environmental departments that have taken over some of the responsibilities – for example, pollution control. In some cases this has as been in response to a perceived unresponsiveness of health departments in addressing local environmental health needs.

Environmental control initiatives, even where these are located within health departments, are often based on regulatory command-and-control approaches, with little basis in public health principles. While it is not in the scope of this chapter to discuss in any depth organizational structures for environmental health services at the national or sub-national level, it would be normally unmanageable (and undesirable) for the full ambit of environmental health services to be delivered centrally in one department. Internationally, a shift has occurred towards organizational diversification regarding environmental health services (EHS). In the context of the development of primary healthcare services and district health systems in many countries, and the parallel development outside of the health sector of environmental management systems, the placement of EHS is a fundamental issue that needs addressing. What is required is a precise division of sectoral responsibilities in environmental and developmental health at different tiers of government, based on a multi-sectoral policy.

Ultimately, it may well be the case that one will see an increasing trend moving towards sustainable health management: a more integrated approach that clusters personal health and healthcare services with related community services, and that of environmental health services with environmental protection and planning/development departments. Regardless of how sustainable health services are structured in any one country, setting or locality, sufficiently trained personnel will be required to deliver the service. There is a need for much better information to be obtained on the nature and composition of personnel necessary to carry out functions. In many cases there is a lack of information on human resources and approaches to training of staff. It is thus necessary to think about the qualifications required for health personnel in a changing organizational model, and to ensure that education systems and curricula are adapted to the changing requirements. Capacity development needs to be oriented to a wide range of professionals in a wide area of disciplines.

Role of the UN and other international bodies

In order to support actions at country level, increased and more efficient coordination between various agencies of the UN system is vital. A large number of agencies in the UN system deal with various aspects of health in relation to sustainable development – some directly and others more indirectly. The World Health Organization is the lead agency on international health and is also the task manager for Chapter 6 of Agenda 21 on protecting and promoting human health. A large number of technical and normative functions are carried out in collaboration with other UN agencies and institutions.

Other agencies, such as the United Nations International Children's Fund (UNICEF), are responsible for a number of activities and programmes in health that focus on children. As a field-based agency, UNICEF implements mother and child survival programmes, as well as those related to micronutrients and immunization, for example. While several UN programmes have responsibility for various aspects of HIV/AIDS, UNAIDS provides high-level global advocacy. The United

Nations Population Fund coordinates UN activities in relation to reproductive health services, while the World Bank finances and facilitates health infrastructure as part of its overall development agenda. Other UN agencies have health mandates in specific areas, such as the International Atomic Energy Agency (IAEA) (health aspects of radiation) and the FAO (agriculture policy in relation to food and nutrition). The ILO addresses health- and safety-related issues in the work environment, UN-Habitat deals with health aspects of human settlements, and UNEP deals with the health components of many environmental issues, including chemical safety and hazardous waste. In addition, the regional commissions have important roles to play in the area of technical cooperation, policy advice, research and analysis, regional coordination and integration, networking, and training (UN, 2002b).

An inter-sectoral perspective is required on health not only within the UN, but also in terms of its relationships to other international bodies. For example, the current debate on the Trade-related Intellectual Property Rights (TRIPS) Agreement with the WTO will have a bearing on the ability of countries to reproduce patented drugs and pharmaceuticals, which they say are essential to be produced generically and cheaply. The UN needs to learn from and encourage wider implementation of good practice at national and local levels by providing guidance, training and exchange programmes.

Conclusions and lessons learned

During the past decade, a number of lessons have been learned, which are key to ensuring healthy sustainable development at all levels, global to local (von Schirnding and Mulholland, 2002). The first and foremost lesson is that in order for development to be sustainable, it must benefit the health and well-being of both present and future generations. Development policies and economic strategies must be aligned to health objectives, as sustainable development is not possible where health is sacrificed for short-term sectoral or economic gains. It is also clear that political commitment in support of the health sector at all levels of government is a prerequisite to success. Where there is such commitment, health and sustainable development issues may move higher up on the international development agenda. Successful strategies and policy measures have been shown to have a number of elements in common – namely they:

- focus on major diseases, health conditions and risk factors, both present and future, which threaten sustainable development;
- focus on the broader causes of health and disease;
- focus on good governance and sustainable health systems, at local to global levels;
- forge partnerships with groups outside of the primary health sector.

Fundamental to ensuring healthy sustainable development are the following factors:

- *Making vertical linkages*: environment and development issues need to be addressed at all levels simultaneously so that national policy-making is informed by what is happening on the ground, and local initiatives can move forward in a supportive policy and legislative environment. International collaboration is necessary so that good practice can be studied, exchanged and encouraged.
- *Making horizontal linkages*: many of the examples in this chapter show that environment and development issues, and disease conditions cannot be addressed successfully in isolation. Linkages between sectors, between initiatives and between government and civil society are key in broad-based, integrated and cross-sectoral approaches that address the underlying determinants of health and sustainable development.
- *Strengthening capacity at national and local levels, building on and working with local knowledge and expertise*: while there is more acceptance now of links between health status outcomes and the determinants of health, particularly those arising from the activities of sectors other than health, there are still problems in acting upon this knowledge. Greater attention needs to be paid to developing managerial, administrative, institutional, human resource, legal and financial capacities to address health, environment and development linkages, and to work in an integrated fashion both between and within sectors.
- *Using tools to track progress and identify emerging health priorities*: a wide range of epidemiological and social science tools are available to assist countries and communities in assessing environment and health situations, in monitoring progress in implementation and evaluating process and outcomes. These include integrated databases with indicators that are understandable and usable by a wide range of sectors and by communities, which are essential for effecting change and tracking progress, as well as for building the evidence base for effective health, environment and development policies. Multiple stakeholders need to be involved from the beginning in developing and using different tools and indicators. In addition, stakeholder involvement should be even broader in order to increase transparency, improve outcomes and facilitate implementation of sustainable health policies.

References

Annan, K. (2002) 'Towards a sustainable future'. American Museum of Natural History's Annual Environmental Lecture, New York

Brundtland, G. H. (2000) 'Statement delivered at the Summit on Roll Back Malaria'. Abuja, Nigeria

Brundtland, G. H. (2002) 'Address to the 55th World Health Assembly'. World Health Organization, Geneva

Buch, E. (2001) 'Poverty and health in the context of sustainable development'. Paper prepared for the World Health Organization meeting on Making Health Central to Sustainable Development: Planning the Health Agenda for the WSSD, Norway

McGranahan, G. (2001) 'Environment, health and the pursuit of sustainable development in human settlements'. Paper prepared for the World Health Organization meeting on Making Health Central to Sustainable Development: Planning the Health Agenda for the WSSD, Norway

UN (United Nations) (1993) *Agenda 21: Programme of Action for Sustainable Development.* UN, New York

UN (2002a) *Johannesburg World Summit on Sustainable Development Plan of Implementation.* From the Report of the WSSD, 26 August to 4 September 2002. A/Conf.199/20, available at www.un.org/jsummit/html/documents/summit_docs/131302_wssd_report_reissued. pdf

UN (2002b) *A Framework for Action on Health and Environment.* WEHAB Working Group, UN, New York

UNAIDS (Joint UN Programme on HIV/AIDS) (2001) *Report on the Global HIV/AIDS Epidemic.* UNAIDS, Geneva

UN Millennium Assembly (2000) 55th Session. UN, New York, September 2000

von Schirnding, Y. (1997a) *Intersectoral Action for Health: Addressing Health and Environment Concerns in Sustainable Development.* World Health Organization, Geneva

von Schirnding, Y. (1997b) 'Addressing health and environment concerns in sustainable development, with special reference to participatory planning initiatives such as Healthy Cities'. *Ecosystem Health*, vol 3, pp220–228

von Schirnding, Y. (2000) 'Integrated strategies for improving health and environment conditions in low income urban areas'. *City Development Strategies*, vol 2

von Schirnding, Y. (2001) 'Health in the context of Agenda 21 and sustainable development: Meeting the challenges of the 21st century'. *Sustainable Development International*, vol 3, pp171–174

von Schirnding, Y. (2002) *Health in Sustainable Development Planning: The Role of Indicators.* World Health Organization, Geneva, WHO/HDE/HID/02.11

von Schirnding, Y. and Mulholland, C. (eds) (2002) *Health in the Context of Sustainable Development.* Background Document prepared for the World Health Organization meeting on Making Health Central to Sustainable Development: Planning the Health Agenda for the WSSD, Norway, WHO/HDE/HID/02.6

WHO (World Health Organization) (1998) *Health-for-All in the 21st Century.* WHO, Geneva

WHO (2000) *World Health Report.* WHO, Geneva

WHO (2001) *Macroeconomics and Health: Investing in Health for Development - Report of the Commission on Macroeconomics and Health.* WHO, Geneva

WHO (2002) *Health and Sustainable Development: Key Health Trends.* WHO, Geneva, WHO/ HDE/HID/02.2

Yach, D. and Bettcher, D. (2000) 'Globalization of tobacco industry influence and new global responses'. *Tobacco Control*, vol 9, pp206–216

9

Agriculture: Improving Governance for Food Security and Agriculture

Robert L. Paarlberg

Introduction

The 2002 World Summit on Sustainable Development (WSSD) did not shy from discussing problems of governance at the level of national institutions and policies. The Johannesburg Plan of Implementation (JPOI) that emerged from the summit correctly emphasized in section I (4) the lead role of 'good governance within each country'. It elaborated this point in section IX (146):

> *Each country has the primary responsibility for its own sustainable development, and the role of national policies and development strategies cannot be overemphasized. All countries should promote sustainable development at the national level by, inter alia, enacting and enforcing clear and effective laws that support sustainable development* (WSSD, 2002).

This emphasis on governance solutions country by country is particularly important in the area of food security and agriculture. Globalization has increased the need for global governance in most sectors; but despite globalization the causes of hunger and low farm productivity remain more local than global. The causes of environmentally unsustainable farming are also primarily local or national, rather than global. The improved governance that is needed to solve these problems must therefore be primarily local or national as well.

In the area of food security, the Millennium Development Goals (MDGs) call for reducing the proportion of people living on less than US$1 a day to half the 1990 level by 2015, which is to say from 29 per cent of all people in low- and middle-income economies down to 14.5 per cent, and to reduce by half the proportion of people in those countries who suffer from hunger. These goals will be particularly difficult to achieve in regions such as South Asia and sub-Saharan

Africa, where poverty and hunger rates are high and, in some cases, actually on the rise. Figure 9.1, based on data from the Food and Agriculture Organization (FAO) of the United Nations, maps today's concentration of very high hunger rates in Africa, in particular.

In most developing country regions the prevalence of poverty and hunger has been declining; but in Africa the percentage of the population who suffer from poverty (surviving on an income of less than US$1 a day) is actually higher today than it was in 1990, and since 1975 the total number of children in Africa suffering from malnutrition has roughly doubled. In the drylands of South Asia, rates of rural poverty and malnutrition are just as high. These severe rural poverty and hunger problems are directly linked, in most cases, to the low productivity of farming. Low farm productivity, in turn, is frequently a cause of environmental degradation. In this chapter we show that the improved governance institutions needed to address these problems of food insecurity and unsustainable farming must be built primarily within the poor countries themselves, at the local and national level.

The local nature of unsustainable farming

The most obvious causes of rural poverty, hunger and environmental damage in the developing world include racial and ethnic marginalization, landlessness, gender bias, unimproved production technologies, and poor access to markets, roads, electricity, education or public health services. Such conditions tend to be highly localized. In many villages in South Asia, for example, the female children of landless laborers will go hungry even while the local markets may have abundant supplies for purchase, and while most male children in the village are well fed. In many countries in Central America, commercial farmers in fertile valleys with irrigated land can prosper even while neighbours struggling to farm on the dry hillsides above the valley remain poor and hungry. The causes of outright famine also tend to be local rather than global. Famine threats usually arise today from isolated outbreaks of internal warfare (for example, in Sudan), or from localized natural disasters such as drought (for example in Southern Africa), or from the mistakes of a specific governments (for instance, policies in North Korea that cause famine, versus policies in South Korea that do not).

The rural environmental damage that can block sustainable food production in poor countries also tends to be local rather than global, both in origin and in impact. Serious rural environmental problems in poor countries, such as soil nutrient depletion, the plowing or overgrazing of fragile rangeland, deforestation and habitat destruction, usually reflect a combination of rapid local population growth plus political weakness among the rural poor. When growing numbers of destitute farmers have access to resources such as marginal lands or forests, but do not have enough political or legal power to control those resources, unsustainable resource exploitation is the predictable result. When rural dwellers sense that their own local control over a resource base is breaking down under population pressure or is being lost to a distant authority, such as a government forestry department,

Measuring and monitoring prevalence

Prevalence of undernourishment is measured by the share of a country's total population that is undernourished. The higher the prevalence, the more widespread the problem. To help analyse and monitor progress, the following five prevalence categories have been established.

Category	% undernourished	Description
1	< 25	Extremely low
2	25–4	Very low
3	5–19	Moderately low
4	20–34	Moderately high
5	35	Very high
		No data

Figure 9.1 *Rates of undernourishment across the globe*

Source: FAO (2003), available at www.fao.org/FOCUS/E/SOFI/IMG/map-e.pdf

an irrigation ministry or a land-titling agency, they will try to get as much as possible from the resource base before it is taken away (Durning, 1989). The resulting environmental damage is a problem of local and national governance more than global governance.

Poverty and environmental damage in the farming sectors of poor countries also tends to be associated with the continued use of unimproved farming technologies. Consider the plight of the rural poor in Africa, where the incidence of child malnutrition is now projected to grow to 40 million by the year 2020, a 30 per cent increase compared to the 1995 level (Pinstrup-Andersen et al, 1999). Africa's rural dwellers remain poor and hungry because their numbers have grown, while their means to be productive as farmers have not. Africa's dominant farm technologies continue to be shifting (slash and burn) cultivation and open-range grazing. These techniques do not return much to human labour, so they have not been able to produce an increase in rural wealth. These techniques have also become environmentally unsustainable due to the growing numbers of people and animals who now must be fed. With more people on the land, the length of time that any one piece of land can be left fallow has declined (limiting the replacement of soil nutrients). With more animals to graze, the protection of fragile rangelands from overgrazing has broken down. As soil nutrients decline on traditional farming lands it becomes necessary to invade the forest margin to clear new lands, leading to a loss of valuable habitat. As traditional rangelands degrade, animals must be moved onto still more fragile lands, speeding the process of desertification. At this point new farming technologies must be adopted in order to protect the rural environment, as well as to escape poverty. In particular, technologies must be found that return more per unit of land and labour. Technologies that boost production on land already cultivated will reduce the need to cut trees and clear new land. And technologies that boost production per unit of human labour will increase the income of farmers and reduce poverty and hunger in rural areas.

Many farmers in Asia have successfully upgraded their technologies since the 1960s to increase land and labour productivity, allowing them to escape poverty and slow a further expansion of cropland and rangeland. In India during the 'green revolution' between 1970 and 1994, the share of cropland planted to high-yielding seed varieties (HYVs) increased from 17 per cent to 55 per cent. Where HYVs were planted, yields per hectare more than doubled. In 1964, India was producing 12 million tonnes of wheat on 14 million hectares of land. By 1993, thanks to this technology upgrade, it was producing 57 million tonnes of wheat on 24 million hectares of land, more than a doubling of yields. To produce this much wheat at the 1964 level of yield, India would have had to plant roughly 60 million hectares, so the shift to HYVs in effect protected 36 million hectares of (fragile) land in India from damaging cultivation (CIMMYT, 1992). HYVs also provided more income per unit of labour, so rural poverty in India declined. Prior to the mid 1960s, the percentage of the rural population living below the poverty line fluctuated between 50 to 65 per cent; but by 1990 only about 34 per cent of the rural population remained poor (Fan, Hazell and Thorat, 1999).

China likewise introduced new farming technologies at the end of the 20th century, resulting in great advantages for the rural poor. Some of these technologies, such as hybrid rice, were independently developed by Chinese scientists. These new technologies, when combined after 1978 with a revolutionary set of post-Maoist institutional reforms, allowed the productivity of the average farm worker in China to increase in real terms by 90 per cent between 1980 and 1997. An estimated 250 million people escaped poverty in China during this period of unprecedented farm productivity growth, the single largest mass escape from poverty ever recorded in human history (Berg and Krueger, 2002).

These technology- and policy-driven gains in farm productivity in India, China and the rest of Asia also helped to reduce food insecurity by boosting rural incomes. In South Asia, between 1975 and 1995 the prevalence of child malnutrition decreased from 68 per cent to 49 per cent. In the developing countries of East Asia the prevalence of child malnutrition decreased from 33 per cent to 23 per cent (Smith and Haddad, 2000).

Africa has not yet taken this path. In Africa, food insecurity and poverty remain and extensive rural environmental damage from farming persists in large part because farm productivity remains low. The rate of adoption of new high yield varieties of crops (as a percentage of area) is now 80 per cent in Asia and 52 per cent in Latin America; but it remains only 26 per cent in sub-Saharan Africa (Tuskegee University, 2001). This helps to explain why in Africa, between 1980 and 1997, average agricultural value-added per farm worker actually declined by 10 per cent (World Bank, 2000, Table 8, pp288–289). As farm worker productivity has declined in Africa, rural incomes have stagnated, and with population growth the number of hungry people has increased. Between 1975 and 1995 the number of malnourished children in Africa increased from 18 million up to 31 million (Smith and Haddad, 2000).

Africa's failure to boost the productivity of its farmers is also a principal cause of the rural environmental degradation now running out of control in the region. Because so few African farmers use fertilizer, and because population growth is forcing traditional low-yield farmers to shorten the times during which they leave crop land fallow, nitrogen and phosphorus are being mined from African soils (and not replaced) at an estimated annual rate of roughly 44 million tonnes and 12 million tonnes respectively. All but three countries in Africa now show negative balances of nutrients of more than 30 kilograms of nitrogen, phosphorus and potassium per hectare annually (UNDP, 2002). As a result of this soil nutrient depletion, crop yields in much of Africa are not only low; they are actually falling (IFDC, 1992). This is in stark contrast to most other parts of the developing world where the green revolution took hold, and where crop yields are high and still rising.

The unhappy combination in Africa of high population growth and low-yield farming also devastates forests and wildlife habitat. Largely due to an expansion of low-yield farming, deforestation in Africa is proceeding at a rate 30 times faster than reforestation, with roughly 5 million hectares lost every year. In West Africa, roughly 4 per cent of the closed forest is razed every year, undercutting biodiversity and threatening endangered species. The fragile tropical soils exposed in Africa when tree cover is taken away are rapidly degraded or lost to erosion, so any gains to farming are only temporary. Because of population growth, traditional animal grazing practices have also become a source of environmental damage in Africa. An extension of animal grazing to poorly suited dry lands has led to a depletion of ligneous vegetation and increasing desertification. On the southern edge of the Sahara, some 650,000 square kilometres of once-productive land (an area the size of Somalia) have become desert over the past 50 years, and the FAO has estimated that an average of 50,000 to 70,000 square kilometres of land in Africa go out of production every year (Paarlberg, 1994).

Low farm productivity is not only a problem in Africa. In India, dryland farmers without irrigation still represent 40 per cent of the entire population. These farmers find it difficult to use green revolution seeds, so their average grain yields per hectare are only one third as high as those on the nation's better watered lands. Among these locally disadvantaged farmers, poverty and hunger persist. Environmental damage persists as well, since the only way of increasing production has been to expand cropping onto fragile grazing and sloping lands or into shrinking forest habitats. In Central America, the continued use of low-yield farming practices by poor communities who are experiencing rapid population growth likewise devastates the rural environment. Wealthy commercial farmers on good lands in Central America are harming the environment by over-irrigating and spraying too many chemicals; but the vast majority of farmers in the region do not irrigate or spray. They struggle on poor lands with traditional methods to produce enough corn and beans to keep families fed. As population has continued to increase, these poor lands have become exhausted, so farmers cut more trees, move higher up the hillside and invade more wildlife habitat. Since 1961, Mexico has lost about 36 per cent of its total forested area, and more than half of the soil area in Mexico is either eroded or undergoing accelerated erosion. In large parts of rural Mexico where impoverished peasant farmers have been trying to use traditional techniques to produce more on dry hillside lands, all of the trees have now been cut, the thin soil has washed away and the terrain resembles a lifeless moonscape.

The solution to farm productivity problems in the developing world should never be a simple copying of the farming techniques in use in developed countries. In today's developed countries in Europe, Japan and North America, farming practices have been distorted by production subsidies that have led to excessive applications of chemical fertilizers and pesticides, resulting in environmental hazards of a different kind. Some of the Asian developing countries that originally used green revolution seed varieties to escape rural poverty are now, unfortunately, following in the policy path of rich countries by providing production subsidies and trade protections to farmers that generate excessive chemical input use. Farmers in Africa may be using far too little chemical fertilizer, but farmers in most of East Asia are now using far too much.

While governments in Africa need to help their farmers increase the adoption of more productive technologies, governments in the industrial world therefore need to remove the subsidies and trade protections that are leading in their own countries to excessive production and input use. High-productivity farming is possible without excessive chemical use. For example, in rich and poor countries alike growing numbers of farmers have learned to control insect damage by adopting the techniques of integrated pest management (IPM). These techniques permit the spraying of chemical insecticides only if more benign strategies (for example, natural biological controls) have failed, and only after pest populations have exceeded critical threshold levels.

Good governance for food and agriculture in poor countries: Providing rural public goods

Good governance is defined most often in terms of institutional traits (for instance, accountable, transparent and democratic). When thinking about improved governance for the rural poor, it is more useful to consider the essential services that governments must provide, rather than the kinds of institutions needed to provide them. Good governance for food security and agriculture must start with the provision of rural public goods. Economists define public goods as those with benefits that are available to all ('non-excludable') and still available even when consumed ('non-rival'). A traffic light at a busy road intersection is one example: all can use it and the safety it provides is not diminished by that use (Kaul et al, 1999). A number of public goods are needed in poor countries to promote farm productivity, food security and rural environmental sustainability. These include internal peace so that farming is protected from violent conflicts; the protection of property rights (including traditional community-based common property rights); the provision of rural social services, such as education and public health (without discrimination on the basis of race, caste, ethno-linguistic or gender); and investments in basic rural infrastructure (roads, water, power, communications and agricultural research). Where national governments have provided these basic public goods, the rural poor have become productive enough to escape poverty and hunger, and have become conserving enough of their own resources to control environmental damage and degradation.

Rural public goods such as these are unlikely to be provided in sufficient quantity either by private business firms or by voluntary non-profit non-governmental organizations (NGOs). Profit-motivated companies lack the commercial incentive to produce a non-excludable non-rival public good because there will be no opportunity to earn money by rationing use. The private sector depends heavily upon the availability of public goods for its own prosperity; but it does not provide such goods. Voluntary agencies such as NGOs deliver many services; but they are also limited as providers of public goods. These agencies may want to produce such goods; but they seldom will have either the resources or the authority to do so. NGOs do many good things; but they seldom build national power grids and trunk roads, or create criminal justice systems to protect life and property, or establish the laboratories needed to carry out basic scientific and medical research. Only governmental institutions have both the financial means and the exclusive sovereign right to provide such goods within their own jurisdictions. They have the means precisely because of their exclusive sovereign right to impose taxes on their own societies. National governments should also have an incentive to provide these public goods, even if they are not democratic. They should want to provide public goods in order to increase the growth of wealth within their own societies in order to maximize available tax revenues over the long term (Olson, 2000).

The provision of public goods is, admittedly, only the first task of good government. Progressive reformers should also insist that good governments undertake wealth redistribution (for example, through progressive taxation) and provide safety net systems to guarantee minimum standards of welfare for the poor. In the area of food and agriculture, redistribution might imply government policies to equalize the ownership of farmland, and a safety net system might be a subsidy to reduce food costs for the poor. Such progressive measures have been hallmarks of good governance in many cases; but they are, nonetheless, secondary. Redistributive measures and safety nets have never been sufficient by themselves to increase the productivity and reduce the poverty and hunger of the rural poor. Governments attempting these more progressive measures must first take care to provide basic rural public goods.

In Africa, the region where agricultural productivity, food security and rural environmental protection are least assured, the greatest governance deficits are precisely in the area of basic public goods supplies. Internal peace is a basic public good; yet national governments in Africa have done a poor job of protecting farmers from violent conflict. Between 1975 and 1995, 12 countries in sub-Saharan Africa (representing a quarter of the region's population) were war torn, often for prolonged periods (Freeman and Lindauer, 1999). These internal conflicts displaced farmers from their work, undercutting food production. One study of food production in nations at war versus nations at peace in Africa has shown that internal peace continent-wide could have added 2 to 5 per cent each year to Africa's total food production since 1980 (Messer et al, 1998).

African governments also do a poor job of protecting private and community property. Soil and water projects developed and implemented by central government ministries too often take resource control away from traditional farming communities. Government land titling schemes frequently take resource ownership away from current users and give that ownership to politically powerful supporters of the ruling party. Ownership is taken away from the current users; but the users initially retain access, which results too often in heedless resource abuse. Governments in Africa also discourage investment by providing little assured protection to private wealth. Because property protections are so weak, Africans themselves have recently opted to locate 37 per cent of their wealth outside of the continent (Collier and Gunning, 1997).

Public investments in rural infrastructure are also inadequate in Africa. More than 91 per cent of Africans in the poorest income quintile live in rural settings; but few of these poor rural households enjoy the basic infrastructure needed for a healthy and productive life. Only 2 per cent have in-house water, only 1 per cent have sewers, and total road density for rural dwellers in Africa is only one sixth the average of Asia. Rural transport infrastructure in Africa includes so few paved roads that 87 per cent of all household travel is still on foot. Without access to all-weather roads and vehicles, African women must learn at an early age to head-carry heavy loads over punishing distances (Barwell, 1996). The high transport costs that result from this inadequate road infrastructure are a key barrier to higher farm productivity. Fertilizer use is discouraged because the cost of fertilizer at the farm gate in Africa is two to six times higher than in Asia, Europe or North America. Diversification into higher-value commercial crops is discouraged because the cost of getting the product to market takes away so much of the profit.

African governments have also done a poor job of investing in the public good of agricultural research. While international policy experts advise that low-income developing countries should spend a minimum of 1 per cent of the value of total agricultural output on agricultural research, most of the low-income countries of Africa have spent less than half that much (Alston et al, 1998). Between 1971 and 1991, public spending on agricultural research and development in Africa increased at only one fifth the average rate for the rest of the developing world. As a consequence, Africa today has only 42 agricultural researchers per 1 million persons economically active in agriculture, which is only 2 per cent the intensity of farm research found in the industrial world. African governments have also skimped on their investments in agricultural development overall. In 1985, the Organization for African Unity (OAU) governments pledged to increase the agricultural share of their public spending up to 20 to 25 per cent of the total; but the pledge was never fulfilled. Governments in Africa today typically spend less than 5 per cent of the state budget on agricultural development.

What is the evidence that larger public-sector investments can boost farm productivity and reduce poverty? In India, where farm labour productivity gains linked to HYVs helped to reduce rural poverty and hunger, state spending on rural public goods played a large role in making this technology upgrade possible. Between 1970 and 1995, state spending on schools helped to increase the literacy rate in rural India from 23 per cent up to 40 per cent. State spending boosted the share of villages enjoying electrical power from 34 per cent up to 90 per cent. State spending also increased the density of rural roads in India at a 3 per cent annual rate, growing from 2614 kilometres per 1000 square kilometres of geographic area in 1970 up to 5704 kilometres per 1000 square kilometres by 1995. Public investments in agricultural research were considerable as well. Economic modelling has now shown how important these public goods investments were to increasing both farm labour productivity and total factor productivity in India, and to removing people from poverty. Fan, Hazell and Thorat (1999) estimate the numbers of people in India removed from poverty by various categories of public goods spending. For every additional 1 million rupees (approximately US$200,000) invested by the state in rural education in India, 32 poor people are lifted above the poverty line. For every additional 1 million rupees invested in agricultural research and development, 91 people escape poverty. And for every additional 1 million rupees invested in rural roads, 165 people are raised above the poverty line. Investment in roads reduces rural poverty through farm productivity growth, but also by increasing non-agricultural employment opportunities and boosting rural wages (Fan, Hazell and Thorat, 1999).

Public-sector investments in rural public goods have also been key to China's success in boosting farm productivity. A model of China's rural economy, using provincial-level data for 1970–1997, indicates that production-enhancing public-sector investments – agricultural research and development (R&D), irrigation, rural education, roads, electricity, and telecommunications – raised farm production, reduced rural poverty and also reduced regional inequalities. In China rural education investments and agricultural R&D investments even ranked ahead of investments in roads as significant contributors to rural productivity gains and poverty reduction (Fan, Zhang and Zhang, 2002).

The insufficiency of emphasizing democratization or anti-corruption

Most contemporary advocates of good governance do not focus on the delivery of public goods. It is more common to focus on desired governmental traits (such as decentralization, devolution, democratization, less corruption, greater transparency or greater participation by civil society) and then assume that good governmental performance will follow. Focusing on traits rather than performance has two drawbacks. First, it takes us one step away from the essential problem of what governments must do with their resources and their authority (for example, deliver public goods). Second, the traits most commonly identified with good governance in wealthy countries may not be either necessary or sufficient to enhance food security for the rural poor in developing countries.

Democracy is a widely recognized trait of good government, desirable on its own terms and now prevalent in rich and well-fed countries; yet the evidence suggesting that democratization by itself can bring economic prosperity to poor countries is still quite weak. According to a 1995 review of 20 separate empirical studies, half of the studies found no significant relationship between democracy and economic growth. Three studies did find a positive relationship, and five found a conditional positive relationship; but two actually found a negative relationship (Brunetti and Weder, 1999). A subsequent review of 12 additional studies uncovered a slightly stronger link between democracy and growth – but only slightly stronger. Of these 12 more recent studies, only one found a negative correlation, while seven found a positive correlation. But the remaining four showed results that were either inconclusive or mixed (Goldsmith, 2001). In Africa specifically, no studies have yet found the few emerging democracies in the region since the 1990s to be any more prone than their predecessors to adopt economic reform programmes, or do better than authoritarian regimes in the region in terms of economic growth, stable prices or balanced budgets. African democracies in the 1990s, on the whole, did neither better nor worse than non-democracies (Goldsmith, 2001).

The important case of China under Deng Xiaoping after 1978 suggests that it is entirely possible to provide a dramatic increase in food security without democracy. South Korea and Taiwan did the same during the 1960s and 1970s under military rule. There is evidence that democracies are more likely to provide food relief in famine emergencies when subject to stronger accountability through regular elections that are held under the scrutiny of a free press (Sen, 1985). Yet, the statistical link between democratization and sustained hunger reduction is simply not strong enough to focus on this one trait of governance alone. Of the several independent variables offered and examined by Smith and Haddad (2000) in a multiple linear regression to explain reduced child malnutrition in developing countries between 1970 and 1995, democracy had the weakest correlation to hunger reduction. Other underlying determinants, such as women's education, per-capita food availability (linked to production), women's status relative to men, improvements in the public health environment (such as access to safe water), and per-capita national income, all emerged as more powerful contributory factors (Smith and Haddad, 2000).

An absence of corruption (theft from the state or bribe-taking) by government leaders and officials is another trait of good government that is highly desirable on its own terms, but once again not convincingly linked by evidence to hunger reduction or sustained economic growth. Developed country governments certainly tend to be less corrupt than governments in poor countries; but there is little evidence from the history of development that corruption must end before economic growth begins. Considering cases such as South Korea, Indonesia or China, these high-growth developing countries exhibited levels of corruption not significantly different from their low-growth counterparts (Khan, 2002). We do know that economic growth eventually reduces corruption in government; but we cannot be certain that ending corruption is a necessary condition for economic growth.

Nor does the international community have a proven method for ending corruption in government. Paying higher salaries to government officials may not reduce the incentive to take bribes; it may only give corrupt officials an income bonus while the bribe-taking continues. Decentralization is not a guaranteed strategy either, since local-level corruption is often no less and is sometimes proportionately much greater than corruption at higher levels (Goldsmith, 1999; Treisman, 2000). Nor is insisting upon civil society participation or democratization a sure path to clean government. Voters in democratic elections can sometimes find it rational to support corrupt machine politics patrons or mafia bosses if those corrupt leaders have a proven ability to deliver payoffs or protection, compared to clean politicians with an unproven capacity to deliver the same (Khan, 2002). Treisman (2000) finds no evidence that corruption is lower in democracies when other factors such as level of wealth are held equal.

Defining good governance in terms of governmental traits rather than governmental performance is thus an uncertain approach to securing sustainable food security in poor countries. It is better for practical reasons to focus on what governments do, rather than on what governments are. The governmental actions needed to achieve food security – actions that deliver rural public goods – are easier to agree upon than the various governmental traits that might eventually lead to this desired result. These actions might even be easier to secure, given that governments in poor countries will probably be less resistant to changing actions than to changing traits, and since international lenders such as the World Bank still technically prescribe conditioning loans on the adoption of specific forms of government.

Need for more public goods at the global level?

If we can agree to define good governance in terms of performance rather than traits, and if we can agree that delivery of public goods is a key performance requirement, then we must still consider one alternative to a focus on rural public goods delivered by national and local governments within the developing world. In the modern age of globalization, an improved provision of public goods at the global level might be more urgent or more important. Upon consideration, global public goods are important; but in domains where improved global governance can make a difference for food security, global institutions with significant capabilities to deliver most of the necessary public goods already exist.

In the area of famine early warning and emergency food aid, a substantial global governance capability already exists within institutions such as the FAO and the World Food Programme (WFP), and also within some regional institutions, such as the Southern African Development Community (SADC). This international food aid system has performed well in most emergency situations, most notably the Southern African drought crisis of 1991–1992. This system tends to break down only in cases where recipient-country governments conceal problems (as did Ethiopia in 1984), or block international access (North Korea after 1995), or in cases where an internal war is underway (for example, in Sudan).

Global governance in the area of international agricultural research is also quite well developed through the Consultative Group on International Agricultural Research (CGIAR). The research centres of the CGIAR have been operating for several decades now to generate scientific and technical innovations that can be used by poor farmers in developing countries. At the international level, this system has a strong record of performance. Unfortunately, the national agricultural research systems (NARS) of many poor countries have not been supported or funded adequately by their own governments to function as capable partners to the CGIAR centres.

Global governance of international food and commodity markets has been somewhat less effective, as these markets have a history of being distorted and destabilized by the agricultural subsidy policies of rich countries in Europe, North America and industrial East Asia. Here, to be sure, improved global governance would be helpful. But it would be a mistake to expect a reform of agricultural policies in rich countries to be decisive for the food security of poor countries for several reasons.

First, the greatest economic damage from farm subsidies in rich countries is absorbed within the rich countries themselves, specifically by the taxpayers who must pay the budget costs and by the consumers who must pay more for food in the marketplace. Secondary damage is then done to farmers in other countries; but these are not primarily poor farmers in the developing world. Subsidized production of wheat, corn and soybeans in the US principally damages the competing commercial producers of these same crops in countries that subsidize less. But most of these producers are relatively well-to-do farmers in Canada, Australia, Argentina and Brazil, rather than poor subsistence farmers in Africa or

South Asia. Many of the poorest farmers in the developing world are producing tropical crops (coffee, tea, cassava) that do not compete directly with subsidized temperate zone farm production, or they are cut off from the world market by the restrictive 'self-sufficiency' policies of their own governments, or by high transport costs resulting from their land-locked status plus inferior road systems. Only in a minority of cases do rich country farm subsidies seriously harm genuinely poor farmers in the developing world. This minority of cases certainly includes Japan's high protection for rice (harming growers in South-east Asia), US subsidies for cotton (harming small cotton farmers in Central and West Africa), and US and European Union (EU) protection for sugar beet production, harming tropical cane sugar producers in both Africa and the Western Hemisphere.

Most poor farmers in the developing world are not so deeply integrated within international commodity markets. It is the world's poorest countries that use international food and commodity markets the least. On the import side this is often a conscious policy choice, in pursuit of what is called 'national self-sufficiency' in basic food supplies. The poor and still hungry nations of South Asia have used steep tariff rate quotas and duties to keep foreign grain out of their domestic markets in the name of national self-sufficiency. This is why South Asia's ratio of grain imports to grain consumption is only 2 per cent, the lowest in the developing world. This makes it hard to blame South Asia's continuing hunger problems on whatever might be happening in international grain markets. Africa is slightly more dependent upon imported grains than South Asia, but more as a recipient of food aid than as a commercial importer. Grain imports into Africa including food aid still account for only a modest 6.5 per cent of total calorie consumption in the region (Ingco et al, 1996).

These poorest and hungriest developing country regions have therefore cut themselves off from agricultural commodity export markets. Sub-Saharan Africa was once a major cash-crop export source; but this earlier integration within global commodity markets has now weakened. World commodity markets continue to grow overall; but Africa's volume of exported coffee, groundnuts, palm oil and sugar has actually been shrinking; it was smaller in 1997 than it was in 1970. We can't blame this shrinkage on protection policies by rich countries, as undesirable as such policies may be, because other nations in South-east Asia and in the Western Hemisphere continued to realize export gains during this period. Africa was seeing its competitiveness in the market decline, not its access to the market. Between the early 1960s and the early 1990s, Africa's *share* of exports in some key international cash crop markets (for example, for vegetable oils, palm oil, palm nuts and groundnuts) fell by 50 to 80 percentage points. This African retreat from international commodity export markets occurred even though African exporters faced lower average tariffs than other developing country exporters, and faced export barriers lower on average today than the barriers faced by earlier developing country exporters during the 1960s (Yeats et al, 1996). Africa's shrinking share of world trade reflects less the hostility of the international marketplace towards Africa, and more the ineffectiveness of African government policies towards stimulating agricultural productivity at home.

We should hope for improved global governance of international commodity markets within the context of the current Doha Development Round of multilateral trade negotiations within the World Trade Organization (WTO). But even if these negotiations should succeed in inducing substantial farm subsidy reductions in rich countries, farmers in poor countries will continue to face the serious national-level governance deficit noted earlier in the form of inadequate supplies of essential rural public goods.

How to induce the delivery of more rural public goods by national governments

We have identified the central governance challenge in the area of food and agriculture as one of improving the performance of national and local governments in delivering public goods to the rural poor. When governments fail to deliver such goods, what can outsiders do to correct the resulting governance deficit?

In some cases the options available to the international community are quite limited. In cases of internal violent conflict, when national governments fail to provide the public good of internal peace, outsiders may be restricted from intervening by long-standing norms and laws of state sovereignty. These norms have recently weakened, to be sure. Beginning during the 1980s, the United Nations Security Council became more active in authorizing states to intervene in the internal affairs of other states in at least three circumstances: when a state engages in systematic human rights violations; when a breakdown of state authority removes protections against human rights violations; and when a government in power is unlawfully constituted. When these conditions are present, the Security Council is now more likely to consider the situation a threat to peace and to exercise its legal powers to authorize international enforcement under Chapter VII of the United Nations Charter.

Unfortunately, this weakening of the state sovereignty norm has not yet been accompanied by any significant strengthening of the institutional or military capacity of legitimate international institutions (such as the UN Security Council) to carry out enforcement actions to preserve or restore internal peace. The resulting inability of the United Nations to operate independently of the preferences of the great powers has blocked timely peace-preserving interventions, as in Somalia between 1988–1991 (Sahnoun, 1994) and in Rwanda in 1993 (Jones, 1999). As currently constituted, the UN is also poorly equipped to restore peace after internal fighting breaks out. Once hostilities are under way, the international community has usually intervened only for the purpose of extracting foreign nationals from physical danger or delivering emergency relief. Discussions continue within the international community over the legal and institutional innovations that might be required to empower the UN to conduct successful peace preservation and peace restoration missions within sovereign states; but this problem remains unsolved at the global level (Smith and Naim, 2000).

While public goods such as internal peace will remain difficult for outsiders to provide, the international community can and should do more to assist in providing those rural public goods that require expenditures of resources. It costs money to build rural roads, provide rural health and education services, and invest in agricultural research. Governments in the developing world are under-investing in these things, in part, due to a lack of adequate resources. The resource-rich international community can help to make up this financial gap through well-constructed assistance programmes. In fact, foreign assistance to governments that are willing to make public goods investments has a strong record of success. Consider the use that Taiwan made of the US$5.6 billion in aid it received from the US after 1945. This assistance helped Taiwan to finance the state investments that were one key to subsequent economic growth.

Unfortunately, traditional assistance programmes designed to finance state investments have been out of fashion for several decades now. The emergence, after 1980, in both Washington and London of a new political consensus (a so-called 'Washington Consensus') emphasizing market-led rather than state-led economic growth dramatically changed the foreign assistance policies of international development institutions, such as the World Bank. Following publication of its *Berg Report* in 1981, the World Bank converted itself to the view that economic performance in regions such as Africa could rapidly be improved by a greater reliance on market forces, plus a parallel reduction of state interventions and expenditures (Sender, 2002). The World Bank thus began lending to poor countries for the explicit purpose of reducing rather than expanding state investments. Bank lending for agricultural investments, as a consequence, went into a particularly steep decline. During the 1980s, the share of World Bank lending worldwide that was invested in agricultural and rural development projects fell nearly by half, while the share that went for the purpose of inducing 'structural adjustment' (deregulation of markets and a down-sizing of the state) increased from almost nothing to more than 20 per cent (Lipton and Paarlberg, 1990). There was a legitimate goal here to shrink wasteful public-sector spending on unneeded consumer and producer subsidies, inefficient state enterprises and large state bureaucracies. One unintended side effect of this structural adjustment lending strategy was collateral shrinkage of state spending on much-needed public goods investments in areas such as rural health, education, infrastructure and agricultural research.

The World Bank's use of loans to induce governments in Africa to do less rather than do more has, for two decades now, produced disappointing results (Sender, 2002). In part, this is because so many governments in Africa, while accepting structural adjustment loans from the Bank, withdrew the state from market regulation only partially, or only temporarily, or not at all (World Bank, 1994; Kherallah et al, 2000; Devarajan, Dollar, and Holmgren, 2001; Jayne et al, 2001), so the intended benefits of structural adjustment seldom had a chance to be realized. Meanwhile, state investments in rural public goods were cut or stagnated. In Ghana under structural adjustment, the index value of real development expenditures on agriculture – mainly capital investment outlays – dropped by 40 per cent between 1981 and 1984 (Sarris and Shams, 1991). In Kenya, between 1982 and 1988, spending on rural roads declined by more than 40 per cent (Grindle, 1996). Kenya was receiving a great deal of money from the international community during this period; but under structural adjustment too much of that money went to buy (or rent) market-oriented policy reforms, rather than toward investments in rural public goods such as roads, schools, clinics or agricultural research labs.

A sustainable food security strategy: Is it possible?

If the goal is to pursue sustainable food security in poor countries, the foreign assistance community should return more of its resources to a public investment-based lending strategy. Lending (and debt relief) should be conditioned not on states doing less, but on states doing better, and in some instances on states actually doing more.

This will be a difficult challenge for institutions such as the World Bank. After two decades of lending for structural adjustment and macro-economic policy change, the World Bank finds itself overstaffed with macro-economists and trade economists who know how to do nothing else. The Bank is now significantly short of in-house talent trained in the fields that will matter most for rural public goods delivery, such as engineering, agricultural science, education and health. Ironically, environmental NGOs may be another source of resistance to investment-based lending by the Bank. Since the 1980s, environmental NGOs have come to see World Bank loans for road construction or other rural infrastructure projects as a threat to the environment. This may be an accurate perception in the interior of Brazil, where penetration roads into the virgin forest did little more than accelerate the spread of poorly managed logging, ranching and farming schemes. But this is a poor reason to resist feeder road construction in semi-arid rural Africa, where existing rural communities desperately need better transport connection to market towns.

Environmental NGOs need to reconsider their opposition to the infrastructure investments necessary in rural Africa. Inside the World Bank, this opposition has recently had a limiting effect on what can be done. It has been five years since the World Bank created its independent 'Inspection Panel' to give NGOs greater voice in the approval of Bank projects. During those five years, Bank lending for infrastructure has declined sharply – for electric power and energy from US$2 billion down to just US$.75 billion; for transportation by 28 per cent over the same period; and for water and sanitation by 25 per cent (Kapur, 2002).

A first step: Measuring the delivery of rural public goods

An international strategy of providing assistance to governments that deliver rural public goods requires, as a first step, a better way of measuring and monitoring public goods delivery in the countryside. Data on public goods expenditures by governments need to be broken down along rural versus urban lines. The World Bank currently collects country-level data on more than 800 'World Development

Indicators': everything from gross domestic product and the female share of the labour force to numbers of international tourist arrivals every year. Included in this list are state expenditures for a variety of public goods such as roads, education, health and research. Yet, nowhere on this list can we find disaggregated measures of public investments in *rural* roads, *rural* education or *agricultural* research.

The World Bank collects data on 44 different indicators of educational expenditure and performance, all broken down by age and sex, but never by urban versus rural. The Bank maintains 21 different indicators to measure transport, power and communications infrastructure (roads, telephones, electric power); but none is broken down as urban versus rural. Twenty-three information technology indicators are provided – but, again, as national averages only, ignoring the urban–rural divide. Only in the case of access to improved water and sanitation facilities does the Bank provide data on public goods delivery broken down along urban versus rural lines (World Bank, 2002).

The rural poor continue to receive inadequate governance services, in part, because of their political weakness relative to urban dwellers (Lipton, 1977). For urban elites in the capital city, the rural poor are physically remote, seldom well organized, politically inarticulate and, hence, easy to ignore. By failing to compare urban to rural public goods delivery, the development indicators used by the World Bank perpetuate the political invisibility of the rural poor. On the theory that governance systems cannot work to change what they cannot measure, it is time for numerical measures of rural public-goods deliveries to be presented separately from national average measures. The Inter-agency Committee on Sustainable Development (IACSD), which is mandated to develop indicators for sustainable development, might logically play a role in demanding such data at the international level.

Conclusion

In defining the good governance needed to achieve sustainable food security, we have found that the traits of governments are less important than the actions of governments. We have argued that the governmental actions most needed are those that will deliver basic public goods to the rural poor. This is a job for national and local government, more than for global government. Global public goods are important; but the key governance deficits in the area of sustainable food security are to be found at the national level, not at the global level. We sometimes hear that it is necessary to 'think globally and act locally'; but in the area of sustainable food security it is often more appropriate to begin by thinking locally, and then act nationally. The international community can and must assist in meeting local and national governance challenges, particularly by redirecting more of its assistance activities back into the support of actual investments. Governments in poor countries must be encouraged by the international community to invest more in rural roads, rural schools, rural clinics and in agricultural research. To encourage this redirection of assistance and investment efforts, a first step is to recalculate official data on the public goods activities of governments, measuring separately the public goods provided to rural versus urban areas. The JPOI that emerged from the 2002 WSSD provides a strong framework for insisting upon the delivery of these rural public goods.

Questions to be addressed

- In developing countries, how much government spending goes towards the creation of public goods in rural areas? Too often data are collected on public goods investments without clarifying the small share going to rural farming communities. Where governments do not invest in rural health, education, roads, power, communications and agricultural research, farming remains non-productive, perpetuating poverty and often leading (as population grows) to environmental degradation.

- Do farmers in developing countries have access to a wide range of technology choices? If population increases while technologies remain stagnant, cropping and grazing can expand in ways that damage natural resources.

- In rural areas, when farmers have access to lands for crop production or grazing, do they also have secure control over those lands in the form of individual or communal property rights? Resources tend to be abused when farmers have access but lack control. It is the job of government to help farming communities control the resource base upon which their livelihood depends.

- In countries where women make up the majority of farmers, particularly in Africa, are the interests and perspectives of women adequately represented in government policy and policy-making? Too often in Africa, agricultural ministries and extension and research services are dominated by men.

- In the Doha Development Round of multilateral trade negotiations, will significant new WTO disciplines be imposed upon the trade-distorting agricultural subsidy policies of the developed countries? Will these disciplines extend to the product markets of greatest interest to farmers in tropical countries, such as sugar, rice and cotton?

- When different institutions of global governance in the area of food and agriculture send conflicting signals, how should developing countries respond? For example, should developing countries adopt the precautionary approach towards genetically modified (GM) crops endorsed in the new Cartagena Biosafety Protocol, or should they follow the more standard risk-based approach endorsed by the WTO?

- As more food and agricultural problems in Africa come to resemble complex humanitarian emergencies in the years ahead, will traditional food and farming institutions such as the FAO or the WFP be able to respond? Will these institutions be able to incorporate issues such as law and order, public-sector collapse and HIV/AIDS within their work programmes?

References

Alston, J. M., Pardey, P. and Roseboom, J. (1998) 'Financing agricultural research: International investment patterns and policy perspectives'. *World Development*, vol 26, no 6, pp1057–1071

Aymo, B. and Weder, B. (1995) 'Political sources of growth: A critical note on measurement'. *Public Choice*, vol 82, nos 1–2, pp125–134

Barwell, I. (1996) *Transport and the Village: Findings from African Village-level Travel and Transport Surveys and Related Studies.* Sub-Saharan Africa Transport Policy Program, The World Bank and Economic Commission for Africa, SSATP Working Paper no 23

Berg, A. and Krueger, A. (2002) *Trade, Growth and Poverty.* Preliminary draft presented at 2002 Annual World Bank Conference on Development Economics, Washington, DC, April 25

Brunetti, A. and Weder, B. (1999) *Explaining Corruption.* University of Basel

CIMMYT (International Maize and Wheat Improvement Center) (1992) CIMMYT in (1992): *Poverty, the Environment, and Population Growth, the Way Forward.* CIMMYT, Mexico City

Collier, P. and Gunning, J. W. (1997) *Explaining African Economic Performance. Working Paper 97–92.* Centre for the Study of African Economies, Institute of Economics and Statistics, Oxford University, Oxford

Devarajan, S., Dollar, D. R. and Holmgren, T. (2001) *Aid and Reform in Africa – Lessons from 10 Case Studies.* World Bank, Washington, DC

Durning, A .B. (1989) *Poverty and the Environment: Reversing the Downward Spiral.* Worldwatch Paper 92, Worldwatch Institute, Washington, DC, November

Fan, S., Hazell, P. and Thorat, S. (1999) 'Linkages between government spending, growth, and poverty in rural India'. Research Report no 110, International Food Policy Research Institute (IFPRI), Washington, DC

Fan, S., Zhang, L. and Zhang, X. (2002) *Growth, Inequality, and Poverty in Rural China: The Role of Public Investments.* International Food Policy Research Institute (IFPRI) Research Report 125, Washington, DC

FAO (2003) Map from *The State of Food Insecurity in the World 2003: Monitoring Progress Towards the World Food Summit and the Millennium Development Goals.* UN Food and Agricultural Organisation, available at www.fao.org/FOCUS/E/SOFI/IMG/map-e.pdf

Freeman, R. B. and Lindauer, D. L. (1999) *Why Not Africa?* NBER Working Papers 6942, National Bureau of Economic Research, available at www.nber.org/papers/w6942.pdf

Goldsmith, A. A. (1999) 'Slapping the grasping hand: Correlates of political corruption in emerging markets'. *American Journal of Economics and Sociology*, vol 58, no 4, pp866–883

Goldsmith, A. A. (2001) 'Foreign aid and statehood in Africa'. *International Organization*, vol 55, no 1, winter, pp123–148

Grindle, M. S. (1996) *Challenging the State: Crisis and Innovation in Latin America and Africa.* Cambridge University Press, Cambridge

IFDC (International Fertilizer Development Center) (1992) *Fueling Sustainable Growth in African Agriculture.* IFDC, Muscle Shoals, Alabama

Ingco, M D., Mitchell, D. O. and McCalla, A. F. (1996) *Global Food Supply Prospects.* Technical Paper No 353 prepared for the World Food Summit, World Bank, Washington, DC

Jayne, T. S., Govereh, J., Mwanaumo, A., Chapoto, A. and Nyoro, J. K. (2001) 'False promise or false premise? The experience of food and input market reform in Eastern and

Southern Africa', in T. S. Jayne, G. Argwings-Kodhek and I. Minde (eds) *Perspectives on Agricultural Transformation: A View from Africa.* Nova Science Publishers, New York

Jones, B. D. (1999) 'Military intervention in Rwanda's two wars: Partisanship and indifference', in B. F. Walter and J. Snyder (eds) *Civil Wars, Insecurity, and Intervention.* Columbia University Press, New York

Kapur, D. (2002) 'The changing anatomy of governance of the World Bank', in J. R. Pincus and J. A. Winters (eds) *Reinventing the World Bank.* Cornell University Press, Ithaca, pp54–75

Kaul, I., Grunberg, I. and Stern, M. A. (1999) 'Defining public goods', in I. Kaul, I. Grunberg and M. A. Stern (eds) *Global Public Goods: International Cooperation in the 21st Century.* Oxford University Press, New York

Khan, M .H. (2002) 'Corruption and governance in early Capitalism: World Bank strategies and their limitations', in J. R. Pincus and J. A. Winters (eds) *Reinventing the World Bank.* Cornell University Press, Ithaca, pp164–184

Kheralllah, M., Delgado, C., Gabre-Madhin, E., Minot, N. and Johnson, M. (2000) 'The road half traveled: Agricultural market reform in sub-Saharan Africa', in *Food Policy Report,* International Food Policy Research Institute (IFPRI), Washington, DC

Lipton, M. (1977) *Why Poor People Stay Poor.* Harvard University Press, Cambridge

Lipton, M. and Paarlberg, R. (1990) *The Role of the World Bank in Agricultural Development in the 1990s.* International Food Policy Research Institute (IFPRI), Washington, DC

Messer, E., Cohen, M. J. and d'Costa, J. (1998) *Food From Peace: Breaking the Links Between Conflict and Hunger. 2020 Brief 50.* International Food Policy Research Institute (IFPRI), Washington, DC

Olson, M. (2000) *Power and Prosperity.* Basic Books, New York

Paarlberg, R. L. (1994) *Countrysides at Risk: The Political Geography of Sustainable Agriculture.* Overseas Development Council, Policy Essay No 16, Overseas Development Council, Washington, DC

Pinstrup-Andersen, P., Pandya-Lorch, R. and Rosegrant, M. (1999) 'World food prospects: Critical issues for the early twenty-first century'. *2020 Vision Food Policy Report* (October), International Food Policy Research Institute (IFPRI), Washington, DC

Sahnoun, M. (1994) *Somalia: The Missed Opportunities.* US Institute of Peace Press, Washington, DC

Sarris, A., and Shams, H. (1991) *Ghana Under Structural Adjustment: The Impact on Agriculture and the Rural Poor.* New York University Press, New York

Sen, A. (1985) *Commodities and Capabilities.* North Holland, Amsterdam

Sender, J. (2002) 'Reassessing the role of the World Bank in sub-Saharan Africa', in J. R. Pincus and J. A. Winters (eds) *Reinventing the World Bank.* Cornell University Press, Ithaca, 185–202

Shantayanan, D., Dollar, D. and Holmgren, T. (eds) (2001) *Aid and Reform in Africa: Lessons from Ten Case Studies.* World Bank, Washington, DC

Shenggen, F., Hazell, P. and Thorat, S. (1999) *Linkages Between Government Spending, Growth, and Poverty in Rural India.* International Food Policy Research Institute, Research Report 110, Washington, DC

Shenggen, F., Zhang, L. and Zhang, X. (2002) *Growth, Inequality, and Poverty in Rural China: The Role of Public Investments.* International Food Policy Research Institute, Research Report 125, Washington, DC

Smith, G. and Naim, M. (2000) *Altered States: Globalization, Sovereignty, and Governance.* International Development Research Centre, Ottawa, Canada

Smith, L. C. and Haddad, L. (2000) *Overcoming Child Malnutrition in Developing Countries.* Discussion Paper 30 (February), International Food Policy Research Institute (IFPRI), Washington, DC

Treisman, D. (2000) 'The causes of corruption: A cross national study'. *Journal of Public Economics*, vol 76, pp399–457

Tuskegee University (2001) *Lessons Learned on Rural Development and Economic Performance in Africa.* Tuskegee University Workshop, 19–21 April, Atlanta, Georgia. Tuskegee University, Tuskegee Alabama

UNDP (United Nations Development Programme) (2002) *Sustainable Development in a Dynamic World: Transforming Institutions, Growth, and Quality of Life.* World Development Report 2003. UNDP, and Oxford University Press, New York

World Bank (1994) *Adjustment in Africa: Reforms, Results, and the Road Ahead.* Oxford University Press, New York

World Bank (2000) *World Development Report 2000/2001: Attacking Poverty.* Oxford University Press, New York

World Bank (2002) *World Development Indicators 2002; List of Indicators.* World Bank Group, available at www.worldbank.org/data/wdi202/cdrom/loi.html

WSSD (World Summit on Sustainable Development) (2002) *Johannesburg Plan of Implementation*, available at www.un.org/esa/sustdev/documents/WSSD_POI_PD/English/WSSD_PlanImpl.pdf

Yeats, A. J., Amjadi, A. and Reincke, U. (1996) *Did External Barriers Cause the Marginalization of Sub-Saharan Africa in World Trade?* World Bank, Washington, DC

10

Biodiversity: Biodiversity Governance after Johannesburg

Andrew M. Deutz[1]

Introduction

The World Summit on Sustainable Development (WSSD), held in Johannesburg, South Africa, in 2002 marked the tenth anniversary of the United Nations Conference on Environment and Development (UNCED), or the Rio Earth Summit. Johannesburg was an opportunity for the international community to review its progress in implementing the ambitious blueprint spelled out in Agenda 21 ten years earlier and to facilitate its implementation. The Johannesburg Summit therefore dealt with a wide array of old and new issues, ranging from the promotion of renewable energy, to AIDS in Africa, to sanitation; from over-fishing, to agricultural subsidies, to women's reproductive rights. In fact, the WSSD was occasionally criticized in the popular media for taking on too many issues. Such is the messy business of sustainable development, which is, after all, fundamentally about integrating social, economic and environmental options into coherent actions to improve the lot of humankind. Despite this cacophony of issues and ideas, the United Nations (UN) put forward five key themes for the summit and its follow-up – water, energy, health, food and agriculture, and biodiversity, popularized by the acronym WEHAB.

This chapter assesses the outcomes of the Johannesburg Summit relating to one of the WEHAB themes – biodiversity – and then considers the implications for biodiversity governance at different levels. The central challenge for biodiversity governance is to ensure coherence and consistency[2] with other governance[3] structures. At the global level, this means ensuring both coherence within the UN system and, more importantly, coherence between other political and economic governance structures. At the regional level, this means supporting regional political processes that can facilitate the implementation of biodiversity goals. The challenges at the national level closely parallel those at the global level – ensuring coherence and consistency within and between separate ministries, as well as with competing political and economic priorities that impact upon biodiversity. At the local level, this means empowering institutions and stakeholders to negotiate sustainable outcomes among conflicting priorities and pressures and to take action to manage the natural resource base.

The biodiversity-related outcomes of the WSSD

Biodiversity was something of an afterthought on the WSSD agenda. Throughout the first few PrepComs, to the extent that there was a coherent agenda, the central themes commanding the delegates' attention were water, energy, health and food security. These were generally linked to a subset of the Millennium Development Goals (MDGs),[4] as well as the ongoing politics of the Kyoto Protocol. At the time, there was criticism coming from some corners of the environmental movement that environmental concerns were slipping off the agenda and that the WSSD was going to focus disproportionately on the economic and social pillars of sustainable development. The WSSD was, after all, the tenth anniversary of the Rio Earth Summit and the 30th anniversary of the Stockholm Conference on the Human Environment. Fortunately for the environmental movement, Kofi Annan addressed that imbalance in a speech on the eve of PrepCom4 in May 2002, spelling out his vision of the Johannesburg agenda, which he articulated as water, energy, health, food and agriculture, and biodiversity, or WEHAB.[5] A draft negoti-ating text of the Johannesburg Plan of Implementation (JPOI) already existed at that point, which dealt with each of these points and many more. Annan's speech did not significantly affect the negotiating text; but it did serve to crystallize the key themes for the summit in a way that could easily be communicated to the media and the public at large. The five WEHAB themes also provided a framework for the UN Secretariat in organizing many of the key WSSD inputs and sessions of the formal summit.

Biodiversity issues were mainly dealt with in a single paragraph of the JPOI text within the chapter on 'Protecting and managing the natural resource base of economic and social development' (Chapter IV). Additional references are also peppered throughout the text in the chapters on natural resources, Africa, Small Island Developing States (SIDS, Chapter VII) and 'Other regional initiatives' (Chapter VIII). The central issues under negotiation throughout the Johannesburg process concerned the clarification of the target on biodiversity loss, the development of a new international regime on access to genetic resources and sharing of the benefits arising, the use of the ecosystem approach, and references to the precautionary principle.

The biodiversity target became an issue in the WSSD process following the sixth Conference of the Parties (COP-6) of the Convention on Biological Diversity (CBD) in The Hague in April 2002. Reiterating the target adopted a few months earlier by the CBD COP in its strategic plan for the convention, the JPOI set a target of achieving a significant reduction in the rate of biodiversity loss by 2010.[6]

The JPOI also called for the establishment of an international regime to safeguard the fair and equitable sharing of the benefits arising from the utilization of genetic resources.[7] This regime is to be developed within the context of the CBD and to build on the CBD's existing Bonn guidelines on access and benefit-sharing.[8] Also of note from a governance perspective is the fact that the proposal was originally put forward by Mexico on behalf of the so-called group of mega-diverse countries, a new negotiating block comprised of a small group of developing countries. This marked the emergence of a new negotiating coalition explicitly created around a common set of biodiversity characteristics and objectives.[9]

The ecosystem approach also proved to be a difficult issue in the negotiations of the JPOI. The concept was originally developed within the context of the CBD and refers to principles and guidelines 'for the integrated management of land, water and living resources that promote conservation and sustainable use in an equitable way'.[10] It therefore seeks to blend ecological, economic and social concerns in decision-making about resource use and conservation. The JPOI contains several references to the ecosystem approach in the sections on oceans, biodiversity and Africa.[11] However, in the final negotiating sessions, references to the use of the ecosystem approach were deleted in the introductory text of the chapter on natural resources (Chapter IV).

One last element of the JPOI was particularly important for biodiversity issues – the treatment of the precautionary approach in the negotiations. The precautionary approach provides guidance for political decision-making under circumstances of scientific uncertainty, and states that 'where there are threats of serious or irreversible damage, lack of full scientific certainty shall not be used as a reason for postponing cost-effective measures to prevent environmental degradation'.[12] However, the precautionary approach has also come under attack on two fronts. Some developing countries, in particular, fear that the precautionary approach could be used as a trade barrier, while some developed countries have proposed alternative formulations relying on risk assessment, which are generally seen as a weakening of the precautionary approach. During the negotiations in Johannesburg, there were multiple references to the precautionary approach in the context of chemical safety, natural resource management and means of implementation. Various proposals would have represented a restatement of the principle from Rio, a recognition of the development of the principle through international treaty law since Rio, or a weakening of the principle. In the final compromise, the entire text of the principle was reiterated in full, but accompanied by the gloss that this should support science-based decision-making.[13]

The JPOI did succeed both in clarifying the somewhat muddled 2010 target on biodiversity loss and in raising the profile of issues related to access and benefit-sharing (ABS) of genetic resources within the CBD. The JPOI did not make much headway in expanding the application of the ecosystem approach beyond the CBD itself, with the exception of the marine context. The ABS work should now be carried forward within the CBD regime itself by further developing guidance on both producer country measures and user country measures, as spelled out in the so-called Bonn Guidelines.[14] However, the WSSD plan of implementation did not go far enough in linking up the conservation and sustainable use issues within the CBD with the broader summit issues of poverty alleviation and the MDGs.

The Johannesburg Declaration on Sustainable Development made a similar attempt at establishing that conceptual linkage. The first draft of the political declaration contained several paragraphs on each of the WEHAB themes. In the end, these were reduced to a single paragraph in an effort to reduce the length of the document.[15] In relation to biodiversity, the first draft of the political declaration stated that 'the significant reduction in the rate of current biodiversity loss at national and global levels is a priority to achieve sustainable livelihoods for all'.[16] The draft thus referred to the biodiversity target and, more importantly, articulated the linkage between biodiversity conservation, on the one hand, and sustainable livelihoods and poverty alleviation, on the other hand. This linkage was also implicit in the CBD's Strategic Plan; but seeing it incorporated within the summit's Political Declaration would have been a significant conceptual leap, given the summit's larger concerns with poverty alleviation and the Millennium Development Goals.

The biodiversity governance implications of the WSSD

Global-level governance

The biggest challenge of biodiversity governance is not so much the governance of biodiversity *per se*,[17] but rather ensuring that governance systems in other sectors that impact upon biodiversity take biodiversity into account. The leading causes of biodiversity loss are generally taken to be habitat loss or conversion, invasive alien species and direct exploitation. These impacts result from any number of direct and indirect drivers, including agricultural and land-use policy, fiscal policy and economic incentive policies, urban sprawl, non-renewable resource extraction, unsustainable forestry, the globalization of commodity production and transportation, and the list goes on. Decisions in each of these policy arenas can and do affect biodiversity, necessitating policy and market feedback mechanisms to mitigate the impacts of spill-over effects on biodiversity. Establishing and maintaining these feedbacks in order to ensure coherent policy outcomes is a major challenge of biodiversity governance. Of course, looked at more broadly, ensuring coherence and consistency among the interconnected goals of economic development, social advancement and environmental sustainability is, in a nutshell, the central challenge of global governance. From this perspective, it is worth examining what Johannesburg contributed to both this larger global governance objective and the more specific case of biodiversity governance.

The Johannesburg Declaration on Sustainable Development calls for more effective, accountable and democratic international and multilateral institutions (JPOI, 2002, para 31), as well as for strengthening of multilateralism in general (para 32). However, the declaration dropped the language calling for efforts to promote coherence and consistency across policy arenas that was proposed by Emil Salim, chair of the preparatory process.[18] This is a disappointment since in the Millennium Declaration, adopted in 2000, the United Nations General Assembly specifically resolved to ensure coherence between the UN system, the Bretton Woods institutions and the World Trade Organization (WTO) in order to promote peace and development.[19] This omission should be seen in light of the continuing efforts of many governments (and some ministries within governments) to weaken the international regime for environmental protection vis-à-vis the trade liberalization agenda. The JPOI did a little better in its section on the institutional framework for sustainable development, calling for enhanced effectiveness and coordination for the implementation of Agenda 21, as well as the outputs of Johannesburg, Monterrey, Doha and the Millennium Summit.[20] While the Johannesburg political declaration may not have been bold in this regard, the UN General Assembly was when it considered the results of the summit; the General Assembly decided 'to adopt sustainable development as a key element of the overarching framework for United Nations activities, in particular for achieving the internationally agreed development goals, including those contained in the United Nations Millennium Declaration'.[21]

Within the UN system, this will require establishing clear connections between the MDGs and the sustainable development agenda, which may be quite an institutional challenge. The MDGs emerged directly from the UN General Assembly (GA) debate and it is likely that the GA will play a central role in monitoring their implementation. In contrast, Agenda 21 and the Johannesburg Plan of Implementation emerge from GA-established mega-summits and their implementation is monitored through the UN Commission on Sustainable Development (CSD). The early indications, measured in terms of political support, donor interest and intergovernmental attention, are that the MDGs will be much more significant benchmarks for the UN system over the next decade than the targets contained in the JPOI. If that proves to be the case, then the relevance of the sustainable development agenda within the UN, and therefore its status as part of the overarching framework of the UN, will require that this agenda is debated and monitored in unison with the MDGs. The CSD would be one possible forum for this conjunction. However, any mention of the MDGs is conspicuously absent from the revised mandate for the CSD, which emerged from Johannesburg.[22] If the CSD only deals with Agenda 21 and the Johannesburg Plan of Implementation, then the UN system risks putting sustainable development into a ghetto, while it gets on with the business of the MDGs elsewhere – to say nothing of trade and finance and peace and security. Ensuring the integration of sustainable development and the MDGs within the CSD, or some other UN body, will be a pivotal governance challenge within the UN system.

Biodiversity and the poverty agenda

Outside of the UN, a similar governance challenge of ensuring coherence and consistency exists for the bilateral and multilateral aid agencies. The donor agenda has shifted over the last few years towards a much more focused interest in poverty alleviation.[23] This shift has meant, in practice, that many donors are focusing on 'basic human needs' issues of healthcare, food security, basic education, and women and children's issues.[24] Biodiversity conservation and natural resource management issues are increasingly dropping off the agenda, especially at the programmatic level where project decisions are made.

Connecting the dots between Doha, Monterrey, Kananaskis and Johannesburg, the development agenda appears to be increasingly mainstreamed in global policy debates, but based on a rather narrow conception. Doha launched the so-called development round of trade liberalization; but within the context of the WTO, development is simplistically conceived of as increasing wealth in developing countries measured in Gross National Product (GNP) growth, without a sophisticated understanding of the distributional aspects of that growth, and thus of the poverty alleviation benefits of trade liberalization.[25] Monterrey did produce commitments to real increases in Official Development Assistance (ODA),[26] after a decade of declining ODA levels. Unfortunately, environmental concerns in general, let alone biodiversity, were scarcely discussed in Monterrey. Instead, there appears to be a trend to undermine the legacy of Rio – which sought to conceptually bridge environment and development under the mantle of sustainable development – and instead treat sustainable development as a boutique issue, related only to Millennium Development Goal 7 on ensuring environmental sustainability, rather than as an integral part of the whole development agenda. The lack of institutional integration between the CSD and the MDGs, discussed above, is a further indication of this trend. The discussions of the New Plan for African Development (NEPAD) in Kananaskis and Johannesburg were worrying as well: African civil society critiqued NEPAD as offering a 1970s model of development based on large-scale infrastructure projects and minimal environmental concerns. The principal development negotiation at Kananaskis was about how much of the Monterrey aid increment would be targeted specifically at Africa, not about the nature of the development model being put forward or accepted. Johannesburg tried to conceptualize sustainable development as being comprised of three interdependent sets of issues: poverty alleviation; natural resource conservation and sustainable use; and sustainable production and consumption. Much of the debate in Johannesburg focused on the first of these issues – and very little attention was focused on the third. Nevertheless, Johannesburg did provide fertile ground for underlining the linkages between poverty alleviation and biodiversity conservation and sustainable use.

The challenge for biodiversity governance in the context of aid is to demonstrate the fundamental centrality of biodiversity to poverty alleviation. It is not a hard case to make, especially in relation to rural poverty. A few statistics clearly demonstrate how biodiversity provides for the energy, nutritional and healthcare needs of the world's poor:

- About 2 billion people use fuelwood and charcoal as their main or only source of energy for cooking and/or heating.
- Wildlife, including wild fish, provides a significant source of protein in the diets of rural populations in many poor countries – an estimated 20 per cent of the animal protein consumed in at least 62 developing countries. Rural households may also consume dozens or even hundreds of different species of wild plants.

• About 70 to 80 per cent of the developing world's population meet their primary healthcare needs through traditional medicine, mainly medicinal plants. Globally, rural households use an estimated 10,000 to 20,000 different plants for medicinal purposes.[27]

In addition, natural resource activities provide direct employment opportunities for millions of people in poor countries and provide supplemental cash income for tens of millions more. Biodiversity is thus an essential component of the asset base of the poor. It is also often a critical form of insurance for poor. In looking at the importance of non-timber forest products for livelihood security, David Kaimowitz (2003) has observed that:

> *Wild plants and animals are especially crucial to poor rural households in times of hardship. These may be recurrent situations, such as the 'hungry' seasons between crops, or they may be crises such as droughts, economic downturns and violent conflicts. During such periods, forest foods often become the households' main sources of sustenance and their most important safety nets.*[28]

This implies a double responsibility for the donor community regarding the conservation and sustainable use of biodiversity. First, development interventions, in general, and poverty reduction strategy processes (PRSPs), in particular, must ensure that they recognize and safeguard the existing natural asset base of the poor. Second, poverty reduction strategies must take much greater account of opportunities to enhance that asset base as a poverty reduction strategy.

The financial implications of WSSD for biodiversity conservation are somewhat uncertain as they depend upon which of two countervailing forces will prevail in the short to medium term. There is a dynamic relationship between the level of political support for the conservation agenda and the level of resources that can be mobilized to support that agenda. These two phenomena tend to reinforce each other such that they can either lead to a virtuous cycle of increasing political support and increasing funding and, therefore, increasing political support, or they can lead to a vicious cycle. Assessing the situation after Johannesburg, it appears that they are headed in opposite directions. The 2002 Monterrey Conference on Financing for Development produced significant pledges from donors for billions' worth of increased ODA levels over the next few years. The countervailing trend is that Johannesburg appears to have marked a decline in global geopolitical interest in the environment, *per se*. In other words, the amount of funds out there to be disbursed by aid agencies might be increasing; but the political salience of the conservation agenda appears to be fading. There is also a real risk that geopolitical instability will significantly redirect ODA flows away from sustainable development programming towards humanitarian assistance and post-conflict reconstruction. The short- to medium-term challenge for biodiversity governance, therefore, is to position biodiversity conservation within that increased funding envelope by making the linkages between conservation, sustainable livelihoods, poverty alleviation and human security. Articulating this agenda in terms of the Millennium Development Goals will be an important mechanism to facilitate this. It is also important to recognize that there is still a lot of work to be done to articulate the critical importance of natural resource management and conservation as the *sine qua non* for sustainable livelihoods and poverty alleviation, especially in rural landscapes.

Biodiversity and the trade agenda

Another critical area where biodiversity governance must grapple with coherence and consistency concerns trade. Well over a decade old, the trade and environment debate is fairly well defined, if less well resolved. There are numerous sub-issues to this debate specifically related to biodiversity governance arising from the CBD and its Biosafety Protocol, and their interfaces with the WTO and the World Intellectual Property Organization (WIPO). Within this context, the issue of ensuring coherence and consistency between the biodiversity and trade and intellectual property rights treaties is captured by the notion of 'mutual supportiveness'. The phrase first appeared in the preamble of the 2000 Biosafety Protocol and has been reiterated in the preamble of the 2001 International Treaty on Plant Genetic Resources for Food and Agriculture. Similarly, in the WTO's Doha Declaration of November 2001, trade ministers stated their conviction 'that the aims of upholding and safeguarding an open and non-discriminatory multilateral trading system, and acting for the protection of the environment and the promotion of sustainable development can and must be mutually supportive'.[29] Given the consistency of the language between various trade and environment instruments, one might have expected that the discussions on trade and sustainable development would have been an opportunity for progress. After all, Doha was an opportunity for trade ministers to give their perspective on the trade–environment debate, and Monterrey was an opportunity for finance ministers to weigh in, as well. Johannesburg should have been the forum for environment ministers to add their perspective and complete that debate. Instead, the language of Doha became a textual straightjacket for negotiators in Johannesburg and circumscribed every nuance of the discussions. By the end of the summit, the environment and development non-governmental organizations (NGOs) had to content themselves with the knowledge that Johannesburg had not resulted in significant conceptual or legal backsliding and that textual proposals in the draft JPOI, which could have implied the subordination of multilateral environmental agreements to the WTO, were deleted.[30] Even without this concrete language being adopted, the so-called 'chilling effect' of the trade regime on environmental diplomacy was very much in evidence in Johannesburg.[31]

Looking ahead, the trade agenda as spelled out in Doha will focus largely on the service sectors as well as subsidies, making agriculture a particularly hot topic. This is also supposed to be the 'development round', focusing on raising the concerns of developing countries around issues of market access. The countervailing issues of labour and environmental standards, which in WTO parlance are often understood to mean Northern non-tariff barriers, will likely loom in the background, making for contentions and drawn-out negotiations. The trade and finance regimes have shown little interest in taking environmental issues into account, and the one place where all of the sectoral issues of trade liberalization, development, the environment, human health, human rights and global finance were supposed to come together – the WSSD – proved to be a disappointment in this regard. The irony is that trade liberalization should not be an end in itself, but rather a means to an end. Presumably, the goal is sustainable development, and trade liberalization should be judged by the extent to which it contributes to that goal. However, the political world is likely to continue to view environment as marginal to the larger economic agenda around which powerful domestic special interests coalesce. Johannesburg sent very telling signals of the direction of things to come regarding the potential consistency and coherence between the sustainable development and trade liberalization agendas.

In terms of biodiversity governance and managing the interface between the biodiversity treaties and the trade regime, the conservation community will continue to fight an uphill battle, and the fight will largely be on trade turf. Indeed, the question of turf, or, more precisely, who will have the 'home court advantage', is at the heart of the governance dispute between trade and the environment. The relationship between trade and Multilateral Environmental Agreements (MEAs), in general, and the legitimacy of trade measures within MEAs, in particular, remains a hotly contested issue. The problem from the environmental perspective is that that contest takes place within the WTO negotiating process and within the WTO dispute-resolution process. Having trade experts deliberate on trade issues may make sense; but it does not make sense to use sectorally specialized tribunals to adjudicate cross-sectoral issues, whether the issues concern trade and environment protection or trade and human health protection. Likewise, it would not make sense to establish environmental dispute processes to adjudicate matters where environmental protection measures impinge on other sectors. Instead, the solution to dealing with cross-sectoral disputes, such as balancing trade and environmental concerns, should be to use existing general fora, such as the International Court of Justice and the Permanent Court of Arbitration in The Hague.

Regional-level governance

One step below the global radar screen, an array of regional processes for bio-diversity conservation and sustainable use appear to be making progress. Regional processes provide a strong basis for practical cooperation compared to global processes because the fewer number of countries involved tend to have common ecological situations, and often share similar political cultures. Indeed, without these characteristics, there would be little reason for the processes to coalesce.

These regional processes appear to be relatively successful in facilitating collaborative political decision-making and implementation for biodiversity conservation and sustainable use, at least when compared to global-level processes. A number of actions should be taken to confirm this hypothesis and facilitate these processes. Regional processes have not received as much scholarly attention as global ones. Comparative studies of regional processes, in particular, would be useful. To the extent that it is not already doing so, the donor community should specifically target funding towards these regional processes, rather than only programmes at the national level. Finally, global-level institutions need to take

---

Box 10.1 Recent regional processes contributing to biodiversity governance

- The Pan-European Biological and Landscape Diversity Strategy grew out of the third Pan-European Conference of Ministers of the Environment in 1995 and encompasses 54 countries of the United Nations Economic Commission for Europe (UNECE). It is establishing a Pan-European Ecological Network to ensure the conservation of ecosystems, habitats and species, as well as their genetic diversity, and includes landscapes of European importance.
- Central America has a dense collection of regional treaties and processes related to biodiversity. These include the Central American Convention on Biodiversity and Protected Areas, which was developed to foster regional cooperation for the implementation of the Convention on Biological Diversity (CBD), as well as the Mezoamerican Biological Corridor, an initiative to establish a regional land-use matrix to ensure biodiversity conservation, including adequate migratory pathways throughout the isthmus.
- Further north, the North American Commission for Environmental Cooperation, established by the 1993 North American Agreement on Environmental Cooperation (NAAEC, the so-called environmental side agreement to the North American Free Trade Agreement, or NAFTA) has, *inter alia*, joint programmes spanning Mexico, the US and Canada to prevent the introduction of aquatic alien invasive species and to create a regional marine protected areas network.
- In Central Africa, the Conférence sur les Ecosystèmes de Forêts Denses et Humides d'Afrique Centrale (CEFDHAC, also known as the Brazzaville Process) was established in 1996. Alongside other activities, it has developed a strategic action plan for forest biodiversity conservation in the Congo Basin among nine governments and, jointly with the private sector, a code of conduct for sustainable forest management.

---

more account of regional processes and institutions, as the latter may prove more effective at facilitating implementation of globally agreed commitments and targets than the global processes that spawned them. Recent proposals by the UN Commission on Sustainable Development and the United National Forum on Forests to incorporate regional initiatives within their formal sessions is a welcome step in this direction and should be expanded.

National-level governance

Biodiversity governance at the national level faces at least two major challenges. The first of these is the proliferation of planning, implementation and reporting processes that national authorities must deal with concerning biodiversity, in particular, and sustainable development, more broadly. These include National

Biodiversity Strategies and Action Plans required under the CBD, National Sustainable Development Strategies (NSDS) following Agenda 21, national forest programmes promoted by the UN's Intergovernmental Forum on Forests (IFF) and its successor body the UN Forum on Forests, as well as the related requirements of the climate change and desertification conventions, and numerous other multilateral environmental agreements. It is not uncommon to hear delegates from industrialized countries complain about the bureaucratic and financial toll that all of these reporting requirements exact, to say nothing of delegates from developing countries. There have been some efforts to streamline reporting requirements across various processes; but these are only likely to bear fruit in coordinating among non-legally binding instruments and institutions.[32] Trying to harmonize across separate legal regimes created by individual treaties is likely to prove extremely time consuming and is highly unlikely to be cost-effective considering how the required creative energies could otherwise be deployed.

The second challenge is to ensure that national-level decision-making processes in other sectors do not adversely affect biodiversity conservation. This requires ensuring effective high-level coordination within and especially between ministries, while avoiding over-coordination and administrative burn-out.[33] This is as much an issue in industrialized countries as it is in developing countries, though it may be even more difficult in the latter given the additional processes that aid recipients undertake. Early evidence suggests that most poverty reduction strategies pay marginal attention, at best, to environmental planning and impacts.[34] If this initial evidence is further substantiated, it would confirm the rather poor track record of mainstreaming the environment into country-level donor assistance frameworks, whether bilateral or multilateral. Clearly, further awareness-raising is needed. At the same time, a major challenge lies within the line ministries responsible for environmental protection and natural resource management. There are significant capacity-building needs if these line agencies are to be able to engage effectively with ministries of finance and planning in national-level poverty reduction strategies.[35]

Local-level governance

Biodiversity governance faces a host of challenges at the local level, but there have been some promising developments since Rio. One of the most significant is caused by the confluence of two related phenomenon – the trend in many countries towards greater decentralization of governmental decision-making and the expansion of strategies for community-based natural resource management.

Many parts of the world, in both industrialized and developing countries, are experiencing decentralization and/or devolution of governmental authority for natural resource management and biodiversity conservation. In some cases, this process is motivated by neo-liberal policies, in others by structural adjustment conditionally, and in still others, it is simply a matter of short-term financial necessity for cash-strapped central governments. In cases where the devolution process is carefully managed and where adequate administrative capacity exists or is built at the local level through the process, devolution can potentially enhance local accountability and enhance biodiversity outcomes.[36] However, where new management responsibilities come in the form of unfunded mandates for local government, the resulting management capacity gap can have negative consequences.[37]

The second side of the local governance equation concerns local communities. Ten years ago, at the Rio Earth Summit, the international community tended to view the poor as part of the problem of environmental degradation. By the time of Johannesburg, the international community tended to view them as part of the solution. This shift in perceptions was due, in large part, to more than a decade's worth of experience with community-based natural resource management strategies, promoted by conservation and development organizations and many donor agencies. Local communities, whether in the North or the South, can be very effective stewards and even restorers of biodiversity.[38] Some of the more celebrated examples include the 5000 or so forest users groups in Nepal, joint forest management approaches in India, and the various communities recognized by the Equator Initiative.[39] Of course, there have been examples of local communities being ill prepared for additional management responsibilities; capacity-building is often required. At the same time, some community-based management systems are starting to face second-generation problems associated with these approaches. These usually concern the mismatch of formal compared to informal rights of access, use and ownership to the resource base, especially after successful community-based management has enhanced the productivity of natural systems, and suddenly government agencies or local elites attempt to reassert authority over the resources.[40]

The greater responsibilities of local communities can actually increase the demands on local officials to facilitate transparency, accountability and participation at a time when they may lack the skills and capacity to respond to these demands. The challenge for biodiversity governance at the local level, then, with attendant implications for national government (and, in developing countries, for donors as well) is to ensure that this capacity gap either does not develop, or where it does, that it is filled.

Conclusion

In terms of the official outcomes, the World Summit on Sustainable Development did produce a clarification of the nature and scope of the key internationally agreed target directing action to protect biodiversity. Johannesburg also put in place the first steps to link biodiversity to the MDGs and the broader poverty alleviation agenda. This conceptual linkage, and the ability of the UN's other institutions to carry it into practice, will be critical factors for the successful governance of biodiversity issues.

The first inklings of these linkages appeared during the first half of 2003. Several international actors, including the United Nations Development Programme (UNDP) and the CBD secretariat, organized a pair of meetings to explore the linkages between the WSSD outcomes, the Millennium Development Goals and the 2010 biodiversity target. These sessions focused on mechanisms for measuring and reporting on biodiversity loss and, thus, evaluating progress towards the 2010 target.[41] In between these two experts' meetings, the CBD convened its own inter-sessional meeting on its Multi-year Programme of Work of the Conference of the Parties up to 2010, which examined, *inter alia*, the relationship between the WSSD outcomes and the MDGs with regard to biodiversity. It adopted a recommendation calling for a report on the relationship, as well as for the creation of a mechanism to ensure that the achievement of the MDGs is consistent with the objectives of the convention.[42] Much remains to be done within the CBD; but action within the semi-autonomous institution of the CBD, while necessary, is not sufficient; the real test of biodiversity governance will depend upon whether and how biodiversity is taken up post-Johannesburg outside of the CBD.

The Commission on Sustainable Development convened its 11th session, its first since Johannesburg in April 2003. CSD-11 adopted it own multi-year programme of work, which included the now almost standard refrain calling for strengthening coherence and collaboration within and between UN agencies and other multilateral fora.[43] Despite these tentative steps, the CSD did not define a clear relationship between its multi-year programme of work and the achievement of the Millennium Development Goals. Its agenda is defined in terms of Agenda 21, its five year review, and the Johannesburg Plan of Implementation, and did not adequately address the connection to the MDGs and their implementation and review processes. As the work of the CSD evolves, it will need to increase its efforts to ensure effective linkages to the implementation and review of the MDGs.

From the foregoing discussion, the main point should be clear: the primary challenge facing the governance of biodiversity is to ensure coherence and consistency of governance structures in different sectoral regimes that impact upon biodiversity, and vice versa. In so far as biodiversity governance is equated solely with the operations of the Convention on Biological Diversity, it will be marginalized in the larger political and economic debates of the day. The task for those concerned about biodiversity, like the other WEHAB themes, and the other goals of sustainable development, such as promotion of human rights and the removal of economic inequities, is to demonstrate the essential interconnectedness of each of these elements of the sustainable development agenda. In the case of biodiversity governance, the challenge is to link the conservation and sustainable use of biodiversity with the large development agenda, especially as currently articulated through the MDGs. It is also necessary to ensure that the MDGs and the narrow conception of poverty alleviation do not supplant the conceptually broader sustainable development agenda. The legacy of Rio was the marriage of the traditional environmental and development agendas into a more coherent whole. Rio also demonstrated that sustainable development, including biodiversity, was as much a local and national issue in the North as it is in the South.

Beyond the development agenda and beyond the rarefied world of UN policy coordination meetings, governance of biodiversity must also demonstrate the relevance of conservation and sustainable use of the benefits and services of genes, species and ecosystems to a much wider range of sectors. The environment–trade debate is fairly well developed; but the interface of biodiversity and financial flows is only beginning to be understood. The linkages between biodiversity and geopolitical security are even less well recognized. Yet the international community is unlikely to solve the problems of wretched poverty, to ensure global economic growth, or to establish peace and security in a world marred by economic deprivation, social dislocation and environmental degradation. Reversing these global failings rests upon the fulfillment of the three pillars of the sustainable development agenda, an agenda of which biodiversity is an essential component. The challenge of biodiversity governance, therefore, is to operationalize these linkages. This will require addressing the following key questions:

- At the global level, how can the UN system better ensure the integration of the sustainable development agenda and the Millennium Development Goals, rather than allow them to go down two independent tracks?
- How can the conservation movement better demonstrate the centrality of biodiversity conservation and sustainable use to achieving sustainable livelihoods, poverty alleviation and human security?
- How can international institutions and processes better ensure coherence and consistency among environmental, social and economic objectives, especially the relationship between trade and the environment?
- At the regional level, how can global institutions better facilitate the work of regional-level institutions for the implementation of globally agreed commitments and targets?
- At the national level, how can governments ensure greater coherence and consistency across different sectors and different ministries?
- And, finally, at the local level, how can different stakeholders meet the capacity needs of local governmental institutions and local communities to more effectively conserve and manage biological resources?

Notes

1   The views expressed in this chapter are the author's own and do not necessarily reflect the views of World Conservation Union (IUCN). The author would like to thank Rosalie Callway of the Local Government International Bureau, Carole Saint-Laurent, IUCN senior forest policy adviser, and Tomme Rosanne Young of the IUCN Environmental Law Centre for their comments and discussions on various drafts of this chapter.
2   The terms 'coherence and consistency' have appeared in a number of UN texts and generally refer to the notion that institutions and policies in different sectors should complement rather than undermine one another. For example, the Canadian announcement during the July 2003 Kananaskis Group of 8 (G8) Summit of Cdn$500 million for the implementation of New Plan for African Development (NEPAD), followed by the announcement at Johannesburg of the removal of all import barriers on goods from least developed countries, are examples of coherent and consistent development assistance and trade liberalization policies.
3   The Commission on Global Governance defined governance as:

> *... the sum of the many ways in which individuals and institutions, public and private, manage their common affairs. It is a continuing process through which*

> *conflicting or diverse interests may be accommodated and cooperative action may be taken. It includes formal institutions and regimes empowered to enforce compliance, as well as informal arrangements that people and institutions either have agreed to or perceive to be in their interests* (Commission on Global Governance, 1995, p2).

4   The Millennium Development Goals were adopted by the UN General Assembly within the Millennium Declaration of 18 September 2000. They consist of 8 goals with 18 targets and 48 indicators. In the context of the WEHAB themes, water corresponded to MDG 7 on providing safe drinking water; health to MDGs 4, 5 and 6 on improving child and maternal healthcare and on infectious disease; and agriculture/food security to MDG 1 on reducing hunger (United Nations Millennium Declaration. A/RES/55/2, 18 September 2000).

5   UN Secretary General (2002) 'Towards a sustainable future', American Museum of Natural History's Annual Environmental Lecture, delivered by Kofi Annan, New York, 14 May 2002, available at www.johannesburgsummit.org/html/media_info/speeches/sg_speech_amnh.pdf.

6   See *Plan of Implementation of the World Summit on Sustainable Development*, para 44, in *Report of the World Summit on Sustainable Development*, A/CONF.199/20.

7   This target reiterated the target set by the CBD in its strategic plan. See Decision VI/26, Annex I, para. 11, UNEP/CBD/COP/6/20. However, at the same COP a more ambitious, but also somewhat ambiguous, target was also adopted, to 'put in place measures to halt biodiversity loss . . . by the year 2010'. This formulation left it unclear whether the date referred to when the measures were to be in place or when the loss was to be halted.

8   See Hague Ministerial Declaration of the Conference of the Parties to the Convention on Biological Diversity, UNEP/CBD/COP/6/20, Annex II, para 11. Some non-governmental organizations (NGOs) criticized this outcome as a missed opportunity to clarify the target adopted by the ministers a few months earlier and set an ambitious target to halt biodiversity loss by 2010. Other NGOs, however, were satisfied with the decision on the grounds that eliminating biodiversity loss by 2010 was neither scientifically justified (there is a natural background species extinction rate that cannot be reduced to zero), nor politically feasible.

9   JPOI, 2002, para. 44(o).

10   Decision VI/24: Access and Benefit Sharing Related to Genetic Resources, UNEP/CBD/COP/6/20.

11   In the framework of preparing for the Johannesburg Summit, the ministers of the environment of Brazil, China, Costa Rica, Colombia, Ecuador, India, Indonesia, Kenya, Mexico, Peru, South Africa and Venezuela met in Cancun, Mexico, in February, 2002 (Bolivia and Malaysia were accepted as part of the group in April 2002). The ministers subscribed to the Cancun Declaration, wherein they defined a common agenda for sustainable development and created the 'Group of Like-minded Megadiverse Countries' as a mechanism for consultation and cooperation. According to the member countries, the group represents close to 70 per cent of the planet's biological diversity, around 45 per cent of the world's population and the richest cultural diversity (Maria-Fernanda Espinosa, IUCN policy adviser on indigenous peoples and biodiversity, pers comm, March 2003).

12   Decision V/6: Ecosystem Approach, reprinted in Secretariat of the Convention on Biological Diversity (2001) *Handbook of the Convention on Biological Diversity*. London, Earthscan Publications.

13   JPOI, 2002, para 30(d), 32(c), 44(e) and 70(b).
14   The CBD's inter-sessional meeting on the Multi-year Programme of Work of the Conference of the Parties took up this issue when it met in March 2003. It requested parties and other stakeholders to comment on their experiences with the Bonn Guidelines and to provide their views to the CBD's *ad hoc* open-ended working group on access and benefit-sharing so that it could make recommendations to the next COP. See Recommendation 5 in the Annex to *Report of the Open-ended Inter-Sessional on the Multi-year Programme of Work of the Conference of the Parties up to 2010*, UNEP/CBD/COP/7/5, 25 March 2003.
15   The Johannesburg Declaration on Sustainable Development, para 18. *Report of the World Summit on Sustainable Development*, A/CONF.199/20.
16   'Draft political declaration submitted by the president of the summit', A/CONF.199/L.6, para. 44.
17   For an examination of the governance of the Convention on Biological Diversity itself, see Le Prestre (2002).
18   See *Proposed Elements for the Political Declaration of WSSD, Presented by the Chairman of the Preparatory Committee, Dr Emil Salim* (on file with the author). This document was released by the chair shortly after PrepCom4 in Bali.
19   United Nations Millennium Declaration, A/RES/55/2, para. 30.
20   See JPOI, Part XI: 'Institutional framework for sustainable development', especially para 151.
21   World Summit on Sustainable Development, A/RES/57/253, 21 February 2003 para 3. This element of the GA resolution is derived from para 142 of the JPOI.
22   See JPOI, 'Role and function of the Commission on Sustainable Development,' para 145–150.
23   For an overview of the logic of this shift and its associated tools, see Maxwell (2003, pp5–25).
24   The Millennium Development Goals, adopted by the UN General Assembly in December 2000, commit the international community to reduce by half, by 2015, the proportion of people living on less than US$1 per day who suffer from hunger and who do not have access to clean drinking water. Maternal mortality and the mortality of children under the age of five are both to be reduced by two-thirds. Universal primary education is to be achieved by 2015, and AIDs, malaria and other infectious diseases are to be brought under control (UN General Assembly, A/res/55/2). The World Bank has estimated that achieving the MDGs will require doubling current Official Development Assistance (ODA) levels from roughly US$50 billion per year to US$100 billion per year.
25   The Doha round is also supposed to address subsidies. Global aggregate subsidies to the agricultural sector amount to about US$360 billion per year, while the energy sector is a close second at roughly US$300 billion per year. A 7.5 per cent reduction in each of these global subsidies would generate the estimated US$50 billion needed to achieve the MDGs.
26   The EU pledged to achieve an average national level of ODA of 39 per cent of GDP by 2006, which, if met, will represent a US$7 billion increase in 2006 over current levels and a US$20 billion cumulative increase over the period 2000–2006. The US pledged to increase its ODA by US$5 billion over three years, leading to a 50 per cent increase over current levels by 2005.
27   See Kaimowitz (2003).
28   See Kaimowitz (2003, p2).
29   Ministerial Declaration, WT/MIN(01)/DEC/1, 20 November 2001, para. 6. The Doha Declaration goes on to say that appropriate measures to protect human health and

the environment should not be prevented as long as they are not arbitrary or discriminatory, and are otherwise consistent with states' obligations under the WTO. This same principle was articulated in the 1992 Rio Declaration on Environment and Development, Principle 12 (*Report of the United Nations Conference on Environment and Development*, Annex I., A/CONF.151/6, vo. 1).

30   On this point, compare the agreed text in the JPOI, para 98, with para 18 of the Means of Implementation negotiating text dated Sunday, 25 August 2002, 5.00 pm (on file with author) The latter stated that countries should: 'Promote mutual supportiveness between the multilateral trading system and the multilateral environmental agreements, as a complement to and in support of the work programme agreed through the WTO'. This implied that countries should ensure that the Multilateral Environment Agreements (MEAs) supported the WTO work programme without necessarily ensuring the reverse. In contrast, the agreed text in the JPOI reads: 'Promote mutual supportiveness between the multilateral trading system and the multilateral environmental agreements, consistent with sustainable development goals, in support of the work programme agreed through the WTO, while recognizing the importance of maintaining the integrity of both sets of instruments'.

31   On this chilling effect, see Thomas (2002, pp200–202).

32   For one such effort, see the Collaborative Partnership on Forests Task Force on Streamlining Forest-Related Reporting, available at www.fao.org/forestry/foris/webview/cpf/index.jsp?geoId=0&langId=1&siteId=2261.

33   For a discussion of various national experiences attempting to coordinate multilateral environmental agreements in Asia, see United Nations University (2002).

34   See Bojö and Chandra Reddy (2001).

35   This observation is based on IUCN's experiences in PRSP and 'debt for nature' swap programme processes in Eastern Africa (personal communication from Alex Muhweezi, country representative, IUCN Uganda Country Office, and Edmund Barrow, forest conservation and social policy coordinator, IUCN East Africa Regional Office, March 2003).

36   There have also been a number of noteworthy experiences in developing and implementing Local Agenda 21s. Nevertheless, no coordinated international network of local initiatives related to biodiversity conservation has yet emerged. See Otto-Zimmermann (2002, p8).

37   See Barrow et al (2002).

38   For examples, see the series of regional profiles by the Working Group on Community Involvement in Forest Management: Poffenberger (1998, 1999, 2000); McCarthy et al (2000); Jeanrenaud (2001); Kigenyi et al (2002).

39   The Equator Initiative is a UNDP-led partnership designed to reduce poverty through the conservation and sustainable use of biodiversity in the equatorial belt by fostering, supporting and strengthening community partnerships. See www.undp.org/equatorinitiative/index.htm.

40   For examples of so-called 'second-generation problems' arising from Nepal's relatively successful experiences with community forest management, see *National Workshop on Learning from Community Forestry: How Can Adaptive and Collaborative Management Approaches Enhance Livelihoods, Equity and Forests*, Workshop Proceedings, 10–11 September 2002, Kathmandu, Nepal (on file with author).

41   For reports of these two sessions, see the sustainable developments reports: *Biodiversity After Johannesburg: The Critical Role of Biodiversity and Ecosystem Services in Achieving the United Nations Millennium Development Goals: 2–4 March 2003*, available at www.iisd.ca/linkages/sd/sdund/, and *Summary Report of 2010 – The Global Biodiversity Challenge: 21–23 May 2003*, available at www.iisd.ca/linkages/sd/sdgbc/.

42   See Recommendation 1 in the Annex to *Report of the Open-Ended Inter-Sessional on the Multi-Year Programme of Work of the Conference of the Parties up to 2010*, UNEP/ CBD/COP/7/5, 25 March 2003.
43   See *The Implementation Track for Agenda 21 and the Johannesburg Plan of Implementation: Future Programme, Organization and Methods of Work of the Commission on Sustainable Development*, para. 17, advance unedited text, as adopted by CSD-11, 14 May 2003, available at www.un.org/esa/sustdev/csd/csd11/csd11res.pdf.

References

Barrow, E., Clarke, J., Grundy, I., Jones, Y-R. and Tessema, Y. (2002) *Analysis of Stakeholder Power and Responsibilities in Community Involvement in Forest Management in Eastern and Southern Africa*. IUCN, Nairobi

Bojö, J, and Chandra Reddy, R. (2001) *Poverty Reduction Strategies And Environment: A Review of 40 Interim and Full PRSPs*. World Bank Environment Department, Geneva, December 2001

CBD (Convention on Biological Diversity) (2001) *Secretariat of the Convention on Biological Diversity, Handbook of the Convention on Biological Diversity*. Earthscan Publications Ltd, London

Commission on Global Governance (1995) *Our Global Neighborhood: The Report of the Commission on Global Governance*. Oxford University Press, New York

Jeanrenaud, S. (ed) (2001) *Communities and Forest Management in Western Europe*. IUCN, Gland, Switzerland

Kaimowitz, D. (2003) *Forests and Rural Livelihoods in Developing Countries*. Centre for International Forestry Research, Bogor, March 2003

Kigenyi, F., Gondo, P., Mugaba, J. (2002) *Community Involvement in Forest Management in Eastern and Southern Africa: Analysis of Policies and Institutions*. IUCN, Nairobi

Le Prestre, P. G. (2002) 'The operation of the CBD convention governance system', in P. G. Le Prestre (ed) *Governing Global Biodiversity: The Evolution and Implementation of the Convention on Biological Diversity*. Ashgate Publishing Company, Burlington

Maxwell, S. (2003) 'Heaven or hubris: Reflections on the new "New Poverty Agenda"'. *Development Policy Review*, vol 21, no 1

McCarthy, R. et al. (eds) (2000) *Comunidades y gestión de bosques en Mesoamérica*. Impresión Comercial La Nación, San José

Otto-Zimmermann, K. (2002) *Local Action 21: Motto – Mandate: Movement in the Post-Johannesburg Decade*. International Council of Local Environmental Initiatives, Toronto, Canada

Poffenberger, M. (ed) (1998) *Communities and Forest Management in Canada and the United States*. IUCN, Gland, Switzerland

Poffenberger, M. (ed) (1999) *Communities and Forest Management in Southeast Asia*. IUCN, Gland, Switzerland

Poffenberger, M, ed. (2000) *Communities and Forest Management in South Asia*. IUCN, Gland, Switzerland

Thomas, U. P. (2002) 'The CBD, the WTO, and the FAO: The emergence of phytogenetic Governance', in P. G. Le Prestre (ed) *Governing Global Biodiversity: The Evolution and Implementation of the Convention on Biological Diversity*. Ashgate Publishing Company, Burlington

United Nations University (2002) *Interlinkages: National and Regional Approaches in Asia and the Pacific*. United Nations University, Tokyo, January

Conclusion

11

Conclusion: Where next?

Georgina Ayre

This book has illustrated that, whether for good or for bad, during recent years global governance as a term and a newly emerging concept has been brought to the fore of international and political dialogue. The collapse of trade talks at the Fifth World Trade Organization (WTO) Ministerial in Cancun, the action of states taking unilateral and bilateral action on international security issues, accusations of corruption in the United Nations (UN) over the Food for Oil Programme, the breach and the improper use of the Universal Declaration of Human Rights, growing criticism of the International Financial Institutions (IFIs) for their lack of transparency and accountability, and a lack of confidence in the role and competence of the United Nations Environment Programme (UNEP) have all, individually and collectively, resulted in calls from all corners of the world for a reform in almost every sphere of global governance.

Multilateralism at a crossroad

As we have read, multilateralism is at a crossroad. While we have imbedded our governance in multilateral processes, with rising frequency their decision-making, accountability and ability to bring about implementation and change is being called to question. As a result, states are increasingly seeking unilateral and bilateral action and agreement.

In some instances, this lack of confidence in countries working together may be justified, particularly at a time where immediate action is required, which does not allow for the often slow wheels of multilateral decision-making to turn. However, just as was argued by Hardin in 'The tragedy of the commons' (1968), the shift of states towards acting in isolation undermines the very structures that have been put in place to protect our collective interests, and instead of bringing about positive change, in fact, leaves countries more vulnerable. The collective case for strengthening and reforming our current processes is a far stronger one than for either the development of new institutions or for states to act independently.

Over the coming years we have a number of opportunities open to us to re-establish and reinvigorate multilateralism. The onus to achieve this not only falls to the multilateral institutions themselves to undertake the necessary reform measures within their own bodies, as well as in the way they interact with others; but it is also the responsibility of national governments to commit to and offer multilateral institutions the political leadership and support that is required to make them functional.

High-level Panel on Threats, Challenges and Change

In response to calls for a fundamental rethink in how global, regional and national systems function, and to gain an understanding of the collective threats and challenges faced by the global community, the UN Secretary General, Kofi Annan, established a High-level Panel on Threats, Challenges and Change. The panel was also born out of the Secretary General's growing concern that the UN system was in need of significant reform to enable it to respond to a new set of global challenges emerging in the 21st century.

The report of the Secretary General's high-level panel, *A More Secure World: Our Shared Responsibility*, was launched on 1 December 2004. The report makes significant proposals on how to approach non-traditional security threats, and usefully highlights the connections between environmental sustainability, poverty eradication and security.

The report recognizes that economic and social threats, including poverty, infectious diseases and environmental degradation, are a collective security threat, and notes that environmental stress caused by shortage of land and other natural resources can result in civil violence. The report also states that environmental concerns are rarely factored into security, development or humanitarian strategies, and that there is a lack of coherence in environmental protection at the international level. It highlights a number of inadequacies in current governance structures, not least the failure to take account of key environmental issues, but also that international institutions and states have not organized themselves to deal with the challenges of development in a coherent manner, and that economic and social structures are inadequate to deal with the challenges ahead.

A number of core recommendations are made in the report, including a call for all states to recommit themselves to the goals of eradicating poverty, achieving sustained economic growth and promoting sustainable development.

Of direct relevance to discussion in this book is the recommendation that 'The United Nations should work with national authorities, international financial institutes, civil society organizations and the private sector to develop norms governing the management of natural resources for countries emerging from or at risk of conflict' (Annan, 2004).

Also embedded within the text is the call for the reform of national, regional and international governance structures in order to enable the challenges of the 21st century to be addressed in a more coherent way. This would, for instance, require UNEP, the United Nations Development Programme (UNDP), national governments and the World Bank to work with one another in a more integrated manner.

If pursued, these recommendations will make a significant and positive contribution to achieving sustainable development through improved governance.

The Millennium Development Goals

During 2000, the global community came together to agree on a set of goals to address extreme poverty, including hunger, education, gender equity, disease and environmental sustainability, by 2015. While progress has been made towards realizing the Millennium Development Goals (MDGs), greater action is required if we are to fully achieve (and even go beyond) them.

Although many approach the MDGs from a purely developmental focus, they are, in fact, a commitment to make significant progress towards sustainable development. Environmental sustainability supports the achievement of all of the MDGs, and as outlined in the report of the Secretary General's high-level panel, environmental sustainability is essential for security and stability.

The report of the Millennium Project, *Investing in Development: A Practical Plan to Achieve the Millennium Development Goals* (2005), provides an indepth analysis of progress towards achieving the MDGs, setting out a series of concrete recommendations for expediting their implementation. The report attributes 'governance failures' as a contributing factor to lack of progress in achieving the MDGs, including the need for better engagement of civil society, more accountable and efficient public administrations, improved governance of the private sector, and the need to protect human rights and to uphold the rule of law, while ensuring equity.

A key recommendation of the report is to develop MDG-based poverty reduction strategies (Millennium Project, 2005). If taken up, this recommendation would have significant implications for sustainable development governance: it would not only alter the way in which national governments manage their development, but also the relationship between donors and recipient countries.

It is important to ask how this might be achieved. Positively, addressing the MDGs directly in the poverty reduction strategy processes (PRSPs) would give them more focus. Negatively, it might not allow for the national flexibility required for countries to define their own poverty priorities – in consultation with their populations – as is currently the approach in PRSP development. A careful balance between national sovereignty, community participation and broad donor guidance is required to ensure that nationally relevant MDGs are addressed by a country's PRSP.

Equally, the industrialized donor countries have to be coherent in their support of the MDGs and sustainability agendas. Internationally, an enabling environment must be provided that allows the Highly Indebted Poor Countries (HIPC) to make progress on poverty and sustainability commitments.

The Three Cs: Coherence, Collaboration, Coordination

The recognition that the international sustainable development governance system is deeply flawed is not new, not least as a result of the fragmentation caused by a plethora of bodies and agencies, both within and outside the UN system, governing the broad aspects of sustainable development. We have long recognized that a disproportionate emphasis is placed on economic development, often to the detriment of society and the environment. Of course, what is required is a significant shift in the global governance architecture to bring about greater coherence in our approach.

As each of the chapters in this book has outlined, reform at one level or in one sector is not going to bring about the change in horizontal and vertical governance that is required if we are to manage our world in a more sustainable way. Strengthening UNEP will, we hope, provide greater authority to protect the environment. Reforming the WTO may also result in a fairer, more equitable and more accountable trading system. Reform of the United Nations Security Council will also encourage collective rather than unilateral action, and reform of the IFIs will hopefully ensure that aid not only reaches those who need it the most, but is also allocated to programmes determined by the recipient countries. But conducted alone, these reform measures will only exacerbate the challenge of achieving sustainable development.

This is not to say that what is needed is a new body to oversee the governance of sustainable development – far from it – although, to some extent, this is what the Commission on Sustainable Development (CSD) does thematically over its two-year cycles. But what is required is a significant change in the way in which different bodies at all levels – local, national, regional and international – interact. No one agency can determine the activities of another; but strengthening the relationship through, for example, the recently signed memorandum of understanding (MoU) between UNEP and UNDP can certainly assist in bringing greater cohesion to the system.

Regular reporting to the CSD may also serve as a useful tool, acting as an accountability mechanism for all institutions, governments and stakeholders to assess progress and highlight further opportunities to enhance governance frameworks towards better implementation of sustainable development.

In order to truly achieve sustainable development, coherent and complementary policies and decisions need to be made at all levels, local to global. To achieve this, what is required is greater coordination between government departments, the UN, the IFIs, WTO and the wide breadth of civil society. Achieving this will require collaborative work, establishing an environment of respect and openness to seek common ground, and the adoption of a shared objective: sustainable development.

References

Annan, K. (2004) *A More Secure World: Our Shared Responsibility*. Secretary General's High Level Panel on Threats, Challenges and Change report, UN, New York, December 2004

Hardin, G. (1968) 'The tragedy of the commons'. *Science*, vol 162, pp1243–1248

Millennium Project (2005) *Investing in Development: A Practical Plan to Achieve the Millennium Development Goals*. UN, available at www.unmillenniumproject.org/reports/fullreport.htm

Index